The
World
Technique

Acknowledgements

Thanks to the Bollingen Foundation, the Institute for Intercultural Studies, Columbia University Research in Contemporary Cultures (ONR nr-552, T.O. 01, MIT W33-038 ac 14105), The American Museum of Natural History Studies in Allopsychic Orientation (NIMH MN-03303- Thanks to Miss Susan Haven for her percipient editing of the Introduction and to Miss Enid Kotschnig for her system of illustrations.* Thanks to the Dr. Margaret Lowenfeld Trust for the financial support without which this book would not have been produced. Thanks to Dr. Michael Hession and Mr. John Hood-Williams for editing and for seeing the manuscript through the various stages of production. Thanks to Mr. Starbuck who designed the layout for the book and the dustjacket.

developed the system being used.

THE
WORLD
TECHNIQUE

MARGARET LOWENFELD

London
GEORGE ALLEN & UNWIN
Boston   Sydney

First published by George Allen & Unwin in 1979

GEORGE ALLEN & UNWIN LTD

40 Museum Street, London WC1A 1LU

© George Allen & Unwin (Publishers) Ltd, 1979

British Library Cataloguing in Publication Data
Lowenfeld, Margaret
The world technique
1. Child psychotherapy   2. Problem children
3. Lowenfeld mosaic test
I. Title
618.9'28'9165   RJ504   78-40722
ISBN 0-04-150067-9

Printed in Great Britain

CONTENTS

Foreword

Margaret Lowenfeld was one of the great pioneers in the discovery of childhood – the discovery was itself an outstanding human and scientific event of the twentieth century – and part of the whole intellectual adventure of seeking for ways to explore children's thinking and feeling. Throughout her long and innovative life, she emphasised the development of new forms of communication with children, especially devoting herself to the diagnosis and treatment of troubled children. In this she was part of the child guidance and child analysis movement, which is taking new forms today, as we speak of child advocacy and the Year of the Child (1979).

But she did even more, because she combined her insights from treating sick children with insights gained from an enthusiastic inquiry into the history of civilisation, the contrasts between different cultures, and the special creativity of artists, poets and great religious leaders. She was one of the first to realise that the special kinds of thought which are manifestations of early childhood perceptions of the world are not only the roots of trouble in disturbed children, but also the precious precursors of the work of genius. From her experience of the horrors of World War I, the atrocities of World War II, and the continuing nightmares of the post World War II period, she derived a vivid sense of the urgency of acquiring greater understanding of the way children in a world of adults, children in particular classes and situations, in particular societies, and at particular periods of history, learn to relate to the real world, or became stunted, apathetic or distorted.

She belongs in the pantheon of those who have enlarged our understanding of children – Erik Erikson, Anna Freud, Arnold Gesell, Melanie Klein and Jean Piaget – and those who have been providing the links between our understanding of the arts, of history and of the experiences of early childhood – Gregory Bateson, Edith Cobb, Geoffrey Gorer, Susan Isaacs, Ella Sharpe, David Winnicot and Martha Wolfenstein.

But unlike most of her illustrious contemporaries, she was most of all preoccupied with the insufficiency of words to express those aspects of childhood thought and feeling which interested her most. Her development of instruments of communication, such as the Worlds described in this book, and mosaics, have become important anthropological research tools; and kaleidoblocs and poleidoblocs are now widely used in introducing children to mathematics and logic. Due to her rejection of words as a medium of communication, unless they are supplemented by visible, manipulatable forms – miniatures of actuality, two dimensional and three dimensional forms with color and texture – she was hampered in her communication with a wider public than those who knew her in the flesh, as teacher, colleague, therapist, lecturer, and always demonstrator. The problem of how to make communicable the detail of nonverbal communication, in a world in which colored reproduction is still ruinously expensive, dogged her footsteps throughout her life, and has been a principal concern of mine since I first became acquainted with her work, in connection with the exhibit she had assembled at the Institute of Child Psychology for the World Congress on Mental Health, in London in 1948.

One of her great contributions was what she called "objective tests" – forms of communication in which the patient or subject, child or adult, would make something out of standardised materials, which was unique, repeatable, and which stood alone to be displayed, realised, analysed over and over again by the same or different investigators or collaborators. But the finished product alone – a set of mosaic designs, or a set of re-produced worlds – even if well reproduced, was only half the story. None of these instruments that she devised were actually meant to be more than half the record; the rest was the participation of the therapist or tester in the process of making a world or many worlds, or making a mosaic design. So *The Lowenfeld Mosaic Test*, which presented a set of finished designs, classified into types, told the waiting world, initially stimulated by some public presentation or private consultation with Margaret Lowenfeld, very little.

It has taken almost twenty years of active experimentation with methods of recording the process as well as the finished product, to devise a method of showing the process in the making of mosaics and the ways of linking the process and the finished designs to other aspects of culture, as has been done in Monserrat in the work of Rhoda Metraux and Theodora Abel, among the Manus by Lenora Foerstal, and by Rhoda Metraux among the Iatmul.

Communicating the possibilities inherent in the Worlds was even more difficult. Students from distant places came to England to study with Margaret Lowenfeld and went home to their own countries to reproduce the World cabinet of miniatures from real life, in local forms. The shape and proportions of the tray changed, or children were permitted to take home one miniature as a present from each session, and the cabinet became depleted! But how to represent the Worlds themselves? We tried photo-graphy, but the result often looked like a box of toys dumped indiscrimin-ately in a sand pile, instead of what it really was – a representation of the way in which the child was coming to grips with relating inner perceptions, proprioceptive intuitions with the realities of the external world. We tried paintings, which combined with the protocols of process and gave a better rendering of the world-making experience, but added the complications of introducing an artist into the recording of a process for scientific purposes. And Margaret Lowenfeld, trained in the rigors of the physical and biological sciences was acutely aware of the importance of non-interpreta-tive faithful and unadorned reporting. Finally, the method of presentation used in this book was developed by Enid Kotschnig. When colored reproduction becomes economically viable, they may perhaps replace this more schematic representation.

But for the present, we have the chapters prepared by Margaret Lowenfeld herself, representations she approved, and an attempt by her students, collaborators, successors and colleagues to put those chapters into a perspective; we have the introduction which represents selections from her lectures and papers over a long period of time, special material provided by Ville Andersen, editing by John Hood Williams, and my own deep appreciation and enthusiasm for her work.

She was a vital part of an emerging new world of understanding of individual human thought processes, their implications for particular troubled human beings and a troubled global population – caught between two worlds, "one dead, one powerless to be born." By understanding and using the tools she developed, we can experience, and so partake of her insights, and go on from there.

Margaret Mead
The American Museum of Natural History
New York, New York
March 4, 1977

References

Bonaparte, Marie F. *The Life and Works of Edgar Allan Poe:* A Psychoanalitic Interpretation. London: Imago Publications, 1949.

Cobb, Edith. *The Ecology of Imagination in Childhood.* New York: Columbia University Press, in press.

Erikson, Erik H. *Childhood and Society,* 2d rev. ed. New York: Norton, 1964. (First published in 1950.)

Foerstal, Lenore. "Cultural Influence on Perception," *Studies in the Anthropology of Visual Perception,* in press.

Gesell, Arnold and Frances Ilg. *Infant and Child in the Culture of Today.* New York: Harper, 1943.

Gorer, Geoffrey and John Rickman. *The People of Great Russia.* New York: Norton, 1962. (First published in 1949).

Isaacs, Susan, *Intellectual Growth in Young Children.* New York: Harcourt Brace, 1931.

Klein, Melanie. *Contributions to Psycho-Analysis,* 1921–1945. London: Hogarth, 1948.

Lowenfeld, Margaret. *The Lowenfeld Mosaic Test.* London: Newman Neame, 1954.

Mead, Margaret. "Some Relationships between Social Anthropology and Psychiatry." In *Dynamic Psychiatry,* Franz Alexander and Helen Ross, eds. Chicago: University of Chicago Press, 1952. 401–448.

Mead, Margaret. "Cultural Determinants of Behavior." In *Behavior and Evolution,* Ann Roe and George G. Simpson, eds. New Haven: Yale University Press, 1958, pp. 480–503.

Mead, Margaret and Rhoda Metraux. *Themes in a French Culture: A Preface to a Study of French Community.* ("Hoover Institute Studies," Ser. D, Communities No. 1.) Stanford: Stanford University Press, 1954.

Mead, Margaret and Martha Wolfenstein, Eds. *Childhood in Contemporary Cultures.* Chicago: University of Chicago Press, 1955

Metraux, Rhoda. "Eidos and Change: Continuity in Process, Discontinuity in Product." In *Socialization as Cultural Communication*, Theodore Schwartz, ed. Berkeley: University of California Press, 1976, pp. 201–216.

Metraux, Rhoda and Theodora Abel. "Normal and Deviant Behavior in a Peasant Community," *American Journal of Orthopsychiatry*, 27, No. 1, (1957), 167–184.

Metraux, Rhoda and Theodora Abel. *Culture and Psychotherapy.* New Haven: College and University Press, 1975.

Piaget, Jean. *Language and Thought of the Child.* Cleveland: World Publishing, 1960. (First published in 1926.)

Piaget, Jean, *The Grasp of Consciousness: Action and Concept in the Young Child.* Cambridge: Harvard University Press, 1976.

Sharpe, Ella F. *Collected Papers on Psychoanalysis.* Marjorie Brierley, ed. London: Hogarth Press and the Institute of Psychoanalysis, 1950.

Tanner, J. M. and B. Inhelder, eds. *Discussions on Child Development*, 4 Vols. New York: International Universities Press, 1957–1960.

Soddy, Kenneth, ed. *Mental Health and Infant Development*, 2 Vols. New York: Basic Books, 1955.

Winnicot, Donald W. *The Family and Individual Development.* New York: Basic Books, 1965.

Wolfenstein, Martha. "Analysis of a Juvenile Poem", *The Psychoanalytic Study of the Child*, Vol 11 (1956), pp. 450–472.

Wolfenstein, Martha. *Children's Humor: A Psychological Analysis.* Glencoe, Illinois: Free Press, 1956.

Wolfenstein, Martha and Nathan Leites. *The Movies: A Psychological Study.* Glencoe, Ill.: Free Press, 1950.

Historical Note on the Manuscript

In the autumn of 1956 Dr. Margaret Lowenfeld received a grant, procured by Dr. Margaret Mead, from the Bollingen Foundation, New York, to enable her to write a book on the Lowenfeld World Technique. The work began that autumn and stretched over some three years, as it could only be accomplished in her spare time. The first part of the book was completed by 1959, but for certain reasons it was never published. The manuscript remained in my care as I hoped an opportunity might arise for publication of the three cases, dealing with children under treatment and followed by the chapter "On the Subjective Making of a World". Till now no detailed description showing Dr. Lowenfeld herself at work with Worlds has been available.

I was fortunate to assist Dr. Lowenfeld in this work, my main part being to collect and sort the material, check her writings in regard to references, numbers, etc. But the by far most interesting task I undertook was to try to find out how and when the "World" arose and was recognised as a psychotherapeutic tool.

On October the 28th 1928 Dr. Lowenfeld opened a "Clinic for Nervous and Difficult Children" at 12 Telford Road, London W.10, a district with small shops and identical brick houses mostly occupied by industrial workers. A printed leaflet was circulated to the local shops and pasted in the windows of the Clinic. One copy of the original leaflet was found, and it is reproduced overleaf.

Playroom equipment consisted of two tables and five chairs, some toys such as plasticine, building bricks, coloured paper, bead-mosaics, stencils, dolls, puzzles, crayons and paints, painting books, a bowl of water with rubber toys. At admission a careful case history was taken. During attendance at the Clinic detailed playroom reports were made and all was put together in very well designed case sheets, one for each child. Those early case sheets were still available for study and examination, and after careful research into that material I wrote a report, the relevant part of which will be found on pages 277–281.

During the time of producing the manuscript for the World book in the late 1950s we were fortunate to have the American artist, Miss Enid Kotschnig, with us. She had herself made a series of Worlds and was therefore familiar with the material. In regard to the illustrations of the following cases she developed a very ingenious technique of presenting the serial Worlds in a simple, stylised way as described by Dr. Lowenfeld in Case 1. Only three of the Worlds in Case 3 are drawn in perspective. As the procedure at a therapeutic session is to draw a sketch of the World in the child's presence and to have these sketches filed in the case sheets, it was possible for Miss Kotschnig to draw the simple Worlds straight from them; more complicated Worlds were set up

CLINIC

FOR

NERVOUS AND DIFFICULT

CHILDREN

12 Telford Road, Ladbroke Grove, W.10

('Bus No. 15 or 52 down Ladbroke Grove, or 'Bus 18 or 46
down Harrow Road to Ladbroke Grove.)

All children are difficult sometimes, but
Some children are difficult all the time.

Some children seem always to be catching
something and never to be quite well.

Some children are nervous and find life
and school too difficult for them.

Some children have distressing habits.

This Clinic, which is in charge of a
Physician, exists to help mothers in these
kinds of trouble with their children, and
also to help the children themselves.

TUESDAYS   THURSDAYS
10 a.m.   2 p.m.

NO LETTER NECESSARY.

again before being drawn.

The cases of Charles Robinson (2) and William Carter (3) were written before Case 1, Mary Smith. In her comments on Mary Smith's Worlds (section, Symbols for E) Dr. Lowenfeld suggests that the analysis of Charles' series of Worlds be read first. In Case 2 (section, Techniques of treatment) Dr. Lowenfeld explains why she wanted only Worlds illustrated for the book.

As the four chapters were to have been part of a book, I have for this publication reviewed the material, deleted irrelevant references, etc., so Dr. Lowenfeld's descriptions of the cases can stand on their own with due reference to the Appendices.

Ville Andersen
Denmark, Fulden 8330 Beder.

Introduction

For many years I have had as my goal the achievement of an approach to the child's mind which shall be both objective in itself and susceptible of record. I have desired to become able to review freshly the whole question of the child's mental and emotional nature and its development, and to bring to light such manifestations of their nature as will carry their own conviction and be themselves grounds for further study.

I wish to put before you some of the results I have obtained. These form part of a considered point of view about the nature of the mind, a point of view which embodies particular pieces of apparatus and their use, and certain deductions drawn from the material produced by children with this apparatus as to the structure of the mind in childhood.

Shortly following the close of the European War of 1914–18 and while the Russo-Polish War still continued, I went with a Typhus Mission to Eastern Europe. Some discrepancies then existing in the nationality laws of this country and of Poland enabled me for a time to function in two ways: – as a medical member of certain missions of help to the East and also as a landowning citizen of the new state of Poland. This dual identity brought with it certain consequences.

My work when in khaki was to assist in sanitary provisions for Prisoners of War Camps, and in the welfare side of work for troops on a four hundred mile front. To this was later added a share in the attempt to feed and clothe many thousands of demobilised Polish students. The 1917 revolution in Russia was only three years behind us and the consequences still flooded the country.

On the other side, once out of khaki and in a different part of the country, one was a powerless and indistinguishable unit of a disintegrated countryside. In this district typhoid, dysentery, cholera, tuberculosis and epidemic influenza raged, with no medical stores. The larger number of the population had the waxy transparency of famine, fuel was short and transport almost non-existent.

Taking the two together was like being at the same time a haunted man and the ghost that haunts him. To this later, was added a third identity by a period in what would now be termed, "the underground", an "underground" of social rather than political activity.

The reason why I trouble you with this experience is that it posed neatly two problems which are problems which face us today. The living of several distinct mutually incompatible lives did for me what the preliminary analysis does for the therapist-to-be, that is, it opened doors on to an interior world I would not otherwise have reached. Later when reflecting upon this experience, I realised that the living of rôles totally different from and even hostile to each other, in a constant atmosphere of fear, and with a lack of any overall direction is of the essence of the

1

experience of unhappy children and the black misery of prisoners of war is very like the depressions of infancy.

This experience led later to a direct understanding of certain aspects of the inner life of children but simultaneously certain other aspects of it posed two definite problems. The first was the fact that contrary to all expectations, certain children and young adults, deprived of everything that psychiatry considers essential to health and development, nevertheless grew into vigorous and creative people. The second was the query as to what exactly was taking place in individuals who carried out the type of actions which words like Ausschwitz and Ravensbrück have since made too familiar to us.

This period was followed by a time occupied in strenuous four-language interpretation which left me profoundly sceptical as to the possibilities of language as a tool of inter-personal understanding.

The obvious course of action was to seek for the answer in psychiatry; but although personally gaining much from two analyses, they brought no answer to these questions and even more surprisingly, I found that it was impossible to convey in analysis the essence of the experiences out of which the queries grew. Either, therefore, the enquiry had to be abandoned, or some other mode of attack on the problem had to be found. Choosing the latter course, it was while getting training in clinical research methods that the clue to this different approach appeared.

I began to notice in the faces and bodies of the children I was studying, expressions, postures and gestures that resembled those with which I had become familiar in prison camps and famine areas. Language I had already discarded as too uncertain a tool; the manipulation of relationships seemed irrelevant to problems whose essence was the absence of relationships. It then occurred to me to wonder if anything could be done with objects instead of persons, and whether it would not be possible to devise a scientific experiment where one could represent to children by means of small objects what one guessed they might be undergoing.

Taking courage therefore, I set out to try acting before children with objects, what I conceived that they might be experiencing, and with immediate result. The children understood at once and responded with a naturalness that has persisted throughout the investigation. With this experiment a door came open and I found the children and myself in contact with one another.

Now it is perfectly clear that children have played since the beginning of time and archaeological diggings show us that every civilisation has provided toys for their use.

The loving care expended upon these toys in all human groups shows that grown-up human beings since the beginning of historical times have understood that the way to make contact with a child and to understand his way of thought is to play with him.

2

Play in childhood is a function of childhood. Toys to children are like culinary implements to the kitchen; every kitchen has them and has also the elements of food. It is what the cook does with these implements and elements that determines the dish.

The child psycho-analyst uses toys as a means of gaining contact with the child's mind in order that that mind may be dealt with on lines indicated by psycho-analytic theory: the child's use of toys is interpreted symbolically in harmony with that theory. Now without entering at all into the question of the validity of psycho-analytic thought, which is far from my purpose, I wish to point out as clearly as I am able, that this is a totally different dish from that which I aim to cook with approximately the same materials.

We both use toys, as does everyone who plays with children, or children who play alone. My own endeavour in my work with children is to devise an instrument with which a child can demonstrate his own emotional and mental state without the necessary intervention of an adult either by transference or interpretation, and which will allow of a record being made of such a demonstration. My objective is to help children to produce something which will stand by itself and be independent of any theory as to its nature.

My own approach to the use of a toy apparatus with children derives from a memory of H. G. Wells' *Floor Games*, the first edition of which had made a deep impression upon my youth. When, therefore, in 1925, I came from orthodox paediatrics to the associated study of emotional conditions in childhood, I began to put this memory to use. I collected first a miscellaneous mass of material, coloured sticks and shapes, beads, small toys of all sorts, paper shapes and match boxes, and kept them in what came to be known by my children as the "Wonder Box"; with this I began to experiment with my children patients.

My approach to the work was that of a clinician, and my aim was to endeavour to devise a method by which direct contact could be made, without interference from the adult, with the mental and emotional life of a child. I set myself as a goal to work out an apparatus which would put into the child's hand a means of directly expressing his ideas and emotions, one which would allow of the recording of his creations and of abstracting them for study. I had at that date no theory of the mind and was determined to avoid making or accepting one until I should have achieved objective records from which a theory could be built or checked.

The central task of psychotherapy is that of making contact with the whole of the patient's mind, not only by intuition but by direct and conscious knowledge and understanding of the laws of mind.

There are certain points about the nature of children's thought that make this task particularly difficult. A child does not think linearly as the adult is capable of doing: thought, feeling, sensations, concept and memory are all inextricably interwoven. A child's thought is fluid and movement can take place on several planes at once. A child's feeling is absolute in that any emotion, while it is present, holds the whole field of consciousness. Finally, a child's concepts have no relation to what we call in our view of the world, external reality.

An apparatus, therefore, which will give a child power to express his ideas and feelings, must be independent of knowledge or skill, must be capable of the representation of thought simultaneously in several planes at once, must allow of representation of movement and yet be sufficiently circumscribed to make a complete whole, must combine elements of touch and sensation, as well as of sight, and be entirely free from a necessary relation to reality.

Another aspect of the necessity for some such apparatus is that not only child psychotherapy but psychotherapy and psychopathology as a whole suffer from a difficulty not now shared by any other branch of medicine, in that it is impossible to abstract clinical material for independent consideration apart from the circumstances in which it is produced.

We cannot examine the mental and emotional products of other physicians' patients without first understanding in full the psychotherapeutic hypotheses upon which the treatment has been based, and secondly having, by courtesy of the physician, access to the whole of the case notes of the patient. Even then, the personality of the physician must be taken into account in evaluating the facts, since what is available even in these ideal conditions is not the material produced by the patient himself, but this material seen through the eyes of the physician.

Physical science has progressed in strict accord with the development of possibilities of precise investigation and direct record of the facts observed, and their abstraction for study from the circumstances of production.

The dish therefore that I wish to cook with our common implements is one in which all these elements are present and which can be used, if you wish it, as check or proof of any system of psychotherapy, but which, although it is the source from which my own theory of child psychotherapy has been drawn, is independent of it as of other theories.

This apparatus I have called "The World" from the feeling the children have about it. It came into existence in 1929 and has been in constant use since that date both in the Institute of Child Psychology and in my private work. Children of all ages from 4 to late adolescence have worked with it, suffering from complaints including somatic disorders, educational difficulties, personality deviations and social maladjustments.

The equipment for the World Technique is a metal tray approximately $75 \times 50 \times 7$ centimetres, half-filled with sand, for use on tables of differing heights according to the size of the children using them; water should be near at hand; implements for use with the sand such as shovels, funnels, moulds, a sieve; amorphous materials such as plasticine, wooden slats, rubber tubes, tins and oddments of any kind. Nearby there must be a cabinet with drawers containing miniature objects of the following kinds:

Living creatures: ordinary men, women and children; soldiers; entertainers; people of other races; wild and domestic animals.
Phantasy and Folk-lore: figures; animals, including prehistoric and "space" specimens.
Scenery: buildings of any kind, trees, bushes, flowers, fences, gates and bridges.
Transport: for road, rail, sea and air.
Equipment: for road, town, farms and gardens, playground and fairs, hospital, school, etc.
Miscellaneous objects: which may be anything at any time obtainable in shops.

This apparatus has proved as valuable in psychotherapeutic work with adults as with children, and is welcomed by adult patients as an aid to their understanding of themselves and to communication with their therapist.

Children are introduced to the World apparatus in the following way.

It is explained in simple words that there is a gap between a child's world and that of the adults of his environment, and thus a lack of mutual understanding. This leads to a short talk about "Picture Thinking" in which it is pointed out that children have many ideas and experiences "in their heads" which won't go into words and which nobody seems to talk about. Further, that many things are more easily "said" in pictures and in actions than in words ("comics" and advertisements are used as examples). It is explained to the child that this is a natural way of "thinking" and that this is what we would like him to do for us here, and that the work to be undertaken will make a bridge between two worlds – that of the child and that of the adults.

The World apparatus is then introduced and the child invited to make "whatever comes into his head".

When used with adults this introduction is modified into a general discussion of modes of symbolic representation in art, literature, advertisement and satirical cartoons.

Once started on the work, introduction becomes superfluous; the interest of the creation itself is its own explanation.

In the ordinary course of treatment, children use this apparatus as but one among many other possible activities. Sometimes they act, sometimes they play, sometimes they recount dreams or paint, write stories or recount phantasies that come into their heads. The "World" takes its place among other pieces of apparatus and forms of expression as a clinical instrument used in the process of treatment and study of the child, but upon which the whole burden of treatment does not rest.

Some children keep up a running commentary on their work as they do it; some invoke the help of the physician with them throughout; some work absorbedly at their "Worlds" in silence till they are completed and

5

seem oblivious of the presence of any other person.

Some children take immediately to this form of expression and hail it with delight, saying, as did one very verbal boy of 14, "I never expected this to be like that! One really can express oneself in that – it's all living – just like we are". Some come to it later, while some children after the first day do not use it at all.

To get any value out of the material the user must find his way to an understanding of the possibilities of the material and gradually come to "find himself" in the medium, if it is to yield a really rich harvest. Careful record, therefore, of exactly what is done by each child at each use of the world material is very important, and this record must contain the maker's own description of it and his reaction to it, both in detail and as a whole. The record should be made at the time by the worker in co-operation with the child, a diagram being made of the "World", each item in it being carefully noted.

As soon as any observer sets out to make such a record, an immediate difficulty arises. Words used in their ordinary grammatical sense and construction do not always express what has been created, something new is needed. To meet this need a series of terms have been invented, such as "a going-alongness" to describe worlds in which rail, road, and river transport are combined together on a track in the tray, which at one time is said by the maker to be a road and at another a river.

Children use this apparatus in a very large number of different ways, and the main characteristic of their use, once the first strangeness of the material has worn off, is its unexpectedness. No object, therefore, and no arrangement of objects, should be taken at its face value, but careful inquiry made of the child as to what exactly each object in the world is to be recorded as being. It is essential for the proper understanding of the nature and use of this technique that no interpretation be given by the therapist to the child. The purpose is to explore the as yet insufficiently known aspects of a child's inner experience. This can only be done through careful adherence to and study of the meanings and the connections that the child himself has made.

To achieve this end, however, it is essential that certain conditions be observed, namely:

1. A deep tray must be used as the basis of the apparatus.
2. It must be waist high to the individual, so that the "world" can be made in it with his hands.
3. There must be an ample supply of sand and water, so that the maker may model any type of contour, and place objects anywhere in or on this sandy base.
4. There must be a wide supply of objects in ample number, including many of each kind.
5. Understanding of any but the most superficial layers of the child's thought cannot be obtained from a first world, except in the case of mentally deficient or very seriously disturbed children.

One word now as to my own handling of "World" material.

It is perfectly clear that, confronted with this material, any one who wills will be able to read into these "World" representations components derived from his personal conviction, and that not merely as a result of wish fulfilment, but because they are almost certainly to be present there. A psychoanalyst will find sexual themes, sometimes overtly, sometimes symbolically represented there, for the reason that sexuality does play a part in a child's "World" picture. The Adlerian will undoubtedly find the power complex and its derivatives represented in this hyponoic language. The "World" apparatus should appeal to the heart of the Jungian, seeing that the "World" cabinet is richly furnished with already completed archetype symbols.

My own direct use of the material in the presence of the child is to treat it like a cipher language, and concentrate my attention on an endeavour to discover what exactly the objects used represent to *the child who uses them*. Thus I explain to each child that a horse for example may be to one child a representation of a thing it fears, to another its dearest friend, to a third, as one said, "A strong thing which runs", to another "What Daddy rides", and so on; and then we imagine I am a South Sea Islander having never seen Europe and the child explains to me what each object actually is, that is, is to him.

Having drawn the "World" we then substitute in it the *qualities and concepts the child has given*. When these are reassembled together the result is a picture of affect, concept, memory and experience inextricably woven together into the presentation of a total state.

The uses to which children put this material range from photographically accurate transcripts of known scenes of ordinary life through every possible modification of this, to the most complex and interwoven incoherence. I am going here to give some indication of these varieties.

With enough experience with the Worlds we can divide them into categories.

The first group are the *realistic or representational Worlds*, complete or incomplete.

A Complete Representational World is a realistic reproduction of a known or imagined world. The purpose of the child is to present certain scenes with such realism as the material available will permit. In a world of this kind every detail is of considerable importance; everything is practical and objective. See figure 1, page 8.

This world was built by a boy of 11. It represents a scene in a town. Everything is shown as it would be in real life. Street traffic, a railway station on the left and a house on the right. The world is composed very cleverly and makes a colourful and lively impression.

An Incomplete Representational World is the result of an attempt by the child to create something real. If the scene is discussed with the child in

7

Figure 1

detail, the child notices that it has not succeeded in achieving complete reality. Parts of the picture remain unreal.

A second group is formed by the Worlds in which *real objects are put together in an unreal fashion*. The child has no clear idea of what it is building before the work is finished. When the work is finished, the child experiences a feeling of completion, gives a sigh of relief and calls out, "I have finished". It cannot explain what it has done; it is satisfied but cannot say why. See figure 2.

This world was made by a schoolboy of 13, who was sent to me on account of a phobia. When he had finished, he said, "I don't know what it means, but I feel that it has to be like this".

In front is a round hill, with a small valley in the centre. There is a house in the valley and a man, instead of sitting in the house, sits on the roof. Other houses are put on the hill, some the right way up, some with the roof in the sand and the foundations uppermost. Traffic is crossing the roofs; people are jumping from car to car; everything is moving in the

Figure 2

same direction.

The circle of houses has an entrance, not on the left, where there is a projection, but on the right. In the centre of the entrance a man is stuck into the sand by his head and an ambulance is running over him.

Both in the foreground and in the background a man is being run over by a car.

A further group can be called "*Demonstration of a Phantasy*". Here the most important thing is the phantasy by which the child is governed while it is working. See figure 3, page 10.

This world was made by a girl aged 17. She had studied music on the continent but was sent back to England owing to improper behaviour. The World represents a day in the life of the snake. One picture shows the snake surrounded by important people, singing into a microphone. On top, a committee is debating the snake's birthday present; on the right, a tortoise has invited his musical friends. Above this scene the snake is seen going home past a wood where the Horror lives.

Figure 3

THE COMMITTEE
DEBATING THE
SNAKE'S BIRTHDAY
- PRESENT -

THE HORROR
IN THE WOOD

THE SNAKE
GOES HOME

IMPORTANT PEOPLE
LISTEN TO THE
SNAKE SINGING INTO
THE MICROPHONE

THE TORTOISE
IS AT HOME TO
HIS MUSICAL
- FRIENDS -

A fourth group is formed of worlds of a *Mixed Type*. Children with a confused intellectual or emotional life or children of sub-average intelligence, tend to make worlds combining all the three types described. In such cases the tray can be divided into various sections, each of which shows a different scene. The various scenes correspond to various layers of the intellectual and emotional life of the child.

Figure 4 is an illustration of such a World.

This world was made by a boy of 18 during the third consultation.

On the left we have a village with a pond and a river. Everything is normal and straightforward. But on the right we have a war. There is a square, guns being fired on three sides. In the background we can see military aircraft and in the foreground dead horses, a dead man and a broken tree.

When I asked the patient whether he saw or felt an enemy, he said, "No" – he did not have the feeling that there was an enemy. The dead figures in the foreground were purely the result of the guns.

Figure 4

When I asked him whether the village people knew that a war was going on, he said, "No, they don't know and don't feel it either. Neither do the soldiers know that the village exists".

Children of low intelligence, very young children and those under great pressure use unrelated material. They take pieces out of the World cabinet at random and put them down anywhere without any relation between one piece and another. A few neurotic children display a tendency during treatment to give their worlds a certain degree of composition. In such cases the later worlds show a clue to the nature of the first apparently disjointed worlds.

The time taken on the construction of a world may be 20 minutes or 2 to 3 hours. "Worlds" may be unitary and stationary in that the whole afternoon may be given up to the elaboration of a single scene; they may be vivid and moving suggesting a cinema film more than anything else for the rapidity of movement. The "Worlds" of many weeks may show a continuous story, each successive afternoon's work being the development and continuation of the previous one.

There remains to be considered the central question which may perhaps be stated thus: Of what nature is the thought depicted in "Worlds"? The first question concerning this material that clearly needs an answer is, "is it possible, with such an objective, non-relationship approach to children to reach any but the more superficial layers of the psyche"?

Children's material is too diffuse for this question to be answered economically. I propose, therefore, to take for this point, material from two young adults which are presentations of the body scheme.

11

*Illustration lost**

This is a spontaneous drawing made during treatment by a young woman suffering from multiple phobias, and represents herself as she felt herself to be.

Here, the place of eyes in the face is taken by one breast and one buttock, a penis replaces the nose and the mouth is a worm. Further down, squinting eyes appear where the breasts should be, a small mouth replaces the umbilicus while a relatively normal face, lacking an upper lip and with massive teeth appears lowering in the lower abdomen. A kettle replaces one foot and a pail the other. For arms appear sticks producing noise, said by the patient to be "perpetually in action".

Illustration lost

Actually drawn earlier, this drawing shows the impact of noise on the patient. The parts of the body are in normal position, but grossly distorted. In the abdomen is a window with curtains, and entering the ears are every possible kind of noise. The black spot on the cheek is putrefaction.

This patient is now a successful and cheerful young woman responsible for the work of her household and leading a vivid social life.

Illustration lost

Here is a drawing of a World made by a young man suffering from a devasting sense of inability to make use of his excellent abilities.

You will see that this World is at one and the same time, a queer shaped island in an inland sea with gun boats about and also a human body. The eyes are on antennae and from the collection of houses on the base of the neck,steps go down to a tunnel, which leads through the head and out at the left ear. The right ear is absent. The left axilla is also a harbour and collections of houses with paths between them appear at different places on the body. The maker said the face was semi-sentient and was the religious centre of the island people. In this World, the patient expressed his feeling of hardly being a person at all, but instead, something other people overran.

During the war, this patient rose from a humble position to charge of the administration of an important section of our war organisation.

The question that next arises is of the possibilities this material offers for the representation of emotion. See figure 5.

This is a painting of a World done by a boy with asthma. You will note the appalling position of the figure on the ground, as the focus of fierce animals and that three of the other animals have a human figure to maul

---

*Editor's note: this and the next two illustrations have been lost, but the text is retained since it is not too difficult to reconstruct in imagination the two drawings and the World that are described.

12

Figure 5

and devour.

This illustration may give you some idea of the capacity of the material to depict emotion.

The essential feature of the conditions for which psychotherapy is sought by or for a patient, is a state of distress which the patient is unable to understand, to control, or to communicate. While, therefore, evaluation of the nature of the patient plays an important part in the preliminary stages, it is communication which forms the essence of therapy; communication of unknown aspects of the patient to himself and to the therapist, and explanation from the therapist to the patient of what is revealed. It is as an agent of communication that the World apparatus plays its invaluable part in the process of psychotherapy. Patients, whether children or adults, feel that with these tools expression can be given to states of being and happenings within the psyche which they find impossible to express in any other way.

I would like to consider what are the qualities of the World apparatus from which its power of expression derives.

1. Its Multi-dimensional Nature

We are all aware of the fact that many processes – and often processes at variance with one another – take place simultaneously within us. If these are to be expressed in words, or even in drama, descriptions of one aspect must *follow* another and their interactions cannot be presented.

Not only is this true, but processes occurring within the psyche take place at different levels, are of different orders of significance, and often appear to cancel each other out.

The World apparatus, with the range of possibilities offered by its mouldable sand, amorphous objects and World cabinet, makes possible the simultaneous presentation, within a single framework, of processes and concepts going on at different levels in the psyche and consisting of differing elements.

2. The Dynamic Possibilities it Offers

Worlds can be static or dynamic and it is this second possibility which is of such value with children. The life of a child, both externally and interiorly, is one of action. Their own experiences and those of the constituents of the world around them are seen by children as stories: stories which can be endlessly repeated or varied and whose endings on one occasion, even if this ending be total destruction of all constituents, have no effect upon the next beginning. These can be directly represented in the World tray, played out, analysed with the therapist, and the contents realised as they appear in endless repetitions.

3. The Power of the Apparatus to Present States of Mind Hitherto Unknown

All schools of psychological thought agree about the importance of the pre-verbal stages of interior development, and also as to the great difficulty of arriving at an understanding of their nature and content. With the World apparatus states of being of the greatest complexity and processes of perception and of phantasy of the highest degree of unexpectedness and confusion can be, and are, directly presented.

4. Its Independence of Skill

While, at times, young adolescents make constructions in the World tray which display a very considerable degree of manual skill, for the most part the fact that no technical ability of any kind is demanded for the making of a World constitutes a strong appeal. Anything in a World cabinet can be utilised to represent anything else and plasticine used to supply what is missing.

I would submit that we have here in this material achieved the first of our tasks, in that we have now an access to the direct register of precognitive thought in the child which can be treated like any other laboratory scientific material.

I should like to present some of the principles of mental life which I have come to formulate as a result of many years study of material such as I have been endeavouring to demonstrate, and which have formed the experimental basis of not too unsuccessful psychotherapy.

We are accustomed to thinking of the mind as consisting of two parts, the conscious and the unconscious. Let us for a moment see what these terms mean and how they came about.

Freud, starting his work and confronted by a human being, took for examination what he saw, the conscious mind, taken at that time as being co-terminus with mind. As he worked however, another structure began to appear which appeared to have none of the qualities of conscious mind and of which the conscious mind was unaware. It was inevitable and fitting that the term unconscious should be applied to this emergent force. This was found to be at its strongest in childhood.

But if we now turn the medal round and instead of beginning with the conscious, that is, by being confronted by the adult in whom consciousness and cognition are fully developed, and in whom one looks backwards to the unconscious, we start with the infant in whom cognitive faculties are not yet developed, and look forward to cognition, then the reverse of the picture arises. The strange part of the mind, the phantasy part, is what confronts us. This is now the norm, and the problem before us now is: "How and why does the cognitive system arise"?

In making his Worlds the child is quite clearly aware of a great deal of what he expresses, but is unable to explain its meaning in words. This thought can not be equated, therefore, with the unconscious of adult life, and to call it unconscious is misleading. Also, clearly, as the conscious or cognitive part in young children is so little developed, it is difficult to see how this can arise by repression out of the consciousness. Psychoanalysis has met this difficulty by calling it the Id, but that is only to dress it up in fancy dress and give the wearer an identity disc. To do so does not explain the underlying process. It is the task of science to examine its material and to examine it upon lines not of an ideology which is self-contained and peculiar to itself, but upon that which holds current in the world outside the dogma.

Once we allow ourselves to move into an ideology which is individual to its subject and has no affinities in the cognate branches of knowledge, we are off the earth and anything is possible, even elaborate cannibalistic phantasies in the recently born.

I suggest therefore that the terms conscious and unconscious are, in these circumstances, misleading – particularly since consciousness, as Spearman has emphasised, is closely bound up with speech and the child has no speech when it begins its mental life. If there is anything at all that our material has shown and shown conclusively, it is that to call a thing not conscious, i.e., outside the individual's awareness, because it is nonverbal, is an abuse of terms.

I wish to propose that we get rid of this difficulty, which is a linguistic one, and substitute the terms Primary and Secondary Mental System for unconscious and conscious functioning.

The Primary System of thought then, describes all mental functioning between the age of 0 and the age when cognitive processes occupy a normal part of the mental field. The Secondary System of thought describes all thought that can be expressed in prose.

The name, Primary System, has been given, since it is a systematised region of the psyche, appears first, and remains for life in the core of the psyche.

Having arrived at this point our next task is to examine the nature of this Primary System.

To make the matter clearer, a parable is set out, the form of which is drawn from Worlds children themselves made.

When we were children, many of us delighted in reading that mixture of fairy story and children's tale in which there was a garden surrounded by a wall, which all the grownups took as being really the end of the garden, but which, at a specially exciting moment in the story, the children of the house found to conceal among the bushes, which grew close up to the wall, a secret door. This door, opened only at midnight, led to a garden of delights, unsuspected by the grownups and peopled with fairies and wise or prankish gnomes. This story has many forms; sometimes it is under the sea, sometimes on an island out at sea, sometimes in a lost valley in the hills. But the essence of the story is the same; the finding of a country near to home but with rules of life within it which are magical and different altogether from those which obtain at home. There are also terrible things in this garden, ogres and man-eating giants and wizards and spells; but in the end it is only the wicked who are consumed, or the careless. If one knows the rules of life in that country, it is exciting and virile, and from it the traveller brings back treasures of gold and jewels.

It is clear that there are many ways in which these stories can be regarded, and Jung and Freud have thrown a great deal of light on them, but here they will be taken quite simply as they stand, and studied in almost a literal fashion so that they may assist the understanding of what we are calling the Primary System.

For instance, there are always certain constant characteristics about these stories. There is always a key to that garden, and the key is difficult to find and to many people altogether invisible; great efforts are called for from those who are bold enough to take the key and open the door, before they can enjoy the freedom of the secret kingdom, and of the strange things that are in it. Within that garden, or that kingdom, there are dangers also, and tests and struggles, and not all come back again. Some die, some lose their way back; perhaps these become some of those people we call insane, who never find their way back again. There are people who, having been once inside, are frightened and spend the rest of their lives denying there is any such kingdom at all; and there are some, like the painter Chagall, and James Joyce and the poet Blake, who live equally on both sides of the wall, and come and go at will; though people find them strange, they do not call them mad.

Two characteristics of that fable must now be considered, which differentiate it in important ways from the concept (either psychoanalytic or of analytical psychology) of the unconscious.

First of all, it is quite a well-defined region, and a wall separates it from the home garden. The rules of conduct and the type of event that occurs on one side of the wall are different from those on the other side. What is to be expected in one garden does not happen in the other, and in the magic garden almost anything may come about. This is not strange, because the idea of the fable has been arrived at directly from study of the actual productions many children have made with the tools supplied to them.

The second important fact about the garden is that though to some extent is looks like the outside world, there is in it neither time nor space. It is this timelessness, and this quality of being able to be at the same time in two places which may actually be far apart, that has given rise to the legends and fairy tales of Rip Van Winkle, the Magic Carpets, Seven League Boots, the little figures that suddenly grow tall as in "Alice in Wonderland", and much of the paraphernalia of fairyland.

We need to ask ourselves, therefore, how is this garden constructed, and what do these strange features mean?

Now it is very difficult to understand this directly; it is too peculiar, and those who are not poets and artists have left it too far behind and grown into too different another world to be able to regain contact with it easily. Some artists keep a dim consciousness of it, and the work of the painter Chagall may be taken to help us in building a bridge.

It is characteristic of Chagall to paint pictures in which figures and objects appear without apparent relation to one another and without the normal relation to gravity. His method of grouping these and his skill in colouring are so aesthetically pleasing that his pictures receive a warm welcome in most countries of the world. Nevertheless, judged from a "rational" standpoint, it is difficult to understand the rules upon which he works, why he selects just those objects that appear in his pictures, or why the ones which are included in any given picture should appear together. Moreover, the size of figures and objects and the place in the picture they occupy seem, judged from the commonsense point of view, to be completely irrational. Figures are painted within other figures and in some, large heads contain whole scenes within them. From the ordinary standpoint, this is very odd. This is not surrealism, which is an attempt to represent and to evoke in the beholder by that representation certain emotional states, but something different that stands by itself. It is, in the main, the painting of the beautiful side of the strange inner region of man, so difficult to reach in adult life but which dominates the experience of children.

As a first step may be considered the way he treated common metaphor in a concrete fashion. For example, it is quite common to speak of a "horse-faced" woman. But in the picture called "Clair de Lune" (1944), Chagall paints a nude female figure in solid texture, and superimposes over the head of the figure a shadow painting of a horse, so that in literal fact the central figure in his picture is both woman and horse.

Figure 6

This is a drawing made by a young woman patient who wished to express early confusion of thoughts about certain aspects of bodies. It is a commonplace of psychoanalytic experience that the teapot with its projecting spout and the breastlike formation of its lid can stand in symbolic fashion for the combination of male and female sexual characteristics. It is also one of the characteristics of the early confusions and identities of the Primary System that the parts of the body which contain orifices into which and from within which substances come and go, stand for and are identified with one another, the head becoming in this way confused with the excretory end of the trunk. This particular patient wished to express a concept into which these ideas had coalesced, and to combine the resultant mass with the idea of struggle for possession of the total qualities conceived of as existing both in the head and in the male and female genitalia.

It will be seen that so complex a conception is impossible to express in words, just as the complex of ideas and feelings behind the impulse to superimpose a horse upon a woman's head cannot be fully expressed in words. Both, however, can be presented in a plastic medium, if the usual concepts of "sense" and "possibility" are rejected. Chagall, being an artist, can blend his concepts into an artistically pleasing whole which has value in itself. This patient, having no artistic ability or desire to do anything but communicate something, has produced a drawing in which teapots formed parts of heads of pairs of people engaged in a struggle with each other. The teapots were of different colours, and the patient stated that each figure was dissatisfied with its particular coloured teapot and wished to change it for another's. The top hat, the cork seen from the side, and the third crude drawing indicating a cork stopping up a hole, fill out the genital significance of the drawing in a manner that will be familiar to all psychoanalysts.

Further, those who are familiar with the paintings of Chagall will remember that, as for example in the well-known painting, "Dans mon Village", Chagall makes use of the device of painting scenes within scenes, small solid individuals within parts of larger figures. In particular, in the painting entitled "La Somnabule" (1945), there appears within and painted upon the crinolone skirts of a female figure a winter village scene, the floating horizontal figure of a man with a cock's head, and a quadruped minus the front legs, and with human legs instead of its back legs. In the same picture a candelabra appears in the top right-hand corner although there is a moon below it, and a man's arm in a coat sleeve is in the region of the ear of the bridal female figure. Once again, because Chagall is an artist, the total result of these compositions is enchanting, and has brought Chagall fame in all countries in which his pictures have been exhibited. But this means only that Chagall, being an artist, has chosen to use as the material for his pictures concepts and plastic forms which many experience. These are a common possession of all human beings, but of which we are at present unaware.

Another feature of Chagall's paintings is the confusion of time and space or, to put it the other way round, the absence of the dimensions of time and space. The materials he uses appear, therefore, to be suitable for the expression of experience in which there is neither time nor space but only immediacy of experience, each experience obliterating the one before it and replacing it with itself.

Now the beauty and the harmony of Chagall's pictures, and the gulf that in that aspect separates them from the productions of patients, gives much material for thought, material which arises equally out of contemplation of the work of Blake, of Coleridge, of James Joyce, of Henry Moore or of Hieronymous Bosch. The great artist works with the same tools as our own experience could make accessible to all of us, but he produces results which are mysterious and act powerfully upon us. Where the work of our patients very often reflects fear, horror and suffering, the work of these artists, even where we cannot understand it with our intelligence, affects some other part of our being in a way peculiar to itself, often calling out responses of which we did not previously know ourselves capable.

Here lies the key to the difference between the Primary System in health and in illness, and this difference will be described in detail later on.

The fact having been established that these strange processes exist, it is now necessary to consider the questions of how they come about, what they convey, and the part these processes play in the total personality. The first idea that will occur to any worker familiar with the technique of free association is that these represent the chain of free association occurring, not in sequence as it usually does, but congested or condensed, as it were into a solid mass as indeed often occurs in psychoanalytic studies.

It will be useful, therefore, to start there and to analyse out some of these combinations. To do so we might take a hypothetical case in which a man walking down a street, undergoing emotional experiences of high significance for him, but of a type liable later to be repressed, at the same time notices idly that a woman on the opposite side of the street, wearing a red hat, is passing a pillar box of exactly the same colour. Further, as she comes toward him, she moves in front of a small front garden to the houses on the street, in which there are some Paul Crampel geraniums. The colour of these, he casually notices, is the same as that of her hat and the pillar box. These three as they come together make, as it were, a column of red topped with a hat and finished with fluffy flowers. It is possible that he would remember that experience exactly as he had experienced it; or the sight, on another occasion, of a component part of the combination would reproduce for him the other part, or even that when some chord in the accompanying emotional experience was touched, it would lead him to associate that with these, or the other way about. But whichever way it happened, he would at all times see the hat as a hat and the pillar box and flowers as a pillar box and flowers. They have displayed themselves before him *as he is accustomed to seeing them*. His ability to keep these distinct while at the same time associating them through a single aspect depends *upon his previous experience*. Had he not had that experience, this would not have been possible for him, or possible only in exceptional circumstances.

But it is just this element which is missing in children, especially young children. It must be emphasised that the one essential characteristic of all

20

children's experience is that it is new to them, and comes, in the larger number of cases, uncombined with understanding of the significance to other people of the sensorial experiences personally experienced.

By what method, therefore, do children classify their experience? This was one of the first questions that it was essential to answer, and the material collected over many years has made it quite certain that the answer is: "By the quality of the personal experience the child has of the thing and event in question". Thus "things which made me feel horrid" go together, as do "things which made me feel warm", etc., etc., up to the greatest refinement of difference, in sensitive children, of all varieties of experience. Moreover, items when grouped together in this way do not become *associated;* they coalesce, the shared quality not combining them in a way that can be separated later by the owner into the component parts, but becoming entirely identified so that the original items now form part of a single whole.

Here is a little story which makes this clearer. A little boy of $3\frac{1}{2}$ with a pretty, social mother, had a green, smooth, shining toy duck to which he was much attached. He used to put it under his cheek when sleeping. This duck quacked. His mother used to go out a great deal in the evening, and so came up to his nursery usually wearing a green silk evening dress, to read him a good-night story. She then sat in a low chair, and being rather tall, her knees came just to the height of his cheek. It was their custom that when he had had his bath he came in from the bathroom to his nursery with his duck under one arm, paused at the door, looked at his mother, then ran forward, stroked his cheek on his mother's knee, said "Pretty Mummy" climbed on her knee and cuddled down, and she read him his story. Every night this little ritual was carried out. But one night his mother came up wearing a red dress. The little boy paused at the door and looked at her very hard before he came forward rather slowly, did not stroke her knees with his cheek, and climbed up rather soberly on to her lap. This happened two nights, and at the third he stood at the door and burst into tears and said, "Oh Mummy, why do you not put on your quacking dress"? That is to say, the whole combination of affection, greenness, smoothness, cheek-stroking, etc., and *quacking* had come together into a whole, and it was a matter of chance which of these composite group of qualities he might hit upon to characterise this whole.

This is the process by which the inner experience of children becomes grouped, and to the results of this process has been given the name "cluster". The strange composite objects in Chagall's pictures are almost certainly clusters, though this could not be finally settled without investigating them with the artist himself. The difference is that Chagall is a great artist and children are just children. There are innumerable clusters in each child's mind. The number and variety depend upon two factors; the sensitivity and the intellectual quality of the child, and the variety of

21

its experience. Clusters are of all sizes and complexity and composed of very various material.

The formation of clusters, it would appear, is an essential process in the development of the individual personality. When the child is sensitive and intelligent, the linking together which takes place in this way in early life, of experiences of intimacy and intensity in ways which are personal to him and which are afterwards forgotten (in a manner to be described later), gives the personality resources to be drawn upon which are of inestimable value. From this region come "five miles meandering with a mazy motion", "Tiger, Tiger, burning bright, in the forests of the night", and so on, that delight us as adults. Since much of our essential experience is similar to that of the poet, musician or sculptor, in whom suddenly a cluster can burst into poetic speech, or dynamic sound, or form, the creation of an artist will express for us similar clusters in our own experience, which are inaccessible to ordinary man. In so doing, they bring about in us discharge of energy and release of tension and the experience of profound inner satisfaction.

Two main characteristics are observable in any large collection of studies of this kind of material. The first is the occurrence in Worlds made by patients who vary in every possible way in age, sex, complaint and intellectual capacity, of the same formations. Take for instance a relatively simple formation, that of the mound surrounded with water which is, at times, a volcano; this can occur with a number of variations in different patients, but with always the same essential features. This is a representation plastically of the kind of experience which in an artist can result, because of his temperament and ability, in the "explosion" of a work of art, but which in a patient expresses only anxiety and neurotic tension. There are a very large number of these constant factors, but we are only at the beginning of the recognition of them and an understanding of their significance, both in themselves and in and for the patient who makes them.

The second characteristic of this type of material is the individuality of each patient's productions, when these are considered as a whole. This parallels to some extent what we all know of human life. We are all born, feed from a mother or a bottle that we suck, and grow in stature with the constant change of relation to the outer world that this involves, come into full possession of our bodily powers, including those of reproduction, and finally die. Our faces and forms are made of the same features, but no two individuals and no two individuals' lives are really alike. In the same way there is a certain likeness in the material produced by patients when it is *itemised*. Were this not so it would be impossible ever to think of understanding it; but there is an infinite difference in the manner in which the material is grouped and in the individual features which are added by each individual patient.

A very striking similarity between the development of Primary System material and of musical themes here appears. The later themes emerge from elaboration of elements of the original design. It is as if the whole system were charged with power which only slowly becomes perceptible as it finds expression for itself, thus once more paralleling the process of artistic creation.

So far, the clusters have only been considered from their sensorial side. But clusters also represent, and in the most powerful way, dynamic experiences.

To return for a moment to the upside-down faces of Chagall. One of the most striking features of the inter-relation of clusters among themselves is the interchange of positions. Clusters are not arranged flat or vertically, but apparently in a massive clumped manner. Children (and also such adults as have been studied so far) often attempt to arrange objects suspended in space above the World trays, and the relation between World and World of the same patient makes it clear that they are conceived plastically. Not only is this true, but confusion between the relation of glove and hand and that of "inside-out" with the "right way out" also frequently occurs.

This leads to a consideration of the relation between the clusters. How is the whole system tied together and what is the dynamic quality?

As far as it is possible to make a statement from what has been observed, it would appear that energy invests the whole of the clusters of the Primary System, but does so in an uneven fashion. Some clusters are very highly charged, some less so; and the question of what happens to this energy, and what part is played in the conscious life of the individual by the presence of these clusters depends on the next feature of the structure of the psyche that has appeared from investigations, which is the formation of the Secondary System.

It appears that the Primary System begins with the first beginning of sensorial experience and continues through life. But *pari passu* with the formation of the Primary System, the child begins to struggle to make contact with and to understand the world that he shares with the rest of his surroundings. To say this is only to say, in other words, what is the common ground and study of all the aspects of child development. Already a great deal is known about this, and there is nothing new to add here. The child as he grows goes through all the stages known to child psychology and shown especially by the beautiful and careful work of Gesell and his school. Through these processes he learns to gain mastery over his own body and gradually to understand and in a practical way to master his environment, adding by about the age of eight the supreme achievement of mankind, the ability to communicate with others, and with his own interior self, in language.

Thus, in every child, there are two systems. The Primary System is personal, idiosyncratic, massive and multi-dimensional, by its nature incommunicable in words to others. Parallel with the development of this goes the development of the Secondary System which is reasonable, practical, governed by causality, shared with other people and to a large extent describable in language. The Primary System is non-rational, peculiarly constructed, entirely individual, and made up of groups of clusters not later separable by free association, all charged with undifferentiated energy. The Secondary System is shared, logical, reasonable and uses language as its tool.

Now the important point is that the contents of the Primary System cannot appear in the Secondary System. Most people are, therefore, totally unaware of their existence and contemptuous about the possibility. These contents are, in this sense, truly unconscious. But they are so, not through repression, either of the Freudian or Jungian type, but for the simple reason that Primary System material as such, and in its crude state, is totally inexpressible in Secondary System terms.

In order to discover the Primary System, material has to be made accessible to the patient in which constructions of this peculiar nature can be expressed. It is the absence of such material which has prevented its discovery hitherto. Similarly, for the expression of music, instruments capable of producing certain types of sound must be available and adequate; and suitable stone must be available for the production of sculpture. What, for example, it is interesting to speculate, would have been the fate of Prokovief or Beethoven had they been born in the Greece of classical times, or to Henry Moore if born in a desert of sand?

For development to be normal, two things are essential. First of all, there is much in the Primary System that is common to many different individuals and groups. Fairy tales, folk-lore, myth and fable embody many of these elements. As the Jungian School of analysis has shown, through enjoyment of these, the energy which charges Primary System clusters can find its way through the Secondary System, to expression in the outside world. Certain of the clusters even become almost tangible in solidity and form the "introjected objects" of psychoanalysis.

The second necessity is adequate opportunity for the child to play and toleration of his play and his difficulties in adaptation, by the adults around him. Gradually then he corrects his interior concepts, through contact with external reality, and the energy with which the clusters in the Primary System are charged passes through to the Secondary System to find expression in the outside world.

If, however, this does not occur, for any of the many reasons that can happen to a child, then four conditions may result and these correspond to the four main disabilities of the children we treat. First, the energy may remain locked up in the Primary clusters. In this case, the child becomes listless and without interest, unable to put energy into any aspect of living; he tends to be conventional, uninteresting as a character and under the domination of outside circumstances. Secondly, if the amount of energy is greater and more concentrated in certain parts of the Primary System, with no outlet through the Secondary System, then the energy, finding no way out, comes to be concentrated in the body. Different organs appear to be associated with different types of cluster; thus arise the asthmas, the eczemas, the catarrhs, convulsions, disturbances of digestive and sleep habits, and so on, which have no organic basis. Thirdly, if, on the other hand, the child takes his clusters for reality and tries to see them in the outside world, they make themselves into phobias and rituals and obsessions. And fourthly, if it be the type of child who cannot achieve a proper development of his Secondary System and a clear distinction between what is outside and what within, the outside world becomes for him mixed up with his inner life and his relation to reality confused. According to the content of his clusters, he may become the dreamy detached child, the child who appears to be suffering from an early psychosis, or the neurotic deliquent. A single child may even develop all four types of trouble, or varying types may appear in turn during the lifetime, or the treatment, of any single individual, depending upon his constitution and upon circumstances.

The use of this approach in the treatment of over two thousand children by a number of workers has made it quite certain that expression of unsuitably-formed clusters in material and their careful analysis by therapist and child bring about in the children release of vitality, with disappearance of symptoms. What appears to take place is that the increase of vitality which release from the domination of pathogenic clusters brings about in a child, so increases his confidence and his knowledge of himself and of the processes going on within him, that he becomes able to work through the tangles of relationships at far greater speed, these becoming expressed through relations between himself and the material he uses and in the material itself. As a result, there comes about an integration of personality. Close contact that has now been kept with a number of these children through into adult life and in some instances, to marriage and parenthood, has enabled us to check this up.

How does this conception throw light either upon the process of survival in impossible circumstances or the appearance of horrific qualities in the apparently normal? I think it does. As one studies the behaviour of children and adults while undergoing this process what seems to take place is a powerful release of vigour, of vitality, the expression of which in creative activities in real life, seems to bring the individual so much satisfaction that previous and existing deprivations fall into the background and cease to exert a limiting effect on the personality.

Conversely, when there takes place an alteration in external social prohibition and permissions to the pathological side, pathological clusters in individuals appear to derive stimulus from this fact and when similar actions take place in reality, they force their way out into action. Such clusters, when expressed in reality, remain distinct from the rest of the personality, as they did when buried in the Primary Processes of the individual.

The study of the atrocious actions of all kinds carried out, either by individuals or in mass, is one of the dreary parts of this research, but essential to it since what we find is that it is these actions which our children in our playrooms, carry out in plasticine and sand, which in certain circumstances, men and women considered by their fellows to be normal, carry out on the living bodies of men and women. Understanding of the one and of the measures which can be taken to arrest them, may well help to prevent the appearance in reality of the other.

Conversely in the poignancy and immediacy of these early clusters and in their richness and originality lies hidden (in sensitive and gifted people) the germ of creative work; absence of the possibility for expression of experienced beauty can be as productive of depression and strain as is emotional conflict.

46646

Clinical Studies

It is our aim to illustrate the brief outline of the theory of E and the proto-system* by a series of extracts from clinical studies. These three cases have therefore a double purpose: on the one hand to show the way in which children use the World apparatus and the part that this use plays in the process of therapy, and on the other to serve as illustrative of the evidence from which these theories have been derived.

These are difficult objectives which entail on the one hand a selection from the very large amount of clinical material available, and on the other such a presentation as will make intelligible both the children's use of the World apparatus and the therapist's interpretation of it.

Children suffering from a great variety of complaints are treated at the Institute, and if the presentation of case material is to be coherent some principle of selection is essential. Three cases have therefore been chosen to illustrate the way in which therapy, based upon the theory of E and the proto-system, actually works out in practice.

The first is a short case of a very ordinary kind: a girl of 10 referred to the Institute by her mother (who was herself under treatment for depression) on account of difficulties in personal relations at home and at school and backwardness in school work. The point of this case is firstly to introduce the reader to some constantly recurring sequences in Worlds and the relation of Worlds to other forms of play, and secondly to show the part played by the therapist in the handling of World material. This child has been followed up for six years and the last report on her was when she was nearly 18 years old.

The difficulties for which the two other children were referred are concerned with the problem of violence. This selection has been made deliberately, since in the opinion of the writer violence rather than sex is the crucial problem of this period of the world's history. Both children are boys, matched as far as possible in age, intelligence, family background, and the nature of their complaint, but differing as widely as possible in everything else. Both were 7 years of age with an I.Q. between 110 and 120; each had a single sister; and each was referred essentially for violent behaviour which thrust them out of the circumstances and routine normal for their age and social class.

The child, Charles Robinson, whose case follows that of the girl, came of ordinary working-class parents in a small rural manufacturing town. He was treated by the writer in bi-weekly half-hourly sessions at the home-school for maladjusted children to which the local authorities had sent him.

The third case, William Carter, came of parents with a traditional upper middle class professional background, who lived in a country town.

---

*See Appendix.

William was treated partly by the writer and partly by other members of the psychotherapeutic staff at the I.C.P.* In both cases contact with the parents was minimal.

Since the whole point of these studies is to enable the reader who has no experience of Worlds to form a visual image of the Worlds composing the series, a set of semi-conventional and stylised, semi-realistic figures have been worked out to represent the objects usually found in Worlds. These have been used as standardised representations of such objects. No attempt has been made at reproducing perspective. The convention has been adopted that objects placed at right angles to the front of the tray are drawn as if regarded from the side of the tray. Plastic sand-mouldings have been reproduced by adaptation of a very simplified use of the usual conventions of pen and ink drawings. The aim of this method is to present to the eye of the reader a drawing which, while enabling him to make an imaginative visual reconstruction of the World described, will at the same time record faithfully the nature and position of the objects used in the World.

The point of view from which the descriptions of the drawings (and so of the Worlds they represent) are made is that of a person looking at a landscape. The terms "nearer" and "further" are therefore used instead of "top" and "bottom", in order to emphasise the fact that the drawings are conventionalised presentations of an arrangement on a horizontal plane. Whenever the sequence in which the different parts of the World were constructed is known, the verbal description of the World follows this order. Where actual remarks of the child are quoted they are put in quotation marks.

The mode of reporting treatment sessions with the children is as follows:—first an account of the making the World with description of the completed World; this is followed by a report of any conversation that took place between the therapist and the child; finally a discussion by the author either of the single World or of a series of Worlds taken in a group.

---

*Institute of Child Psychology.

Mary Smith

Mary Smith

Mary Smith, age 10 years 10 months, I.Q. 118, was the elder of two siblings, the other being a boy of 6½. Our first contact with the family was 1½ years earlier when this boy was brought by his mother to the I.C.P. for unmanageable behaviour at school. It was then decided that Mrs. S. should be taken on for treatment by the parents' physician and contact maintained with the boy's school; but no treatment arranged for the boy himself.

Mrs. S. was found to be suffering from a severe endogenic depression which gradually yielded to treatment. Towards the end of the first year she asked that her daughter should be taken on for treatment at the I.C.P.

Symptoms. Mary was said to be tense, noisy and babyish; to attack her brother; to have difficulties in school work; she wetted her bed occasionally.

Family. Mary came of an upper middle class family, employed in industry and business on both sides. Her father held a senior position in a bank. Her mother returned to work as a journalist with a women's magazine after having successfully completed her treatment. She had had a strict Methodist upbringing, while Mr. S. belonged to the Presbyterian Church. On the whole, it was a normal and successful family, but rather serious.

History. The child was wanted, but both parents were bitterly disappointed that Mary was a girl. Pregnancy was difficult, labour long, though ultimately spontaneous. Birth weight 5½ lbs; not breastfed and early feeding inadequate; screamed constantly for the first 10 weeks, particularly at night; at 7 weeks old she was found to have rolled onto her face and nearly suffocated herself. She was separated from her mother from 6 months old till 2¼ years (the war broke out) and during these winters had frostbite on arms, hands, legs and feet. Severe constipation occurred in early infancy, and at the age of 3 she had measles, jaundice and a persistent cough; she was given enemas for threadworms and screamed violently. "Milestones" were somewhat delayed. From the age of 5 her health improved and seems to have remained good ever since.

Much of Mary's difficulties during infancy was due to her mother's lack of common sense, inadequacy as a mother and complete inexperience. A contributing factor may have been that Mary was born just before the war broke out, had seven changes in environment, and did not have a real home until she was just over 4 years old. Then her father was stationed in India for 2 years and her younger brother was born.

The family situation at the time of Mary's referral for treatment was as follows.

The marital relation between the parents and their personal relations with each other had improved very much during and after Mrs. S's treatment. Mr. Smith was a careful, protective, very conscientious man for whom his family took the central place in his life. Mrs. S., as her daughter saw her, was over-kind, over-gentle, and over-protective, offering nothing which could be met with a healthy resistance. There was some justification for the friction between Mary and her brother, as he remained difficult and during adolescence had a period of pathogenic truculence for which he had a short period of hospitalisation.

Mary was first seen by the writer in November of the calendar year before she was taken on for treatment. Treatment was carried on for a total of 35 once weekly sessions, during a single calendar year, with breaks for the school holidays, by the senior non-medical therapist on the staff of the Institute. Follow-up visits were made three, five and six years after discharge.

Consultation Session

Mary was a thin, brown haired, sulky girl with tight lips and an inhibited manner. She was silent and loath to respond to any advances. After a short talk she was asked to make a *Mosaic*. She settled down to it in a dogged sort of fashion, and starting at the further edge proceeded silently to make a compact abstract pattern covering the whole of the tray. She was exact and careful, and tried hard to make both sides identical, but failed to do so in details, substituting for example a red piece on one side for a similar yellow piece on the other. The pattern as finally constructed used all the colours, but only the simpler shapes. It showed some ingenuity and a fairly good idea of colour balance. Her attitude to it was per-severative. She thawed a little while making it and responded in a mild way to talk about school and home. She was, she said, not happy in either; she felt her brother was preferred to her at home, and she did not get on in school although she did not know why; she agreed that life could be much happier than it was. Feelings of irritation against her mother appeared at frequent intervals as she talked. When half of her Mosaic pattern had been made, work on it was stopped as she would have needed a very long time to complete it. When asked what she would like to be, supposing she could have three wishes fulfilled, she said "a nurse, a butcher or a baby".

The total impression she made was of a child with a great deal of strong feeling bottled up inside her. After the kind of work undertaken at the I.C.P. had been explained to her, including "Bridge" and "Picture Thinking",* she agreed that she would like to come up for help.†

---

*See Appendix.

†At this time the standard consultation technique had not been adopted and it was not until she was admitted for treatment that she was asked to make a World.

31

Treatment of Mary Smith

At her first treatment session Mary was introduced to the World apparatus and was interested in it.

Making an experiment (1st session)

Mary took out some houses and tried how they looked scattered about the tray, tried out the making of a road with paths going from it to the houses. Then made a river and took down a model of the Tower Bridge from the shelves in the playroom and played with it, making the bridge go up and down. She then put some boats in the river and also on the road, added some cars and a petrol pump, found some sheep and cooed over one model where a small lamb lies by its mother.

Having experimented with the material she now removed all the objects from the tray and set out to make a World.

World 1   Figure 7 (1st session)

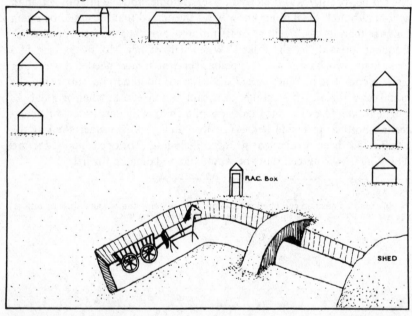

This she said was a village. It had 8 houses and a church placed around the three further edges of the tray. Almost in the centre of the tray she put an "Automobile Club" telephone box;* the nearer right-hand corner she filled with a heap of sand, dug out a hollow in it on the side facing the centre of the tray and said "this is a shed". She then excavated the sand down to the base of the tray in a bent road with a square cut end, and put on it a horse and cart racing towards the right;

---

*Often found by the side of main roads in England.

across this "road" she placed a bridge. She said, "This is the horse's private part". While making this World she talked about her brother and what a nuisance he was; she would not like to be a boy because they had to play football. She had nothing further to say about the World.

Discussion. During the conversation at the beginning of this session about her consultation interview, Picture Thinking was described again. The World makes it clear that Mary had understood this concept and had accepted that attitude to the World tray and cabinet. In a first experimental trial of the material she found out that roads and a river could be easily and realistically represented and that the cabinet contained attractive and appealing objects, like the sheep and lamb. But in her removal of all these objects and in the bareness and curious nature of this first actual World she showed that she was responding to the invitation to use the objects from the cabinet symbolically rather than realistically. The fact that in her experimental try-out she had already put boats on a road was a pointer in this direction. It illustrates one of the constantly recurring characteristics of children's Worlds, i.e., the use of motor and rail transport, horses, carts and ships, rivers and roads, in any combination, without relation to reality, so that they express movement *as such*, rather than a particular form of movement as it occurs in real life. Talking with children about their Worlds in words which approximate as nearly as possible to the ideas and feelings the children are trying to express in them is important. Since it happens that often no actual words exist for many of these, a set of descriptive manufactured terms has grown up among us to meet this need: for example, Mary's use of boats, road and river in her experiment would have been called "a going-along-ness" and this word often proves a useful tool.

In World 1 there is no way of communication between the houses, no general road. The one piece of road that appears, is a small "private" piece with a horse and cart at its beginning and at the end a dark cave into which it can go which is, Mary said, "its shed". There is a bridge over this road from one part of the "general" area to another, but no road or path on either side leading to the bridge. Near the bend of the road is a very special kind of telephone box, only able to be used by grown-ups and always mysterious to children.*

Had this World stood alone and been made at a Consultation Interview the bareness and the curiously cut short road would have suggested the possibility of low inherent intelligence or possibly the pressure of schizophrenia. This illustrates the importance of correlative investigations on other lines. Mary's I.Q. of 118 rules out both possibilities.

---

*These boxes are locked and can only be used by motorists who are members of the Automobile Club and have special keys.

This time Mary came into the playrooms smiling and talked all the time she was making her World.

She put 3 houses together along the further edge of the tray, with flowers carefully arranged on one side and trees on the other (flowers are the one thing she "adores" in nature). Between the houses and the left-hand edge she placed 2 benches, each in front of a tree, a rabbit, a pigeon cote with a single chair in front of it; and a table with four chairs. She then took out sitting figures for mother, father and a child and placed them on the benches with the child in the middle; later they were made to sit round the table as in the illustration having tea. A piece of cut green linoleum surrounding a mirror was placed in front of this to represent a pond, and 2 ducks and a swan were put on it with a dog nearby. In front of the pond fencing was now added, parallel to the front of the tray and extending the whole length of the area of houses and flowers up to a corner where another fence ran back at right angles to the further edge of the tray. The houses are thus shut into a fenced area in which there is a closed gate towards the right-hand side of the front fence. A long path was now made from this gate to the door of the left-hand house, with two other paths leading from it to the other two doors. A cat was later put in beside the tea party, a barrow by the pond, a pump by the right-hand fence, and some flowers in the nearer right-hand corner. On the path a man and a dog are going towards the house, and a woman with a dog behind her coming away from it. (Mary has no animals at home; she likes animals, particularly horses.) Outside the fence a road was vaguely indicated. In front of the fence two cars were put, going in opposite directions, and a man on horseback; two street lamps were placed just outside the fence, and the Automobile Club box against the left edge. The soldiers of a military band were arranged marching from left to right along the road in the centre of the picture. At the back of the tray outside the side fence on what is

34

presumably thought of as a road, Mary placed a cart and a cage with monkeys in it drawn by a horse and led by a man; traffic lights were set at the corner. Right across the road space by the right-hand edge Mary constructed a rectangular enclosure and put in it two bulls and one cow. Running along the nearer edge of the tray, but stopping abruptly in a square end, she made a river and put an Indian in a canoe and two rowing boats on it. Mary enjoyed doing this World and said she thought it was the best she had done.

Discussion. The fenced off portion of the World presents a pleasant friendly domestic scene; the band going along at the front suggests marching and cheerful noise. The monkeys in the cage, about which she said nothing, the two bulls and the cow in the enclosure, and the abruptly ended river are in contrast with the "reality" of the enclosed space. The space within the fences is treated logically and realistically, the space without is not. The Automobile Club box is the one defined object from the first World which appears again, this time in a more appropriate position. The river occupies approximately the same place as the private road in World 1.

This World illustrates a common feature of Worlds made by children under treatment, that is, the combination in the same scene of realistic and non-realistic features. This occurs also at times in the Worlds of children not under treatment. Another interesting feature is the inclusion of noise in the military band. While making the World, Mary said that she loves animals (she has no pets). She did not want to talk further about the World.

World 3   Figure 9 (3rd session)

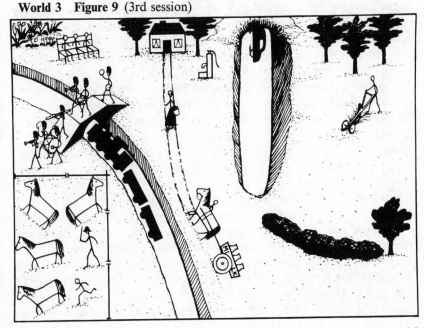

35

At the next session, a few days later, Mary spent the whole hour, in complete silence, constructing World 3.

A somewhat similar arrangement to World 2 appeared, but this time 1 house instead of 3, was placed between two tall trees; in contrast 3 children, instead of 1, were put on a single bench with flowers behind it. The pump was now placed just beside the house. The major part of the tray to the right-hand side she made into a field with 3 trees at the back, and a man ploughing. Between this field and the house, by the further edge, Mary repeated the structure that she had made in World 1 and had then called "a shed"; she now called it "a garage" and put a car in it. Leading from the garage is a short excavated road ending abruptly in the middle of the tray. There are no fences around the house, but an inadequate semi-circular hedge was put stretching parallel to the edge of the tray which marked the boundary of the field and ended with a tree on the right; the other end of this inadequate hedge finished about where the gate was in World 2. At this point Mary put in a milk cart with a man beside it taking milk to the house. On the left a deep railway cutting was made from the nearer edge, a train put in it just going under a bridge and over the bridge the military band marched. The left nearer corner of the tray was occupied by a fenced enclosure containing four horses; in this field a little boy (Mary said) "is being chased by a man for trespassing". Almost in the centre of the picture and at the centre of the path from the house a woman was put walking down toward the milkcart; "she is a widow" Mary said, and "it is her three children who are sitting on the bench".

Conversation. The changes in the family situation from World 2 to World 3 brings the question of families into high relief. From the point of view also of the symbolism of psycho-analysis there is much in this World which is suggestive of an interest in Mary's mind of questions and ideas concerning sex, particularly in the combination on the left-hand side of a train going under a bridge, the military band and the trespassing boy. When the World was finished, therefore, the therapist opened up conversation about her parents. "Her father", Mary said, "is sometimes nice to do things with"; her mother is sometimes nice, she likes going for walks with her on the common, hiding and jumping out on her. Her brother "is pretty awful". As this was the first time such material had appeared, it was not taken any further.

Discussion. We are now in a position to consider these three Worlds together. World 1 is empty of all content except the small piece of sunken road covered with a bridge, with a horse and cart about to drive under this into a shed. The characteristic of this road is its abrupt square end. Nothing goes over the bridge and it does not lead to a road; it is therefore more "something one goes under" than "something one goes over". Beside this is a tool of communication connected with adults and motor cars.

In World 2 this truncated and square ended channel of movement appears as a river; there is no "shed" or bridge and the river is straight. The R.A.C. (Royal Automobile Club) box stands at its end, this time in reasonable relation to a road. The horse and cart on the road, if these are considered as "going-along-ness", are replaced by an Indian in a canoe. (The two empty boats probably only emphasise that this is a river, no water was used). The other element of World 1 which was only sketched in, viz., houses, appears in World 2 as the strongest element in the picture. If the concept of "going-along-ness" is accepted, World 1 is contained in World 2.

To World 1, World 2 adds a domestic enclosure complete with flowers, trees, pond and birds, dovecote, barrow, pump, benches and a family sitting at tea. This family has one child, a boy. A second woman and man appear on the path; and three dogs, a cat and a rabbit complete the scene. A horse and cart appear here also and a man on horseback rides along the road. The ordinary furnishings of a road appear, with lights and motor traffic. The odd parts of this World are an enclosure with two bulls and a cow placed roughtly in relation to the river at the point where in World 1 the "shed" was in relation to the road, and a cart-load of monkeys being led down along the shorter fencing of the "estate" beside the horse and cart. Right in the middle of the road marches the military band.

World 3 falls into two halves.

In the centre is a single house (is this a condensation of the three former houses?). The single seated child of World 2, on the other hand, has now become three children. The pump has moved from beside the fence to just beside the house. There are no fences shutting in the house and garden, and flowers appear only behind the children's bench. There is no road, nor road signs, nor traffic – men have disappeared both from the tea table and from the centre path. Where there was a closed gate in World 2 there is now a milk cart being led up to the house. Instead of the two women in World 2 there is one in World 3, and she holds the centre of the picture. From Mary's remarks about her it appears that it is her house, the three children are her children and she is a widow. The sunken "way" is now on the right of the house and is "a garage" with a car in it. A new feature to the right of this is a field in which a man is ploughing (this recalls Shakespeare's line *speaking of Cleopatra.

> "She made great Caesar lay sword to bed
> He plough'd her, and she cropp'd.)"

The three children on the left are repeated in three trees on the right; and a new feature, a hedge, forms the boundary of the field.

The second half of the picture is formed by a railway-in-a-valley-about-to-go-under-a-bridge on the left with the military band marching over it. Finally in an oblong enclosure, comparable to that of the bulls and cow in World 2 but on the other side, a man chases a boy among horses for trespassing. The monkeys have disappeared, but there is kinship in idea between them and the "naughty boy".

World 3 is of considerable interest because here several "ideas" appear

---

Antony and Cleopatra, Act II Scene 2.

in a number of different aspects. The presentation of the same person or object seen from different angles in one picture, is a very familiar phenomena of dreams, poetry and various forms of modern art. Since dreams occur in sleep the consciousness cannot be said to take any part in their production. Conscious design however is the essential quality which separates art from phantasy, and conscious activity is inseparable from the work of an artist. Worlds stand half way between these two. Part of their "meaning" is deliberately and consciously designed and in this aspect of World 3 Mary negates the father: the woman is a widow, the children have no father. Two other aspects of "men" appear; the man ploughing the field and the man being punitive toward the boy. Whether there is a man with the milk cart or not is debatable, as World objects can only be used in the form in which they exist; thus a human figure is often included as part of an object where, if this were not the case, the maker of the World would not have added such a figure.

World 4 *not illustrated* (4th session)

In the next session the influence of T.V. appeared. Mary made "a circus she had seen on T.V.". This was to a certain extent realistic except for one element; an arrangement of two ladders with a plank across and a clown standing on the ladder; under this Mary placed a man tied to a tree trunk (from an Indian/cowboy set).

Discussion. It commonly happens in our experience that a World containing elements that according to analytic modes of thinking represent sexual symbols, will be followed by a World presenting a circus. In this World the circus carries on the theme of the band. The tied-up man is the first hint of suffering or disaster that has so far appeared. The incongruity of this with the "circus" did not strike her.

World 5 *not illustrated* (5th session)

At the next session Mary made a farm scene. The three houses with the three paths from their front doors, converging on to a single path (as in World 2) with a single dog on one of them reappeared here placed by the further edge of the tray. Between the right end of these houses and the right-hand edge of the tray two prams, a well and a pump were placed in a line along the tray's edge. The right-hand nearer corner and most of that side was filled with a fenced field with cows in it and a haystack at the further corner. Between that and the prams-well-pump line was a hunter and two hounds. Two cars side by side were put between the path and the field and a farm woman was walking down the path away from the houses. A fenced off railway with two engines side by side, said to be in a valley, ran along the left edge. A broad road ran straight from front to back of the tray by-passing the houses and on it was put a milkcart driving towards the further edge of the tray. Between this road and the railway fence there appeared again the pond with ducks, some hens by it, and at the back, in the same place as in other Worlds, a bench and a dovecote, only this time two girls were put sitting on the bench with two dogs at their feet, and their father, a farmer, was put standing by them talking.

Conversation. While she was making this World a conversation developed about a pram: Mary urgently wanted her mother to give her a pram and her mother thought it too expensive. The therapist remarked to Mary that she thought what Mary probably wanted was not a pram but a baby, to which Mary replied that she did not know about that but she loved taking babies out in prams, adding that her father tells her she should go and buy one from the baby shop. Here the therapist asked what Mary knew about babies, and Mary replied "not much but something about a seed which the father gave the mother". The therapist then, in accordance with our standard procedure for preparing the way to discussion of this subject, talked about the body as a whole and how it worked. It became quickly evident that Mary knew a good deal already.

Discussion. This World marks the end of a stage. Parts of the last two sessions had been filled with discussions of the workings of the body, leading up to, but for the present not discussing, sex and reproduction. Mary's response at her next session was to break away from realistic presentation and to make a World which is frankly symbolic. While she was making it she said spontaneously she "knew it was a funny World".

World 6   Figure 10 (6th session)

This World has three parts. Along the left edge Mary placed a line of three large aeroplanes facing to the right, with a good deal of space around them. Two

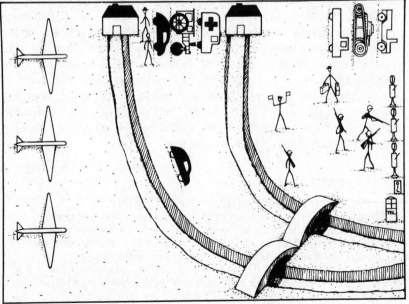

small houses separated by a space were placed in the centre third of the tray against the further edge. Between these two houses in a line along the further edge are an ambulance, a steam roller, a car, a man in city clothes and a hiker. Along the same line at the right further corner she placed two army lorries and a tank. From the front door of each house Mary dug out a stream which flowed across the tray and curved to the right, almost meeting at the right-hand edge. Across these streams two bridges were placed continuous with each other. In the space between them and half-way along, a private car stood facing down stream. Between the army cars and tank and the streams and along the right edge, she placed a row of petrol pumps, a telephone box, four soldiers with rifles, one man with flags and a man carrying luggage.

Conversation. After the making of this World the therapist talked over the fundamentals of sex reproduction as they appear in various kinds of animals.

Discussion. This World is frankly symbolic; streams do not flow from the fronts of houses, nor could the other objects be disposed as they are in this World. Mary is therefore not constructing a realistic scene but attempting to "say something" using realistic objects to do so. In all schemata of symbols houses appear as symbols of femininity, "the home", or, as is probable here – "the body". The three vehicles between the two houses carry with them ideas of accidents (or illness) pressure and movement. The two men beside them, the absence of women from the whole World, and the army vehicles and soldiers on the right all emphasise the maleness of the rest of the scene. Aeroplanes are very male objects to small girls. Apart from the flowing streams nothing but the soldiers and male human beings move in this World; (it was not clear whether Mary intended the single private car between the two streams to be regarded as stationary or moving). From a psycho-analytic point of view this World is a symbolic statement of confusions between impregnation and urination into the female, ideas of erection, coitus and damage, which is in one way more obvious and direct than many attempts made by children and adults to express these ideas and fears in words. Bearing these ideas in mind the therapist said that houses were a bit like bodies and continued discussing the stages of the evolution of reproduction finishing in the following session with the situation in human beings.

World 7   Figure 11 (8th session)

Mary dug out a winding river running across the length of the tray and placed two steamers and two rowing boats on it; a railway crossed this on a bridge at right angles, running from the left nearer corner to the further right edge. This went over the river but under a bridge carrying a road which crossed the tray on the opposite diagonal. A train was put on the railway moving towards the nearer edge. The first road, after going over the railway, went also over the river. In the right-hand nearer corner between the end of the road and the edge of the tray she placed a telephone box opposite a car on the road "running out" of the

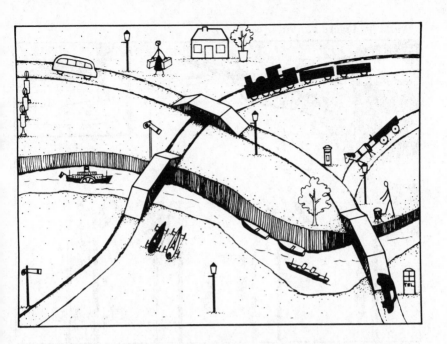

tray. At the centre of the tray against the further edge she placed a house and a tree in a tub beside it. No path leads from the house, but a woman carrying luggage was put going towards a bus on the road, a lamp post between them. In the strip of land between the road and river Mary placed a line of petrol pumps along the left edge and a railway signal by the railway line, a street lamp by the road, and a tree in the angle of road and river. On the other side of the road at this point and where a second road came into it on which were a horse and cart, she put a pillar box. In the triangular space between the new road, the old road and the river she placed a workman's brazier with a man beside it and a street lamp. Finally in the space between the river and the nearer edge she placed two racing cars side by side and a lamp post. A railway signal by the line at the extreme left completes the scene.

Mary enjoyed making this World but had nothing to say about it. At this session she also made a Mosaic.

Discussion. This World was an intricate design of "going-along-ness" – a road with motor traffic, a road with horse traffic, a river with boats, a railway, with crossings over and under each other. The emphasis here is upon movement, all sorts of movement. Only two human beings appear, the woman with luggage walking towards the bus and the man standing by the brazier. In this part of the World however are placed also the letter box and the telephone, both means of communication, and two erect objects, the tree and the lamp post. In the very front, not on the road, a new symbol appears in the two racing cars standing side by side.

This World marked the completion of a stage. For reasons that cannot now be discovered a six-week gap in treatment occurred at this point and the final World of this Spring term was of an entirely different type.

41

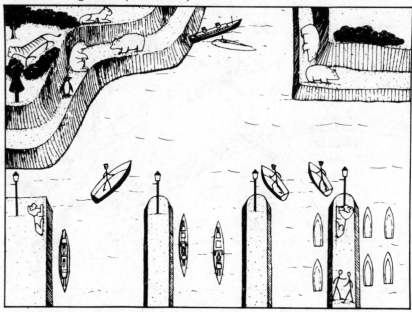

Stretching back from the front of the tray Mary constructed the wharves and slipways of a harbour: she placed stationary ships in each and boats setting out from two of them. The whole of the centre of the tray Mary thought of as water. At the point of each pier a lamp post was placed and on the two outer piers she put what she said were statues of lions. Two men said to be arguing were placed on the base of the right-hand pier.

A different atmosphere informs the further side of the tray; this is said to be the coast of an island. Two bears, a penguin, a tiger and a lioness were placed on terraces at the left-hand further corner; on the top terrace trees and bushes. In the right-hand further corner on two right-angled terraces she put two bears; on the top terrace a bush. A ship was put near the island on the left hand; a submarine was said to be coming up near it to wreck it, while sailors in boats went to the rescue.

Symbolism. With the change of idiom in World 8 we are in a position to make a brief study of the symbolism employed by Mary. Up to and including World 7 all the objects used (except possibily the cage of monkeys) represent items which will have been normally encountered by Mary in her ordinary life. The exceptions to this are the tied-up man in World 4 and the Indian on the river in World 2 but those figures stem directly from the American Indian adventure stories and cartoons read by all children. It is in the placing of these objects on the tray that departures from the normal expectations of arrangements of such objects occurs. The striking fact about Worlds of this nature is the combination of ordinary scenes such as the house and garden enclosure in Figure 11 – with bizarre arrangements of real life objects, such as the abruptly ended river with the Indian upon it in the same World.

If we consider Worlds 1–5 on the one hand and World 6 on the other, two types of "irrationality" appear. Worlds 1 and 2 contain the impossibility of a cut off river and road while in World 6 streams take the place of paths leading from the front doors of houses. An important element in the study and handling of Worlds is the child's perception or lack of perception of the "impossible" nature of elements in his Worlds as this offers valuable indications as to the type of presentation being made and the inherent normality or abnormality of the child's mental equipment. In spite of the fact that Mary's I.Q. was 118 she did not perceive the bizarre nature either of the road in World 1 or of the cut-off river in World 2.

On the other hand, by the time she came to make World 6 two changes had taken place in Mary. She had become aware of the presence in herself of an impulse to produce an irrational scene and at the same time had come to feel "easy" about giving expression to this impulse. Making World 6, she said "I know this is a funny World" and did not mind. World 6 is therefore important. The objects in this World are still part of her normal experience. The relation of object to object however is either impossible or very unlikely. Streams do not issue from houses. It is only supposing that the space between the two houses represents a road that it is even possible that the ambulance, streamroller and car could be assembled together. This possibility is however negated by the approximation of the two streams at the right-hand side of the tray and the blocking of this end by two bridges. It would seem therefore that these objects are being used by Mary in the manner of the drawings of ordinary objects which appear in political cartoons. The difference between symbolism of this nature when it occurs in a World or in a cartoon is that the underlying significance of the objects or figures in a cartoon is known to all the spectators and the contrast between the apparent absurdity and the underlying meaning is the *raison d'être* of the cartoon. In a World however, as in a dream, the significance is personal. Here, however, two classes of symbolism appear. On the one hand, those objects and their use which are absolutely individual to the maker and which will, in all probability, not occur in Worlds made by other people; and on the other, those whose occurrence is so frequent in Worlds of all kinds that a general meaning can be accepted for them. So far no individual symbols have occurred in Mary's Worlds.

How then is World 6 to be understood? It is clear that the World falls into three parts; it is also clear that the way the objects are disposed indicates a vague and very general idea in the maker's mind. The incongruity of the three parts. taken as a whole, suggests that they are preliminary efforts only which will become more explicit as the process of treatment proceeds.

Discussion. World 8, however, introduces a new quality into the series. For the first time a definite and sharply defined incident is represented. This incident, together with the island inhabited by wild animals, are entirely outside Mary's normal life-experience, although, as with the Indian and the tied-up man, submarine attacks on ships have probably formed part of films that she has seen. Although there is nothing bizarre in the separate sections there is no possibility of a grouping of animals, ships and harbour, such as appears in the scene, occurring in the maker's real life. We are therefore in the realm of imagination or phantasy and the ordinary rules for understanding and interpretation of works of phantasy or imagination begin to apply.

The nearer half of this picture combines the idea of boats at rest and boats in movement. The statues of lions to some extent link the two halves. All except one of the animals on the island are potentially dangerous, though, being isolated on their terraces, they do not constitute a present threat. The ship, however, is in imminent danger. Rescue comes from the harbour but there is no idea of a counter attack on the submarine.

The Easter holidays intervened here and afterwards arrangements were made for Mary to attend once weekly.

On the first visit of the following summer term Mary made two Worlds.

World 9 *not illustrated* (10th session)

This was a strictly reality-scene, the first that she has made. It has two parts – an aeroplane field on the right with planes, hangar, waiting cars; the only unlikely feature was the inclusion of a steam-roller among these. On the aerodrome Mary placed four figures which she said were a mother, two children and a porter with luggage going towards a plane. Along the left edge of the tray in the same area as the three planes in World 6, she made a fenced-in railway with two trains parallel with the short side, and a station against the fence dividing it from the aerodrome.

Discussion. It is a common occurrence that children starting treatment again after a holiday break make a realistic World. This, however, is an entirely fresh theme. Mary has not herself been in an aeroplane, nor did anyone in the family leave or arrive by one in the break time. There is no father here as there was none in World 3 and the mother and two children (the number in her family) are about to go away.

44

World 10 *not illustrated* (same session)

In contrast this was said to represent her own garden. She put a house in the middle of the tray and surrounded it with square fenced lawns, a flower garden, a bicycle shed and a summer house. At this session Mary said that she was glad to be going back to school because she was bored at home in the holidays.

NB. Till now Mary had been accompanied to the I.C.P. but two weeks later she came by herself.

World 11 *not illustrated* (12th session)*

This was a World of the kind from which the theory of the proto-system has been deduced. It shows a development in six steps.

Step 1.   Mary made a round castle in the middle of the tray, with a round tower on top, surrounded by a moat with a sand draw-bridge and a tunnel running underneath the bridge.

She tried to tunnel through the castle but did not succeed and did not seem to mind.

Step 2.   She now pressed the substance of this castle down into a single mass which she said was "a cake".

Step 3.   She scooped the centre out of this mass turning it into what she called "a basin".

Step 4.   She now "mixed a cake" in this basin and said it was her brother's birthday and wrote on it "Happy Birthday". On top of this she put, out of the cabinet, a figure of a mother and baby polar bear, very popular at that time.

Step 5.   She cut slices of the cake with a stick, and in doing so made "a slide" and played with this for a bit.

Step 6.   She levelled it all out and kept pushing the stick in and out and began now to squeeze the moist sand in her hands, playing about with it. In doing this accidentally she splashed the therapist's face and was very amused by it.

Discussion.   The round mound, sometimes with, sometimes without a tower upon it, the surrounding ditch, the draw-bridge and tunnel, sometimes called a castle sometimes not, is a form which constantly appears in Worlds. So far it has not been possible to identify whether there is any correlation between age, I.Q., type of child and complaint, and this structure. Most commonly, when it has been constructed and patted into firmness a tunnel is made through the base of the mound. Often a second tunnel is made at right angles to this and then joined with an excavation from the top.

The stages of Mary's play following the making of the castle illustrate

---

*The description of this World is set up differently on account of it being a proto-systematic World and not a scene.

also a typical series, in that, from constructing a round building into which one goes, she proceeds to make a round substance that itself goes into the cavity of one's mouth. When this has been completed, what can be looked upon as the mould of the round cake is made. This mould is next treated as a container and a fresh food substance created in it – this time to act as a present to her young brother. The idea of her brother makes the link between eating slices of cake and using the cutting implement to poke in and out of the sand, this in its turn lending to experiment with sensuous and humorously aggressive play.

The next session showed sharply contrasting forms of behaviour.

World 12 *not illustrated* (13th session)

Mary put a farmhouse at the back of the tray with a big fenced yard, a chicken house in a corner, two pumps and a kennel with a dog. In the further right corner was a large garage and cars, and along the right side two smaller houses each with a fenced garden. On the opposite side she constructed a field in which she placed three cows and a donkey. Between the farmyard and this fence is a milk cart facing right. The centre of the tray was occupied by a playground with swings, a roundabout and a slide, and she put a number of children playing about. When putting in the milk cart Mary said the cow looking towards the milk cart "was very cross when it saw the milk". The therapist pointed out that this "cow" was really a bull and explained why.

At the next session Mary started out to elaborate the playground theme of the last World and made "a fair". After starting on this however she changed her mind and said she would rather make *a zoo*.

World 13 *not illustrated* (14th session)

This was a very bare construction. Four irregular spaces along the two short sides of the tray were fenced in separately; three polar bears were placed in one, three penguins in another, a mother and a baby polar bear (that were much in the news) and a pond in a third, and in the fourth a lion, lioness and cub. The whole of the centre was bare. A pay box and turnstile were put in at nearer edge but no people.

On completion of this World Mary "messed it around" and then made wet sand pies characteristic of the play of a very much younger child.
Discussion. These two Worlds with the one between that was begun and not really completed, form a related series, the central theme being carried on from the children's playground (World 12) to the fair which was begun but not completed and becoming implicit in a zoo-without-visitors. The lay-out of Worlds 12 and 13 is to some extent similar; to the right-hand side of World 12 we have two enclosed spaces with a house in each; in World 13 occupying the same space on the tray are two enclosures, each containing one animal family. There are no people in World 13, and the children in World 12 really only reinforce the idea of a playground. In

46

World 12 one of the two pumps, the milk cart, the bull/cow (who was cross about the milk) are grouped together in a form which would need too much space for description here but which is often met with. In World 13 wild animals appear in these same spaces – not walking about wild on their islands as in World 8, but safely confined within fences. The messing play of World 11 is then repeated with keen enjoyment and no relation to any outside person or object. These two Worlds illustrate a pendulum-like oscillation which frequently occurs in a series of Worlds (as it does in many aspects of human intercourse) when a very significant World which breaks new ground is followed by a realistic one repeating old material.

World 14 *not illustrated* (15th session)

Mary started off to make a dam across the tray and wanted to tunnel through it but the sand was too wet for this to be successful. She added dry sand and asked what she had done last time. The therapist told her and she said "Oh, I am going to make pies again today" and spent a happy time messing wet sand and adding water until she had made it really sloppy and thought it was like lovely ice cream.

Having enjoyed this for a while Mary moved away to water-play with a doll's shower bath, filling and emptying it with tubes, sucking and squirting with water, finally squirting at the therapist. The therapist pointed out the likeness of this to a boy urinating and Mary repeated the squirting play in the garden.

Discussion. As in World 11 Mary had carried out a procedure which occurs very often with children of all ages – here Mary played out another theme which also frequently appears, that of the dam. Although she did not actually put water on either side of the ridge of sand across the tray, the fact that she called this a dam implies the idea of something to be dammed up. When this theme is expressed by boys it is usually in the form of an elaborately constructed dam with water on one side and various devices by which this water is eventually released (expressed here in the abortive tunnel) to flood the other side and ultimately the whole tray. In Mary's case these three aspects: – dam, water held back, water pouring through, mushy sand – were treated separately, the water being manipulated by itself instead of being used in a play of pressure between water and sand. With boys this play usually ends in complete destruction within the tray; with Mary the sand emerged into a sensuous mouth gratification, the theme of which was carried on into the sucking and squirting of water.

The connection she expressed at the end between the "mud" and "lovely ice cream" illustrates another aspect of these World sequences which has led to the hypothesis of the proto-system. The form of play here and at the end of the last session is that of the 3–4 year old child, but the identification of it with the sensuous enjoyment of sweet food of similar consistency belongs to a later stage of development.

To anyone familiar with psycho-analytic work the themes underlying this series will be obvious, and they were certainly in the mind of the therapist. The normal rule, however, of this work, that so long as vigorous development is proceeding from session to session interpretation should be used sparingly, held good here.

At her next session Mary made three Worlds: (15, 16, 17), working very quickly and breaking new ground.

World 15 *not illustrated* (16th session)

An Indian appeared in World 2; in World 4 a tied-up man from the Indian/ cowboy set was put in; these two hints are now developed into a full fledged Indian/cowboy fight. Mary made a row of hedges across the tray where the dam had previously been and put Indians and cowboys along this hedge with the tied-up man behind – one solitary tree toward the nearer edge, and cowboys and Indians on foot and on horse attacking.

Conversation.   When the therapist asked what this was meant to represent, Mary said they were Indians against Redskins, but when the therapist pointed out that there were both Indians and cowboys on either side Mary said they were not supposed to be mixed, they were the good against the bad; bad people are those who want to fight. The therapist remarked this was a very boy-like World and wondered whether Mary wanted to be a boy, to which Mary said "No" in a rather unconvincing manner; the therapist remarked that girls often did want to. Mary then piled the dry sand on her hands and rubbed it about rather violently, to which the therapist said it was nice rubbing things like that and it was nice rubbing yourself.

Mary now decided to make another World.

World 16 *not illustrated* (same session)

This was a school. Mary put six desks at the right facing inwards, a corner cupboard in the further right-hand corner, a mistress' desk facing with the teacher behind and someone coming to speak to her; a blackboard beside on which Mary wrote, "BOAC Travel to America"* and a dunce beside that. Opposite to the cupboard was a Nature table with two chairs beside it and luggage on chairs and table.

World 17 *not illustrated* (same session)

This is a bedroom. It was said to be the bedroom of a mother, a father and three children. One double bed, 3 single beds and 4 night tables were put in, a dressing table, a chest of drawers, a sideboard, a second dressing table, a settle and a

---

*An airline advertisement current at the time.

corner cupboard were arranged in this order around the walls; there was one separate chair and a table and 4 chairs in the middle of the room.

Discussion. A very common sequence in Worlds is for a period of primitive play with sand and water to usher in the theme of good and bad which in Mary's series appears in World 15 for the first time. The form of the Indian/cowboy fight is an example of the use of current cliches to express ideas which are too confused in the mind of the maker for clear individual expression to be possible. This was followed by pictures of the two places where in a child's life ideas of "good" and "bad" are met with most frequently, i.e., at home and at school, the whole being a natural sequence of the messy play of the last few sessions.

World 18   Figure 13 (17th session)

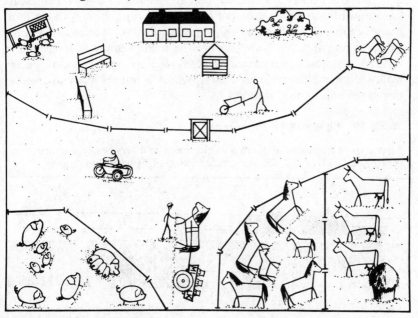

Mary set out to make "a big farm" and said this was a story. She put the farmhouse in its usual place at the centre of the further edge and a fence fencing in a wide space in front of the farm house, taking in about one-third of the whole tray. In the left further corner where the bench and trees have been in previous Worlds there is a large rabbit hutch and three rabbits; on the other side of the house a rockery. Two benches, a shed, and a man with a wheelbarrow were arranged in a rough semicircle in front of the house. There is a closed gate in the fence in front of the house but no path leading to the house. In the right-hand further corner of the tray, continuous with the fence of the farmhouse, Mary made a field and put two calves in it, separated from their mothers, the cows, which, Mary said, always happened. Curved fencing shut off each corner of the nearer side, leaving some space between. Into the left field Mary put a number of pigs and piglets; the right-hand field was divided into two, with 3 cows and a haystack in one field and 4 horses and 2 foals in the other. Moving towards the house from the gap between the two sets of fences is a milk cart with a man leading it. A man with a combination motor-cycle was going along the road to the left.

Conversation.   Observing that young only appeared with animals in this World the therapist took up again the mode of human reproduction and started to discuss the pleasure side of sex.

The session finished with a Mosaic which showed a marked improvement.

Discussion.   This World repeats the themes of Worlds 5 and 12 but now focused on a single house and garden with only the calves, who have been taken from their mother, adjacent to the garden. The theme of mothers and young is heavily emphasised, but with animals only. The milk cart faces towards the garden gate but has no clear connection with the farm house occupants. No human family appears, the only human being in the garden is a man with a wheelbarrow. The road is empty of traffic except for the motorcycle combination. Many feelings and concepts of the reality of the mother/child are clearer but she is not yet ready to consider this in relation to human beings.

World 19   Figure 14 (18th session)

Mary took great trouble about this World, executed it very neatly and was very pleased with herself. She constructed a viaduct, apparently along the

middle of a river, with three archways through it and two trains running along the top. A steamboat was placed going through one arch, and an Indian in a canoe was put in the river parallel with the viaduct (no real water was used). By itself in the centre of the nearer river bank she put an earth excavator; at the right-hand nearer corner, facing at right angles towards the river, a car which she called a steamroller.

Discussion. This is a very interesting combination of a number of previous themes carried out in an almost realistic fashion. The viaduct, although constructed in a realistic manner and competently executed, is identified with the river. Attention is drawn to the fact of arches by the steamer which goes through one of them; the Indian of World 2 reappears on this river.

An interesting element from the point of view of implied movement is the fact that the centre of the river bank is occupied by a road scoop, and the implied action of this instrument is contrasted with that of a steamroller.

If World 7 be considered together with World 19 some interesting points emerge. It is not impossible that a scene such as that presented in World 7 could exist; the fact, however, that this is made by a girl, and a girl who in ordinary life has no interest in trains, boats and cars, suggests that this is a symbolic presentation of an interior rather than an exterior situation. As already pointed out the emphasis is on movement, and although those different lines of movement do not obstruct each other (as they might do were a situation of conflict being represented), yet the movement goes in several directions with a sense of complexity and confusion. In World 19 on the other hand, except for the steamer going under the arch, movement has become simplified and unified in one direction. The confused situation of World 7 has therefore been simplified and resolved in World 19, and these two Worlds explain the reason for our adoption of the somewhat clumsy term of "going-along-mess". It is from the study of many similar resolutions in sequential Worlds that aspects of theory outlined in the Introduction have been deduced.

These two Worlds are part of a series in which powerful machines (such as steamships, trains, motor vehicles) present the idea of force. This series is strongly contrasted with the other and earlier theme of houses, families, farms and animals. These two themes intertwine with one another and elements of both only appear together in World 3, where the train goes under the bridge in a valley in a farm. This separation of content into two strongly contrasted types of symbols and symbolic scenes is very frequently met with in series of children's Worlds.

World 20   Figure 15 (19th session)

Mary said this time she was going to make a railway station like St. Pancras, and set to work with energy and effectiveness, using the big wooden building blocks in a competent construction of a railway terminus with three main

Figure 15

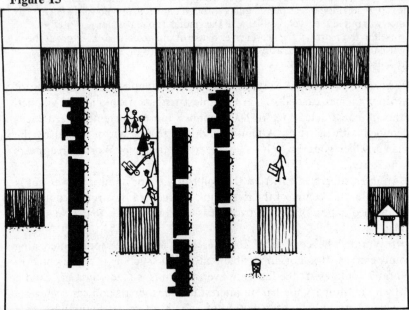

platforms. The platform to the right is empty with a shed at the end of it; on the second is a single man with a brief case, and at the end of it the same workman's brazier which had been used in World 7; two trains, one stationary and one leaving were placed in the second bay, and one stationary train in the third bay to the left. On the platform between the second and third bays were a mother and two children, a porter with luggage, and a guard. The platform to the left was empty.

Conversation. Mary said the trains had come from the far north, but she would say no more until the therapist had drawn the World. During this process Mary found a pop-gun and a shooting play developed between Mary and the therapist. This ended with Mary shooting all people on the platform, who then were put, as dead, in the goods train; after that Mary shot at the therapist. When discussing the family on the platform the therapist asked where father was. Mary replied they had got rid of father, indicating the moment she had shot down the guard. Mary was, however, unable to maintain this position and when it was pointed out to her, denied she had said so.

Discussion. If this World is compared with World 8 it will be seen that the arrangement of the platforms in the station is identical with that of the harbour piers in World 2. The mother and children with a porter on one platform are the same group as appeared on the aerodrome of World 9. We have here, therefore, in these two Worlds, somewhat the same resolution of situation and integration of meaning as appeared in the relation between World 7 and World 19. World 8 presents three separate elements, the coming and going of going-along-nesses (ships) to and from the piers of a harbour; wild animals at liberty and on their own island, and a passenger ship being attacked from below by an engine of war (submarine). As has been pointed out in the comments on World 7, whis is not an *impossible* scene, but Mary has had no reality contact with ships and harbours. The harbour part of the scene, therefore, like the "reality" of World 19 is probably symbolic rather than realistic. The wild animals in World 8 have their conventional significance of wildness and fierceness as experienced in oneself. The submarine attack presents a "hostile" action against the people in the passenger ship, but aggressiveness as such is negated by the presentation of this attack as an incident in war. World 8 therefore presents three elements of interior personality which are held separate from one another. In World 20, when taken together with the play that followed the making of the World all three elements come together and with them is combined also the negation of the father expressed in World 3, and the isolation of mother and two children of World 9. Mary was now able to become aware of hostile and aggressive impulses present in herself and to give expression to them in aggressive play with her therapist.

The three sessions that followed were occupied with the exploration of Mary's aggressiveness which was expressed with paint (in the "Mess" room), with wet sand, in physical activity (in the Gym room), and in playing "school" where an aggressive role was assigned by Mary alternately to herself and the therapist. Since Mary's aggression was now conscious and finding direct impression, the therapist felt the time was ripe for the discussion of the interrelations between herself and her parents. This discussion showed that Mary's depression and unconscious aggression was largely determined by her mother's invincible "sweetness" which produced in Mary a sense of unreality and frustration.

Six weeks summer holiday here intervened.

World 21 Figure 16 (23rd session)

This is a really charming presentation of four houses and gardens occupying the whole of the further edge of the tray and three-quarters of the right-hand edge. Each house is furnished with a well-arranged garden and a bench; a cat in the left-hand one; a dog kennel (no dog) and a sun dial in the next; a rabbit hutch, two rabbits, dovecotes, and another sun dial near the third house; and an owl in the tree of the fourth house. There are no people in these gardens and all the gates are shut. Outside the fencing round the gardens, Mary put two telephone boxes, one by the left edge and one in the right-hand corner; by it a letter box. By the left edge of the tray are petrol and oil pumps and a taxi standing by them. The nearer part of the tray is bare except for two lines of traffic with a wide distance separating them, going in opposite directions, including the milk cart

53

Figure 16

which is coming in at the bottom of the right-hand corner. Mary looked at two figures of girls, put them in a carriage, and was very particular not to have a boy.

Discussion. In her last "village" (World 12) Mary's interest in a single house or group of single houses (Worlds 2 and 5) has begun to break up and other houses appear along the right-hand edge of the tray. This development has gone a considerable step further in World 21.

Besides, there is a certain parallelism between Mary's reaction on her return after the Easter holidays and on her return after the summer holidays. Both Worlds 9, 10 and 21 are made on a strictly reality basis, but where World 9 includes a comment on the family situation, the only comment in World 21 is the absence of all people in the houses and gardens with emphasis on traffic on the road outside. In discussion of this World Mary was able to express her pleasure in the society of her father.

Reality Situation. Between this session and the next the parents reported that in their opinion Mary had become very truculent and difficult at home; when the incidents reported were examined, they proved to be of a very trivial nature and to be instances of the mother's "sweetness" and ineptitude in handling children of which Mary had complained to the therapist. On the next session this was discussed fully between Mary and the therapist.

World 22   Figure 17 (24th session)

Most of this session was spent messing about with wet sand and water.

54

Figure 17

In the middle of the session Mary made this World.

Running along parallel to the further edge Mary placed three trains in a railway cutting, two alongside in the same direction and one separate in the opposite direction. The position of the railway cutting in World 3 is repeated by a canal in World 22; over this canal is a bridge (as over the railway cutting in World 3), but the place of the military band in World 3 is taken here by a group of riders. (Mary had been riding in her holiday); a steam boat was placed on the canal above the bridge, and two parallel lines of small boats across the "harbour" at the base of the canal. On the remaining space of the tray the arrangements of the trains above is duplicated in two horse-drawn vehicles facing to the left, one drawing a cage of lion cubs "going to the fair"; facing the other way are two children in a cart drawn by an ostrich.

Discussion. This World illustrates a principle which has been pointed out in the Introduction, that the same objects – even when used in the same manner – can carry different meanings. As explained before, objects whose essence is movement usually signify going-along-ness, but the fact that Mary called the water here a canal instead of a river and in a way cancelled out the idea of movement through the two parallel rows of boats across the canal, gives us a hint that trains in this World may have another meaning. The fact that the two trains are side by side and facing one direction and the third train going off in the opposite direction, taken in conjunction with the discussion out of which this arose suggests the possibility that the two trains stand for her parents and the third train for herself. This concept is repeated in the three vehicles where the two which

55

face the same way as the two trains are either empty or contain animals, whereas the one facing in the same direction as the single train contains two children; (no grounds appeared for the inclusion of the ostrich). The band which was a visual and acoustic source of excitement, but not one which came actually into Mary's reality life, is replaced by a physical exercise and excitement which she enjoys very much indeed.

In the next session (25) Mary's desire to be a boy, which she had hitherto denied, came to expression. She asked for the mechanical trains, said she would like to play with them on the floor as a real boy, did so, and enjoyed herself immensely.

At the following session Mary made two Worlds of very different character.

World 23 *not illustrated* (26th session)

Mary put a line of hedges across the middle of the tray parallel with the long side, not reaching the right short edge. In the further left-hand corner she placed palm trees and in the nearer left corner a gunboat; this she said was going to be a fight between soldiers and sailors. Army transport was grouped along the left side around the trees, and a cannon put in the middle of the space between the further edge and the centre hedge; a number of soldiers were put facing towards the centre between the cannon and the trees; a group of sailors was placed behind the gunboat; along the centre hedges was an indiscriminate mixed line of soldiers and sailors on both sides, and a monkey among the branches of a tree. Standing by itself by the hedge at the extreme right was a zebra, facing towards the left.

While she was doing this the therapist brought up the question of her liking to be a boy, but today Mary strenuously denied it; the therapist explained that there were many reasons why many girls did in fact wish to be boys; but Mary was firm in her rejection of this desire.

Having finished this World Mary went to another tray and started messing about with sand and water. She said she would make cement and poured in more water until is was very sloppy, then made her second World.

World 24 Figure 18 (same session)

This was a deep crater with high banks around it; water was inside and outside this crater; she said "it is a volcano".

Discussion. Mary's ambivalence towards both the masculine and the feminine sides of herself, and towards both parents had been apparent to her therapist for some time. This now came to open expression. So long as her wish to be a boy remained on the playing level, as in the last session where she could identify with her younger brother, she could tolerate this wish. When, however, masculinity became linked with aggression as in

56

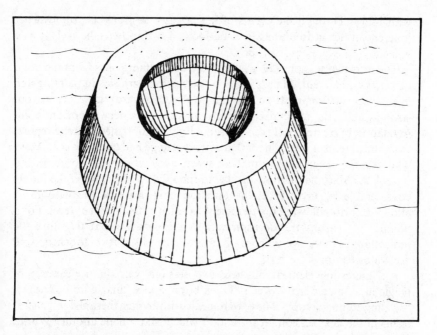

World 23 she became violently repelled from it. World 23 is a very interesting development from World 14 in that while it is a battle between two sides, these are no longer separated into the crude division of "good" and "bad", with aggression identified with badness, but are now stepped up into rational forces which are in conflict with each other. The monkeys from World 2 reappear as a single one placed high up in a tree in World 23. The zebra has not appeared before.

Before making World 24 an idea occurred to Mary which is again one of the standard facts or sequences that constantly recur. Having spent some time, usually on different occasions messing with sand and water, the idea very often occurs to children that this mixture looks like cement; this usually happens in boys who carry out the idea in building; it is less usual in girls, and when it happens it frequently represents – as in Mary's case – the boyish element. When it arises in girls it very rarely leads to building.

The *volcano* is also a constantly recurring feature in World sequences in makers of all ages; we have not as yet examined sufficient case histories to be able to say whether the volcano is more a feature of one sex than of the other. There is a considerable variety in the treatment of the volcano theme; they can be eruptive, or extinct, or, as in Mary's case, they can contain an essential contradiction, in that though called a volcano it contains water. Volcanoes, we find, are made by children and adults at a point in treatment where the projections of interior forces previously made to external persons and objects have been withdrawn, and the pressure of interior drives has become focused but not yet expressed. This is the case with Mary. Through the events of her last two sessions the ambivalence inherent in her attitude has become focused within her; she feels it as a volcano and expresses it as such.

The next two sessions (27 and 28) were determining ones from the point of view of treatment. Mary's mode of expression here was in painting and aggression; self-deprecation and ambivalence towards males came out strongly and from much deeper levels, thus raising a very important point in relation to treatment. From the school reports obtained and the reports from the parents it was evident that a great change had taken place in Mary who was now beginning to make a satisfactory adjustment to home and school. As Mary had a long journey to the I.C.P. which caused the family considerable inconvenience, the question now arose of the wisdom of allowing or not allowing the treatment to reach a much deeper level. For a number of reasons the decision was in the negative and therefore the indications in these two sessions of profound depths, not yet touched, were not followed up.

An interesting element of these two sessions was the appearance of magic in a "magic tree" which "killed boys" and a "magic house" which "swallowed people up". These were dealt with by her therapist in general terms in the next session, at the end of which Mary made another World.

World 25   Figure 19 (29th session)

A river was cut out going the length of the tray nearer the further edge and a bridge put over it to the right, two big trees placed at either side exactly opposite

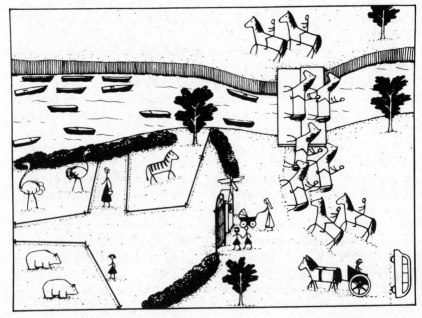

each other near the right-hand edge, and many rowing boats on the river. Mary now took out the long hedges, put one along the nearer bank of the river by the left-hand edge with a tree at its right end; with two other pieces of hedge, a gate, a paybox and a road sign she enclosed a space in the left nearer corner for a zoo. Within this space she fenced off three enclosures, put a zebra in the one near the tree, two ostriches in the one to the further left, and two polar bears in the one at the left nearer corner. Within the zoo were placed a "mother" looking at the ostriches, and a "daughter" looking at polar bears. Just outside the entrance to the zoo she placed a nurse with a pram, and two small girls. At the same level by the nearer edge a fourth big tree was placed. In the extreme right-hand corner a bus was waiting to go off, and the bizarre figure of an old lady in a Roman chariot, said to be "going to the zoo". The World was completed with nine horses and riders (children and grownups) riding across the bridge, two of them having reached the further side.

Discussion. In this World the wildness (as her therapist pointed out) is now manageable, to some extent socialised; the interest of mother and daughter is focused on different aspects of this wildness, mother paying attention to the ostrich whom we have seen before (World 22) completely tame, drawing a cart; the daughter's interest centering upon the polar bears who have played a part several times before. The zebra has appeared in World 23 without Mary making any reference to it. The significance of the bus we do not know, but it is clear that in the riding party adults and children are together sharing a pleasant experience. It was not at any time possible to find the significance to Mary of the little boats.

This was the last World Mary made while under treatment.

The next session (30) was spent in gay, active play, normal for a girl of her age. At the following session (31) the therapist went over with her the drawings of all the Worlds Mary had made, pointing out how early on there had been a boy trespassing, and all along a great deal to do with milk; the therapist then said that this looked as if Mary was expressing a real situation: that her brother came along when Mary was still a small girl and was fed by her mother: that a part of her felt him to be a trespasser and another part would have wanted to rival him by herself being a boy and this she had carried out in a number of boys' kinds of play. At the beginning of this session Mary had had an idea of playing school, but after this conversation she gave it up and did instead a charming drawing on the blackboard of a house with lighted windows, a good tree and a pond that was frozen all the year so they can skate on it; there was a path running from the house to the gate in the fence; in front of the house were three little girls with lanterns, singing carols.

It was now the middle of November. Between this date and Christmas there were four more sessions (32, 33, 34, 35) in none of which Mary made a World, but instead carried out very ordinary active play appropriate to her age. As reports from school ("her work now quite normal and no complaints at all") and home were now satisfactory, at the end of the Autumn term Mary was discharged.

Follow-ups

The I.C.P. kept in touch with the Smiths.

One year later Mrs. Smith reported that she "is finding Mary now a nice child to have about; she is happy, has plenty of friends and enjoys school; she is still not a worker, remains at the bottom of the class but nobody seems to be worrying".

Two years later Mary was seen again. She was now 15 years old, rather stocky, with a somewhat ungainly walk. She said she was "extremely happy", "loves school", where she was now a boarder, "has lots of friends", "doesn't like games much", "doesn't yet know what she wants to do when she leaves school". At this visit she made a World.

World 26   Figure 20

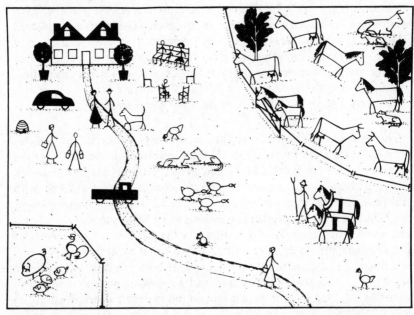

This World is called a farm. There is a manorhouse standing freely near the left further corner of the tray, and a tree in a tub on either side of the door. On the right-hand side three children sit on a bench with four chairs in front of them, on one of which a fourth child is sitting. The path from the house winds down to the nearer edge; the farmer, his wife and a dog are walking down it. A man and a woman, "farm workers", are on the left with a beehive behind them. In the left nearer corner are a pig, piglets and a cock in an enclosure; in the right further corner a curving fence with a gate encloses a large field with two big trees, 5 cows,

2 calves, 3 horses and one foal; in the space between the path and this field a man is leading 2 farm horses; a chicken stands by itself; a cat sits by itself; there are 3 angry geese, 2 dogs, a pecking hen; on the path by the nearer edge a woman is going shopping. One car is placed parallel in front of the house and a lorry further down with its front wheels across the path.

Discussion. The central feature of this World is its freedom and looseness of construction; Mary said it was a fine summer day and the therapist's remark was that the whole made a very pleasant impression. The one bizzare factor is that the lorry has been placed straight across the road.

Five years after termination of treatment contact was again made with Mary. She was now 17 years old. Her school reported that Mary's personal development was on the whole satisfactory, "more assured in the face of adversity"; she is "a very pleasant and willing member of the house and thoughtful of others". On the work side, however, she is 18 months older than the average of her form and not certain of passing any subject at O-level in G.C.E. She has no sense of number, little imagination, finds difficulty in any subject which has not a practical meaning for her, but "is working well and trying hard". She is said to be completely happy at school and so content with the present that she can give no thought to the future. Her interest in riding has waned and her one great interest is music for which she has some degree of talent. She writes a good and interesting letter home and seems to be able to write to her parents about herself and her friendships in a frank and natural manner.

Her father reports, "We as parents are both devoted to her and find her a delightful and happy companion. Her mother has a great longing to give her more demonstrative affection than Mary seems ready to accept. She shows none of the usual teenage problems. We feel Mary is still jealous of her brother and we are told that she talks much more readily and easily when he is out of the way".

Six years after termination of treatment. When seen for a reporting visit at the I.C.P. Mary made on the whole a good impression; she was friendly and free, interested to discuss her present situation and the future; there seemed no doubt that her present adjustment to school and home was good, but it was equally clear that she was somewhat retarded in emotional development and had not yet reached the stage in adolescence parallel with her chronological age.

Review of Mary Smith's Treatment

The theory of disturbance in children upon which treatment is based is briefly that of E* flowing through the various systems of the body/personality and becoming held up at various points where the absence, for any one of a number of causes, of suitable channels through which it could discharge itself, produces symptoms of disturbance. Mary is an example of a girl of normal physique who had passed through a number of painful and distressing experiences in early youth and who at the time of her referral to the Institute was unable to make contact either with her family or her school fellows, and at the same time was failing to achieve a satisfactory standard in school work.

Her treatment during the 35 sessions falls into a number of stages.

Her first World expressed her situation. In a hollow square, houses stand against three edges of the tray; in front a truncated road leads only into a shed at one end and a dead end at the other; a telephone box by it suggests a desire to communicate.

Stage 1. In Worlds 2, 3, 5, Mary made use of objects representative of her ordinary surroundings, and these were grouped in a way which expressed a constellation of ideas and emotions concerned with the family and her feelings toward and about her family. In all of them she obliterated her brother and in World 2 she repeated the picture of a block in E, in a river carrying an Indian in a canoe which came to a dead end at about the same point in the tray as the "cul-de-sac" in World 1. Between Worlds 3 and 5, Mary expressed in the circus of World 4 the tensions, odd physical movements and excitement obscurely aroused in herself by thoughts and feelings about sexual life and the parents. It contains a hint (which comes to fuller expression later) of dimly seen possibilities of oppression and cruelty.

Having achieved a certain degree of expression of these sides of her problems Mary was ready to put on one side the near-reality form of her presentations and embark upon a symbolical World.

Stage 2. In World 6 Mary boldly used the outer forms of her previous Worlds in a frankly symbolic way. Houses here stand for bodies, and some of her perplexities about these appeared in the streams which issued from the front doors and the collection of aggressive and powerful masculine symbols arranged about them. World 7 presented the other side of the picture, that of E. Here all the possible ordinary forms of longitudinal movement (going-along-nesses) crossed and recrossed each other in a weaving pattern, with a woman leaving a house to enter a bus as a central figure.

Stage 3. In the last World of Mary's first term she made a further step. Her sense of security had developed to a point where she could leave these

---

*See Appendix.

"everyday" symbols and embark upon something bolder. In the centre of this World was a disaster: an attack by a submarine upon a passenger vessel. This took place at the edge of terraces inhabited by wild animals, mainly of the fierce kind. This is the first time wild animals (other than the monkeys in the cage in World 2) had been used, and Mary contrasted them with the orderly going and coming of ships in a harbour.

Stage 4. At the beginning of the next term Mary started off with a reality World (9), not this time of anything she had experienced herself but one emobdying the modern idea of power combined with a picture of a mother and two children. She balanced this with a picture of herself – a housing standing by itself in the middle of the tray, in a garden (World 10).

Stage 5. The work that had so far been done now culminated in an outburst of proto-system material. For the first time Mary luxuriated in the possibilities of quickly changing sensorial and pictorial possibilities offered by sand and water (World 11). The making of each of the next two Worlds was followed by handling and playing about with wet sand in the tray. The first of these (World 12) represented her original village scene but this time with the houses as the "surround" to a children's playground. In the second (World 13) animals had been caught and put in cages in a zoo – ready to be visited but so far without spectators.

World 14 carried on the proto-system play and finished with a frankly sensuous oral phantasy of the sand representing "lovely ice cream". In both proto-system Worlds (11 and 14) there is a strong emphasis upon enjoyable foods forming a strong contrast to her own early feeding history.

Stage 6. Having gained so much freedom in sensorial experiment Mary burst out into three Worlds in one session. The first of these (No. 15) was a violent and extremely confused battle scene of cowboys and Indian) (i.e., of "bad" and "good", the bad said to be those who wish to fight, ending with a direct expression of sensuous skin pleasure and indirect reference to masturbation. This was followed by a World representing a school room (No. 16) in which she could now put a figure of herself at school, the dunce; and finally by a World (No. 17) of a parental bedroom shared by a girl and *two* boys (the first time a direct reference to her brother has appeared).

In World 18 Mary returned to her house and farm theme (as this made possible the presentation of animal mothers and babies); between two sets of these was a milk-cart facing toward the single house. Although the milk-cart had been a frequent constituent of the Worlds this was the first appearance of suckling babies.

At this point in her development several themes crossed each other and clear-cut stages no longer appear. World 19 is a powerful presentation of two symbols for E: a railway train and a river identified with one another, the train running down the centre of the river. On the nearer bank she placed an excavator, an almost witty hint of further excavation to be done.

World 20 combined the paralleled arrangement of the harbour of World 8, represented here in a railway station, combined it with the mother, two children and porters of World 9. This started off a bout of cheerfully aggressive play with her therapist in which her relation to her father was obliquely expressed. This World introduced a period of general play in other media, with two sessions of "school" play which finished the summer term.

Mary now sought a means of expressing the "movement" which was taking place within her, and to do so went back to her original type of scene. In the first World (21) of the Autumn session she presented her usual collection of houses and gardens, with, as the main feature of the World, a very wide road upon which every possible kind of large and small vehicles moved to right and left. Her next World (No. 22) is puzzling and gives one an impression of being more an "essay" in the statement of something that is not completed than the actual statement itself. It was made in the middle of a session in which the irritation which her mother caused Mary came to full expression, and later her fondness for her father. The line of water across the left hand corner of the World, with a bridge crossing the middle of it, had appeared in World 3, but it was here a canal rather than a river. Ordinary riders on horses cross the bridge, as individuals, not in a band, and the canal terminated in a wide end with two rows of small boats. Trains like those of World 19 ran along the back, and the space to the right contained a curious collection of vehicles which had not appeared before. This World seems to be preparatory to the two Worlds (23 and 24) made at the next session. In the first of these the theme of fights from World 5 reappeared but this time between the fighting men of her own country – British soldiers and sailors. Finally there appeared the typical basic pattern of the volcano, fully discussed on page 57.

Skipping, painting and drawing occupied the next two sessions together with discussion of the Worlds so far done. One of her drawings was of a magic house "which if you go in swallows you up". Her therapist in the next session discussed with her the different feelings which are connected with mouths, biting, eating and being bitten and swallowed. In the final World (25) the river flowed the length of the tray carrying many small boats. In the zoo which appeared on the left of the tray, a "mother and daughter" were included. Free movement was expressed in a number of riders and horses. There were no houses.

Six sessions after this World came Christmas, and Mary's parents reported that Mary's all-round improvement was so satisfactory that they asked for her discharge.

It is probable that to all experienced therapists many aspects of this treatment will appear superficial, and to some extent we would agree with this judgment. As already pointed out, at the age of 18, Mary's emotional development was to some extent lagging behind normal, and it is yet to be seen how she will face adult life. On the other hand, had the parents agreed that she should continue treatment, it is certain that the Worlds she would then make circling round the themes already expressed, would have brought to light other more interior and profound aspects of her inner experience, and have made possible a complete resolution of her problems.

Review of Mary's Worlds

If we now turn from the question of the psycho-therapeutic treatment of Mary as shown in her Worlds, to consideration of the Worlds themselves, we need, in order to be able to compare the use of this technique by different children, to have some means of analysis and comparison of individual Worlds.

I propose next to consider in reference to Mary's treatment three aspects of Mary's Worlds: – The objects chosen by Mary for use in her Worlds; the themes presented by and through these objects; and the structure of the presentation.

Objects and Content

Study of a large number of Worlds made by children and adults brings out the unexpected point that each individual, unconsciously to himself, selects a certain range of objects and revolves around them in his series of Worlds; rarely moving outside them. Thus, for example, Mary Smith used houses, gardens and traffic, and expressed both her proto-system contents and her interpersonal relationships in these terms; Charles Robinson, on the other hand, as will be seen, expressed family relationships in terms of jungle animals, and blockages to E in terms of varieties of transport. In the matter of the disposal of the objects within the tray, in the moulding of the sand and the making of defined shaped and designs within the tray, a similar individuality appears.

On the other hand, although that is so, yet there is such variety in the forms which are constructed that the task of finding a mode of classification which will enable direct comparison between child and child is a matter of considerable difficulty. Four processes can be distinguished.

1. The making of a coherent story or scene in which each object used and the placing of it, relates in some way to the scene or story.
2. The creation of a definite pattern within the tray, whether through manipulation of the sand or disposal of the objects or both. (The formation of distinctive dimensional forms, such as the mound in Mary's World 11 would be included here.)
3. The creation of a single "moment" in a scene, comparable to a still photograph in a cinematograph series.
4. The selection, placing and manipulation of objects in the tray without the emergence of a coherent scene or story.

These four processes can be present in very many degrees and a wide variety of permutations and combinations between them can take place. For the purpose of understanding the three children presented in this chapter we shall consider only some of these combinations which are presented in Mary's Worlds, and go into the matter in greater detail in the analysis of the Worlds of Charles Robinson and William Carter.

These are:

Coherent Worlds which may occur with or without a definite patterning.
Incoherent Worlds in which no coherent story emerges, but which may appear combined with a definite shape or patterning in the tray or without such.
Composite Worlds which contain a balance of one type with some features of the other which can also be combined with definite patterning or be without such.
Story Worlds which tell a story.
Multi-dimensional Worlds which represent aspects of the proto-system directly.

Analysis of Mary's Worlds
Table 1 shows the grouping of Mary's Worlds into Coherent and Incoherent, together with the categories into which these fall.

Table 1

	Coherent	Incoherent
Country Scenes		
Village	12–18	1
Suburban	2–3–5–21	
Farm	26	
Other country scenes	7–10	6–22
River and bridge		19
Harbour, Airport and Station	8–9–20	
Interior Scenes		
"Circus"		4
School	16	
Bedroom	17	
Fights	15–23	
Wild Animals		
Zoo	13–25	
Proto-system		11–14–24
Total	**18 Worlds**	**8 Worlds**

Patterning
In the sense in which patterning occurs in Charles' Worlds (for example in Worlds 10 and 31) or in William's (for example Worlds 4 and 10) it does not appear in Mary's series. Similarities of arrangement, however, in the disposal of component parts of similar scenes, for example those classified as suburban scenes, occur frequently. Two examples occur, however, of forms which constantly recur in the Worlds made both by children and adults, i.e., World 11 (tunnels and mound) and World 24 (volcano), while

in World 14 an incoherent series of manipulations *in time* expressed proto-system contents.

Symbols for E

As symbols for E occur with much greater clarity in Charles' Worlds than in Mary's, discussion of this type of symbolisation will be found in the analysis of Charles' Worlds. It is suggested therefore that the analysis of Charles' series of Worlds be read first, and the study of the presentation of E in Mary's Worlds be considered after that of Charles' Worlds.

As in Charles' Worlds, so in Mary's, the two main symbols of E which occur are a river and a train (with the addition in World 1 of Mary's of a road with a cart on it). As pointed out already, movement in both Worlds 1 and 2 is blocked.

In contrast to these two, in World 3 a train is in movement. Here a question arises, which applies also to the river and train in Worlds 5, 9, 20 and 25: that since these are coherent naturalistic scenes, can the river and trains be considered as symbols of E instead of essential parts of a coherent scene? Worlds 6 and 22 on the other hand are frankly unrealistic and Incoherent and the streams in the one and river and trains in the other stand in their own right as symbols of E, while in World 19 both train and river as E symbols are identified together in an Incoherent scene. In one remaining instance, World 7, all forms of going-along-ness occur together.

Charles Robinson

Charles Robinson

History: Account of Treatment

This boy has been selected as an illustrative case for the exposition of the place played in the treatment of disturbed children by the World Technique because the nature of this boy's disturbance exemplifies two of the crucial difficulties facing educators: that of inability to make contact with his fellows accompanied by unmanageable outbreaks of violence on the one hand and an almost absolute inability to learn on the other. Such a boy offers a good opportunity for exposition of the part played by the World Technique in the treatment of disturbed children and of some discussion of the meaning to the child of the objects he uses.

Charles was a boy of 7 whose behaviour difficulties were so acute and severe that he had had to be excluded from school, and which formed an urgent problem at home. He had failed to respond to the usual Child Guidance approach and his education and home handling offered a practically insoluble problem.

While, on his father's side, there was on the whole an unexceptional heredity, Charles' mother confessed during the later course of treatment that throughout her life, previous to marriage, she had been terrified of her father's rages and now felt these to be being reproduced in her son.

Charles' intelligence quotient on the Stanford-Binet scale was 118 but his school attainment was so far below average as to make his education a very difficult problem. his social adaptation could be said to be practically nil and he was subject to outbursts of violence of a degree that made inclusion in normal school or home life impossible. His mother's intensely possessive attitude to him and his to her added an additional complication; his father played little part.

In view of this very acute problem the decision was taken that Charles be admitted to a home-school for maladjusted children of an unusual kind, situated in the country at some distance from his home, on condition that psychotherapeutic treatment be undertaken by the author. At no time was it possible to secure any treatment for Charles' mother and contact with her was, by the circumstance, limited to beginning and end of term and half-term visits paid by the family to the school.

Charles Robinson therefore presented an admirable opportunity for the study of E in a boy already disposed by his maternal heredity to outbursts of uncontrollable rage.

History

Charles Robinson, age 7 years 8 months, I.Q. 118, was the younger of two siblings, the other being a girl of 16.

Symptoms.   Violent rages and depression; inability to make contact with other

70

people. Charles was severely mother-tied and timid, with neurotic fears of water and of mechanical toys; occasional bouts of asthma.

Family.   Charles came of a respectable working-class family. His home was in a small industrial country town some miles from the school. His *father* was a porter in a local store, himself an illegitimate child, brought up from the age of 11, when his mother died, by a maiden aunt. His first marriage had been unhappy, his wife having run away with a lodger and left him with a daughter, aged 4½. Some years later he married Charles' mother. He was a quiet, inarticulate man who "never laughed", a rather colourless personality, dependable and "proper", who "had never sworn in his life". His main aim was to avoid anything arousing a display of feeling in the family.

Charles' *mother* came from a working-class family, was one of 12 siblings. Her father was subject to fits of sudden irrational and uncontrollable temper; in one of such outbursts, for example, he threw the family dinner out of the window. He "went to pieces" after his wife died. His wife was said to be "jolly and full of jokes"; one brother committed suicide, the others did well. As a child Mrs. Robinson had had rheumatic fever, and she developed tuberculosis in various organs, and later suffered from premenstrual tension; was frequently in and out of hospital for considerable periods; later her health improved, and she worked occasionally at a restaurant when she wanted to make extra money for acquisitions for her home. Her temperament was emotional, possessive, limited in outlook, with very little understanding of children, but in other ways a practical and capable woman.

Charles' *sister*, Mary (8 years older than Charles), was an intelligent, competent go-ahead girl and popular with young friends. Relations between Charles and herself had always been stormy, the fault sometimes on one side and sometimes on the other.

Charles' *stepsister* (Mr. R's daughter from the first marriage) was married with 2 children about Charles' age, both her social standing and her domestic standards were below those of the Robinsons. She took charge of Charles for a fortnight once, at the age of 3, when his mother was in hospital.

Family atmosphere.   The economic circumstances of the family at the time of treatment were good and nothing that is customary in their social group was at the time lacking in the house. The children were for the most part used as bones of contention between the parents, the father protecting the daughter, the mother the son; the sister was provocative to her brother and to some extent jealous of her mother's pre-occupation with him; relations between mother and father were poor, Mrs. Robinson having a contempt for her husband.

History.   Charles was not wanted on account of financial difficulties at the time; normal pregnancy and labour; birth weight 8 lb. 11 oz; breastfed for 2 months then easily weaned to a bottle; he was a "lazy feeder", a lazy child, sat about and never crawled; development satisfactory except that he would at times hold back his motions for 2–3 days. At age 2½ his buttocks were scalded by hot tea; he was treated in hospital; on return he wanted to get into his mother's bed and was afraid of the cot. Between the ages 3–6 Charles was frequently separated from his mother who was in and out of hospital and he was then sent from pillar to post among relatives. For 3 months he was in a Children's Home; at age of 4 broke his arm, was admitted to hospital and treated unsatisfactorily; he had constant colds; tonsilectomy at 4½; severe attacks of asthma.

Housing conditions were very bad during his first 6 years (no playground and no garden, with lodgers who quarrelled noisily). Then the family was re-housed and conditions improved to the position noted above. At 5 Charles started

Infant school; at 7 he was excluded for uncontrollable behaviour by the Education Authorities and admitted to the residential Home School at which treatment took place.

Summary of History

From the accounts we have of Charles up to the age when he was first seen, there emerges a picture of a brooding obsessional type of child, passionately possessive of both people and things and demanding their exclusive absorption in himself; given to violent rages and with an easily aroused sense of injury: unable to make contact with his fellows and so absorbed in and dominated by his interior emotional life that all that happened outside was dim to him.

Charles' life experience had been most unfortunate and quite apart from a possible predisposition to violence on his mother's side, from the age of $2\frac{1}{2}$ disasters of one sort or another crowded upon him; the frequent absence of his mother, his many changes of background and handling were first reacted to by severe asthma and later by withdrawal from contact with the people around him, passionate possessiveness towards his mother and violent outbursts of temper.

His hospital experiences had been unfortunate and on one occasion, when in hospital for his broken arm he saw, from the ward window, his mother and father come up to the hospital and then through some misunderstanding they were not admitted.

When admitted to the residential school Charles was a child who was almost completely withdrawn into himself; he was silent and unresponsive to all advances and then would suddenly, usually in the middle of lesson time, burst out into such phrases as "my mother is a *pig*," shouting at the top of his voice. At other times he would seize and break the object nearest to him and throw the pieces at anyone within his reach, attack furiously the child or children who had annoyed him, and at other times would creep away and hide under a bed in the house or if outside run away blindly.

His educational attainments were minimal; two years after admission and at the age of $9\frac{1}{2}$ he was not certain of the sequence of the primary numerals.

Treatment

Charles was seen by the writer twice weekly for half an hour during the school terms in a "play hut" in the school grounds. At first this was part of an old brick building left over from war alterations and fitted with water and a sink; later when this was demolished and a wooden hut substituted, running water was missing. Both huts were fitted with the same technical equipment as at the I.C.P.

The case was a long one and the extract chosen extends from the first session to two years later which marked the end of a definite phase. The half hour session was insufficient for optimum treatment of a case of this severity but was all that could be achieved in the circumstances. In any other school this would probably have proved insufficient, but the great patience and understanding of the head of the school, coupled with his skill as a teacher and the atmosphere of security in the school community made possible what would ordinarily have been difficult to achieve. The shortness of the sessions also had a bearing upon the length of treatment.

Techniques of Treatment

As this is a book descriptive of the World Technique and not of psychotherapy as such, the description that follows of Charles' treatment is *focused upon his use of Worlds*. The number of the session at which each World was made is given after the serial number of the World. Charles was introduced to and used a number of other techniques, the choice of what he could do in the vast majority of sessions being left to himself. The exceptions were when incidents had occurred in the school in the periods between sessions which needed discussion with Charles or sessions taken by his bed in periods of physical illness. In the main Charles used three techniques, Worlds, drawings and the Newspaper Game alternating with short periods of construction. A brief statement concerning these is included in the text or as footnotes for the periods between Worlds so the progress of the case can be seen as a whole.

Charles drew with vigour, concentration, and speed. The subjects of his drawings were sometimes chosen by himself, sometimes suggested by me. His drawings were mainly representative of interpersonal relationships and added to or enlarged the content of his Worlds. If this were a description of the complete psychotherapeutic treatment of Charles, considerable space would have to be given to these drawings, but *as the subject we are considering is his use of the World Technique*, this, regretfully, has had to be omitted, a brief statement about each drawing having to suffice.

Charles was silent for most of his early sessions; he would do things with his hands, build with Poleidoblocs, or draw, or fit a wooden engine and rails together, and would listen when talked to but would not talk himself. After his first year at the school an arrangement was made with the Headmaster by which he could get into the Play-Hut when a violent stress arose and make and leave a World. This would be discussed with him at his next session.

His Worlds were made with passionate absorption, accompanied with noises appropriate to the scene, but only rarely with spontaneously spoken comment; when asked about the World, however, in most cases he was able to give detailed information.

Progress of Treatment

At the *first session*, my descriptive note about him says "silent, sullen expression, very withdrawn, mouth breather".

As is customary, Charles was presented with the *Lowenfeld Mosaic Test*. He accepted it readily and set to work slowly to make an irregular outline in diamonds of a large rectangular frame fitting into the nearer right-hand corner and covering half of the tray; inside the frame he fitted together six squares in a horizontal line, superimposed on these three large diamonds composed of putting two equilateral triangles together. He then put a row of equilateral triangles along the further edge using all the colours, with three diamonds in the corner; between this and the rectangle he put an experimental row of scalenes.

This completed the session.*

At his *second session* Charles was shown the World apparatus and was not interested. He accepted instead Poleidoblocs G. He used these first to put together a motley collection of small bricks and tried to "enclose" them and failed. He then tried again and made an oblong enclosure, this time with an "entrance" in front, and the smaller bricks disposed within it. He then, at my suggestion, built "the tower"† and smiled for the first time when it was completed. It was at this session that I first noted a characteristic which persisted throughout his treatment. When sitting at a table and absorbed in concentration he would protrude his tongue to a remarkable length, doubling it over on itself and moving it round his lips.

At the *third session* Charles was very keen to come. As he had appeared interested in colour, another box of gaily coloured pieces was offered to him, with which he occupied himself happily through the half hour constructing what he called "a hat" of a number of colours.

At his next session Charles was prepared to accept the World apparatus and set to work steadily.

World 1 Figure 21 (4th session)

When starting this World Charles said he was going to make a river and cleared away the sand from the tray down to the blue base, leaving bare a looped area of

---

*Description of Charles' further Mosaics will be found on pages 162/3.
†An easy construction which uses all the blocks.

74

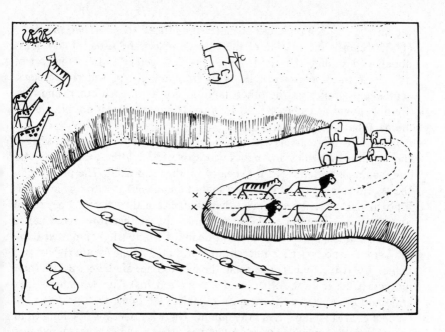

tray as represented in the drawing, with a tongue of land projecting into this from the right. He then looked for, found and took out of the wild animals drawer a large and a small elephant, said to be mother and baby, and then a second large and small elephant, put them at the point of the tongue of land. Three crocodiles were placed in the water facing right and the elephants were made to walk along the tongue to where they are shown in the drawing. A lion and lioness were now taken out and then another lion and a tiger; these were put following each other along the tongue, lion behind lioness and beside these tiger behind lion. A large and a small hippopotamus, said to be mother and baby, were taken out and put "in the water" in the left nearer corner; a big giraffe and two small ones (nothing was said about these) were put across the water on the land near the left edge and a zebra near them; two monkeys were put in the further left corner without comment. The final figure, a man with a rifle seated on an elephant, was then added, the rifle aiming towards the tongue of land.

Conversation. Charles was completely absorbed in the making of this World and was silent until it was completed. In the meantime the arrangements of the animals on the tray was drawn and the usual conversation about these then took place. Charles' comments were that it was a river, that the man on the elephant was aiming first at the lions and tiger and then at the crocodiles; he did not know if they were hit or not; the crocodiles were going off down the water to the right.

Discussion. Charles' first World is in marked contrast to Mary Smith's use of the material. Mary selected reality objects familiar to her from her own environment; the significance of the Worlds lay in the manner of her use of these. Charles, on the other hand, leaped, as it were, straight into

75

the middle of a symbolic use of material and used these on two planes.

(1) The choice and placing of the animals reflect the usual child's ideas about wild animals, i.e., lions and tigers go together and are the sort of animals men shoot; crocodiles are fierce and live in water. Monkeys, zebras and giraffes on the other hand do not harm each other, and they are not sought as game or food by men. Hippopotamuses are big clumsy animals that like living in mud.

(2) The fact that animals are of two sexes and have families somewhat in the way human beings do, makes it possible for children to use large and small animals to represent the idea of mother and child. The presence in the World cabinet of a figure of a man-on-an-elephant-with-a-rifle makes it possible to present a statement that humans are also "fierce", they shoot at the fierce wild animals. What it would appear therefore that Charles has stated in this World is an absorbtion in the relationship of mother-baby in various aspects; the adult giraffe (presumably the mother) has two babies, the two elephants one each, the hippos one; all these are with their mothers (Charles on the other hand is away from his). The elephant mother and child are in danger from the crocodiles; the lions, the tiger, and the crocodiles are in danger from the hunter. There is no means of telling what the zebra and monkeys express for Charles – they may be casual ingredients put to blurr a little the giraffe with *two* children.

To those trained in psychoanalytic and analytica lpsychological schools of thought a number of points about this World will occur and very probably most of them would be correct; but taken as it stands all we know is that it states that there are two classes of human relationships: Mother and child, and male and female – and that both are in danger of direct attack. This World was discussed with Charles in the above terms but not linked to his own situation.

World 2 *not illustrated* (5th session)

This was made at the next session three days later and shows an entire change of scene and reaction to the material. On the left side of the tray he made a vaguely indicated airfield. The sand was cleared away to the base of the tray, and four planes put in it with "a man about to get into a plane". In the right nearer corner he put another plane said to be "about to take off". Charles then got out various motor vehicles, mostly army ones, and moved them about the sand making appropriate motor noises, now and again making pieces of road and putting men in various places without obvious reference to anything else, except for the one man "about to get into the plane". The whole was incoherent and unplanned and every now and then he would take an aeroplane up and make it crash with loud noises. In the middle of this he got a horse and cart out of the cabinet, looked at it and put it on the table – later put it away contemptuously. He was completely absorbed in his play, and did not talk about it at all.

Discussion. This World may be influenced to some extent by the fact that a training airfield is situated some six miles from the school and planes fly fairly often overhead. Charles was at this time quite silent. The main power symbols in this World were placed on the left – (Charles is right-handed) – and a separating sand wall made between them and the rest of the tray. A good deal of the session was spent by Charles in moving these planes with intense concentration up and down and flying around in the air, making loud buzzing noises. At other times the vehicular traffic was moved about with equal violence to and fro on the sand with similar noises, Charles studying intently the tracks they made in the sand. He seemed to be oblivious of any presence and wholly absorbed in his actions. The few notes I have of the significance of the different objects were gained in answer to questions on my part which had to be phrased so that a nod was adequate reply.

On the 6th session Charles painted patterns and on the 7th drew three of the children at the school, two girls and a boy, the boy in the centre with a truck beside them and a lot of scribbles.

During this period the school reported that during one morning at school Charles had suddenly burst out with "My mummy is a pig, my daddy is . . ." calling him various names and shouting and cursing. At the next session he was heavy-eyed and silent with out-pushed lower lip and vacant eyes, pushing one sock up and down. He could give no reason for his outbursts which seemed to come from a separate part of him and his only comment upon this and other outbursts was "I lost my temper".

On the 8th session I suggested he use "pin men" drawings about his family* – this he did, including a rabbit in its cage. The last session (9) of the term was spent in discussion of the outbursts in the school.

The Summer holidays here intervened.

At the first session (10) of the autumn term, according to our usual procedure Charles was asked to make a *Mosaic*. This was a great advance on his first one and showed a balanced vertical "intermediate" structure using all the colours and covering the whole of the left side of the tray.

On the next session (11) he went back to Poleidoblocs and again showed considerable progress, making this time a well-constructed square "house" with a roof, saying, "the centre is where you go when you are hot and the back when you are cold" and there was "a gentleman and lady in it".

At the following session he made a World.

---

*These were in character in that "mummy and daddy" drawn first had prominent teeth: later "mummy pushing daddy in a barrow"; Charles standing between mummy and daddy; Mary by herself (with no teeth); and Charles on a rock "going to jump on Mary".

World 3 *not illustrated* (12th session)

The form of this was very similar to that of World 2, with a cleared area again at the left and in the same place as the previous airfield. Charles lined up four cars along the further edge, made a strongly marked looped road leading out of the cleared area and then turning on itself to end at the left edge of the tray, and put road signs beside it. He then took out a number of cars and ran them to and fro about the tray making so many tracks in the sand that in the end it looked like the snow of a beginners ski-school. By the right edge of the tray he enclosed a square "field" with fences and took out two cows to put in it but did not use them. Suddenly he dashed to the cabinet and got out several policemen and put them at various points on the tray, not, apparently, relevant to anything in it.

On the following session (13) I suggested Charles might do a pin-picture series of "a boy making the mother angry" and he drew two pictures – mummy and daddy and boy "skipping on a carpet" and the boy sitting on a chair and shouting at his mother because she threw away one of his old toys.

Three days after this Charles was reported as having had an attack of vomiting the day before, and when seen was in bed in the middle of a typical, moderately acute, attack of asthma. He evidently enjoyed being in bed on his own and ate with great gusto. Sessions 14 and 15 were taken in bed – mostly spent in drawing and discussing comics he was reading. He reported a dream of being at the seaside with his mother and his father (thus obliterating his sister).

World 4   **Figure 22** (16th session)

This World, made a fortnight after his last one, was made with great swiftness and decision by Charles – he knew exactly what he wanted and chose and acted decisively.

He smoothed the sand flat and made a river which ran diagonally across the tray, clearing the sand to the base, the direction of the water being thought of as flowing from front to back. A bridge was placed across the river in the centre. Then a covered van containing milk was put in on the right bank of the river; on the left at the near corner he made a pond and later very carefully fenced it in. He now occupied himself with the bridge, put two empty lorries on the left end of the bridge and running the milk lorry from right to left attempted to make the lorries run in opposite directions passing the milk lorry, but the bridge was too narrow so a road was made over the bridge to make passing possible. The second lorry was taken off. A bench was placed to the right beside the milk van, with two lamp posts on each side, two cars, one red, were coming in from the far right corner. Three racing cars were parked against the further edge with a road-sign beside them, and a telephone box and a halt-sign nearer the river; at the far right-hand side of the river was a single car. On the left side of the river a hexagonal field was made and sheep put in, then enlarged to make possible the inclusion of a chicken hut into which he put the lambs. Finally a train was put in running along the right-hand shorter edge.

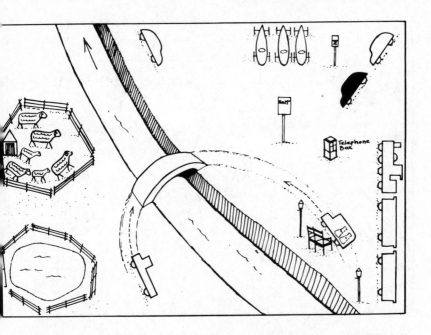

Discussion. When he began World 1 Charles said he was making a river; at the end it had become a small lake. In World 4 a river really appears; it flows he says, from front to back. In World 1 the movement described was *in* the water from left to right. Here the focus of the World is the bridge which is the centre of the picture. A semi-circular road beginning and ending at each side was made by the milk van and empty lorry passing one another across the bridge. The theme of animal mothers and babies appears again, as in World 1, but this time with farm animals of the essentially docile kind. The big lake of World 1 has shrunk to a pool and both it and the sheep are completely and carefully fenced in. There is no hint of danger in this World and the only touch of violence is the three stationary racing cars. World 4 is in fact a kind of summary of what has been expressed in the three previous Worlds, only without noises and without violent movement. There are here two land masses separated by a river each carrying a different kind of object: the feminine symbols (sheep and lambs, and a small pool) on the left and the masculine (transport and objects related to it) on the right. The bridge links the two sides, the milk van being about to move from right (the masculine side) to the left and the empty lorry from left to right.

World 5   Figure 23 (17th session). See page 80.

Charles made a T-shaped river along the further edge of the tray with the stem crossing the centre; at the right-hand further corner the river was made to bend

along the right edge; while when the central river reached the front it turned left and ran along the nearer edge towards the left corner. On the central stream which divides the sand masses into two parts Charles placed a boat carrying a man and a small girl. In the river along the further edge facing left he put a crocodile; there are two trees on the left sand mass and one on the right. At the far left side "a baby giraffe" was put "going down to drink at the water, but stopped when he saw the crocodile"; the giraffe was said not to be aware that there was a lion behind him. Lower down on the same part of the land two rhinoceroses were placed facing to the left; by the left edge towards the front Charles placed a trumpeting elephant and a lioness, both facing towards the right. Just above the boat on the left bank he put a mother and baby elephant; on the right bank further back another elephant was placed facing right, and along the right bank of the river a crocodile on land. On the far right of this sand mass he put a zebra facing towards the river, and lower down in the water a hippopotamus; a tiger was placed coming in on the right.

Conversation. The contrast in Charles' behaviour when making World 1 as against Worlds 2, 3, and 4 appeared again here. In making 2 and 3 he identified himself with the vehicles and acted it all out with intense absorption; in this World as in World 1 he was more the "deus ex machina", manipulating the objects as pawns and talking about them while doing so. "That is a man and his little girl" he said of the people in the boat; "the giraffe has gone down to drink but doesn't because he sees the crocodile in the water; he does not know the lion is behind him. The baby elephant on the left bank belongs to daddy on the other side; he may play on the left side and come back if he wants to, but the edge is too steep and when he tries to get back he cannot, so the daddy comes to fetch him". He had nothing much to say about the other animals.

Since Charles had talked freely while making this World about the parts being played by certain of the animals he used, the time seemed to have come to point out some of the features he had not mentioned and their relations to similar arrangements in the other Worlds; for example, in World 1 where the mother and baby elephant, in the position in which they were first put, were threatened by the crocodiles and moved away. In this World the baby giraffe is on his own and is similarly threatened by the crocodile. I therefore suggested to Charles that perhaps the giraffe represented himself and he agreed. There are a number of other important aspects in this World which were apparent to myself as therapist, but it was too early in treatment for it to be wise to discuss these with him. I therefore went over the material of the previous four Worlds also, pointing out the powerful "going-along-nesses": how water appeared in three Worlds, and the different shapes it took; the positive and negative attitudes of young to the mother, and that in this World the father takes the central place.

Discussion. From the point of view of the understanding of Worlds a great deal more needs to be said, as this World has many features in its use of animals, human beings and configurations of sand and these in relation to water, which are specially characteristic of children's use of World materials.

If the ground-plan of World 1 be compared with World 5 it will be seen that there is a tongue of land projecting into the water on the right-hand side in both. The water in World 5 follows the general position of the river in World 4 and adds to it the two arms of the lake in World 1. On the left in World 1 by the edge of the tray, opposite to the promontory, are 3 giraffes. In World 5 one small giraffe occupies almost the same position, facing the same way, but this time without sibling or mother. This is the only animal whose position in the World is exactly repeated.

As regards the exact objects chosen, mother and baby elephants appear in both (duplicated in World 1); in World 5 a trumpeting elephant and a "father" elephant; in World 1 an elephant is carrying an attacking human being, and a lion and a lioness move together with a second lion beside them; in World 5 the lion and lioness are separated. The zebra and tiger appear in both Worlds; in World 1 the hippo has a baby, in World 5 not. There are three attacking crocodiles in World 1, and two in World 5, one menacing and one on land. The monkeys of World 1 are not repeated in World 5; on the other hand World 5 contains two additional rhinos, three trees, and a man and a girl in a boat.

Themes. World 5 is very important as it illustrates the mode in which several aspects of a personality or of an experience and/or of a situation can be presented simultaneously in a world. The child theme has here 3 versions. (1) The run-away child who gets into danger (a theme which will recur often in the future both in Worlds and in his "acting out" in real life;

it is played here by the giraffe). (2) The baby-mother/baby-father relationship expressed in the elephant family. (3) The explicit father-daughter relationship represented in the two humans in the boat.

The group of 5 animals in the nearer left corner are interesting, for the lion and lioness are here separated by 3 animals whose main characteristics are erect horns and trunk. On the right side appear a single palm, a single male elephant, a crocodile on land, a tiger and a zebra, making the right side appear very masculine and it is possible this use of the zebra indicates Charles' feeling his way towards the horse symbol which he uses a great deal later but which his sense of congruity would not yet allow him to use here. The hippo is this time of unspecified sex, resting comfortably in the water.

The boat on the river is a new and important element; it does not appear again for a long time; it isolates the girl in it from the other embodiments of child/parent by putting her into a separate species. A father therefore appears in two aspects: as the father of the adventurous baby elephant who seems to be thought of as belonging ot the father's side of the river but who has run across to the mother, and as the father of the daughter in the boat. The elephant father is permissive and helpful; the human father is isolated in the boat with his daughter. All these points were observed and noted; but Charles' absorption in the "story" aspect of this World was so complete that to attempt to bring it into contact with his consciousness (or rather lack of awareness) of his actual situation would, I felt, interrupt the developments of his progress towards self-knowledge by means of his Worlds; this aspect of his "real" though unconscious attitude to his father (either at that date or earlier) was discussed with him much later.

These five Worlds belong together; a number of ideas concerning the parent/child relationship have been stated and the World material used to express uncontrolled and controlled force. From now on different symbols appeared.

On the next session (18) in order to link this World with his statements in drawings at the end of last term I suggested he might go on with the pin-picture series he made last term of the nasty mummy, but nothing fresh emerged. I next asked if he would like to do a World out of a fairy tale* but he preferred to continue with drawings and drew a wolf and an empty house of leaves, the people in it have heard the wolf and run to a safe brick house.

The school now reported Charles "blowing up for trouble" and session 19 began with (at my suggestion) stamping on "conkers† to see how strong they were" which was taken up eagerly. Then followed neat work with a many-coloured construction toy. My note runs – "very eager, smiles now, rushes at things".

---

*An exploration to see if the witch symbol would appear.
†Dried horse-chestnuts.

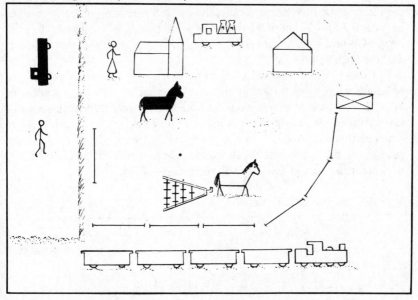

Charles made this World in silence and the scene is quite different.

At the further edge he placed a church and a farm house and cleared away the sand to the left (as in Worlds 2 and 3) to make a "farmyard". Between the church and the house he put an open lorry with milk churns; a woman was placed by the church; a sand wall built on the right extends forward from behind the house to a gate from which fencing completes a roughly square enclosure, the sunken farmyard forming the fourth side. Along the inner side of this fencing a horse and plough were put; a single horse occupied the centre of the picture and a lorry was placed in the farmyard. Painstakingly Charles put together a train and placed it facing towards the right along the nearer side of the tray. During part of the construction of this World Charles began to talk about it, and in doing so made clear that it was very much more detailed and coherent in his head than appeared in the World. (At one point I had, mistakenly, suggested he might put a small person coming out of the house; Charles put a little fat man there but moved him at once into the farmyard.) Charles' account of the scene was as follows:

"The horse was tied up and has broken loose and jumped over the fence; the farmer is afraid he might get run over by the lorry coming round. The woman is saying 'I'll wait for you at the church at 3' ".

Discussion.   The five groups: (a) farmhouse, milk lorry, woman; (b) man and lorry; (c) horse and harrow; (d) church; (e) train, do not appear to have any connection in Charles' mind, except that the statement of what the woman said connects man, woman and church.* The train which appeared

---

*In World Technique no attempt is made by the therapist to probe a meaning or attempt to bring to light connections not stated, as World-making is a process which has to move at its own pace.

in World 4 appears here again and in the same detached way as before. In the place in the tray where the airfield and lorry parking space were made in Worlds 2 and 3 is now the farmyard with the empty lorry in it; the milk lorry of World 4 reappears. The church, the house, the women, the horses and the harrow are new.

For those readers trained in psychoanalysis a great deal of this World will have an obvious meaning and it is essential in the understanding of Worlds that such interpretations be both known and held in the mind of the therapist. When contemplating actual Worlds, the question as to whether this knowledge is made use of or not depends upon the exact relation of the individual World to the whole treatment of the case. No interpretation was at this stage given to Charles.

World 7   Figure 25 (21st session)

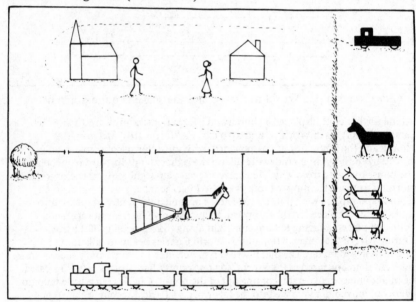

This World made at the next session carried the story further.

First the church and house were put in the same positions as in World 6.
The farmyard, dug out as before, was made on the right of the tray now instead of the left. A train was put in again parallel to the nearer side, this time facing to the left. The horse and harrow occupy the same position in the centre part of the tray as before, now in a fenced-in field with a gate in its further right-hand corner. A haystack was placed in the left further corner of the left-hand field, a man and a woman by the house. Charles now began to tell an elaborate story, while continuing to make the World, which ran as follows (taken down verbatim). "His (the farmer's) horse was outside the church and ran away; the man walked down the road to fetch a lorry and drove it up to get the horse and bring him down to the farmyard. The woman came to ask her husband if it was

time for the horse with the harrow to stop. He said yes so she went back to the horse to take it out". Charles then manoeuvred the horse and harrow out of the gate and down to the farmyard. (It was at this point that the long fence parallel to the train was put in.) He now put three cows in the farmyard, then moved them round the end of the fences and through the gate into the field and went on with his story. "The farmer now goes in the lorry to get the second horse which is a mare, because," he said, "the first horse is lonely"; "two weeks after, the mare has a foal and the farmer thinks he should have a special place for all three" (so Charles put in the short fences). In answer to a question about the train, Charles said the animals did not mind the noise of the trains as they were used to it.

Discussion. Once again, the theme is that of the family expressed directly in human figures and farm animals. The content of this world (a) asks a question concerning procreation and birth through the common child's mode of making a positive statement; (b) presents a "running-away"; the farmer sets out to fetch and bring back the runaway animal; (c) the whole has something to do with food (haystack and cows), with the female, and and with husband and wife.

It is interesting that the milk lorry has disappeared and cows appear instead; all the elements of the marital-situation-cum-birth are in fact represented in symbolic form. Various small points had by now shown that "the farmer" in this and in subsequent Worlds represented the headmaster of the school with whom Charles had now made a trusting relationship. It will seem to some that this World was so clear a statement of a family situation that it should have been immediately linked up with Charles' own position. Two factors operated against this. The first is exactly the clarity of the statement. Charles' disturbance of personality was as severe as ever before and what was stated here partook of too exactly worked out a presentation for it to be wise to move Charles' thought from a pictorial to a verbal mode of expression. The second is that any talk about this World in reality terms would inevitably have brought up questions of sex and birth which I had, at that date, no permission to handle. Charles felt my complete participation in his story and we left it in that medium.

World 8   Figure 26 (22nd session). See page 86.

This was made three days later and the general layout is the same.

On the right is the dug-out farmyard; at the back the church and the house; along the nearer edge the train, running from right to left with the fencing behind. This time Charles told a vivid story as he constructed the world, moving the pieces around as he did so.
The part of the World between train and buildings has become more complex and more animals take part. The haystack appears at the same spot; there are three fields, but with additional smaller fields within the centre one; the harrow does not appear. Charles told the story as follows starting at the point where he had put four cows and the foal in the left-hand field:— "The foal goes to the

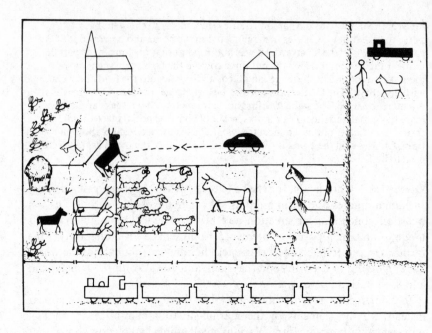

cows, and one cow sees the gate is open and thinks he'll come out; a car coming up to the house does not know in time, he has poor brakes, and runs into the cow knocking him (called so by Charles) over; the farmer jumps into the lorry and drives back to put the cow in a special place for a long time. The farmer has a dog, and goes and buys a sheep dog, and puts in new fences across the field. He comes up to the front of the house in a lorry with two sheep and a lamb. (Here Charles put a ram beside the church with the two sheep, manoeuvred them all into the field and shut the gate). The farmer fetches the sheep dog in case the ram is troublesome; (while unloading the ram Charles' hand went to the fork of his shorts); the farmer fetches 3 more sheep; up came 6 rabbits, the new dog runs around the fences, the rabbits see him and scuttle off and make a hole in the cows' field and a rabbit scuttles through, the dog jumps that fence too, the rabbits get buried, all but one; this one is too busy eating and the dog gets him and kills him and takes him back to the farmyard and goes to sleep. The other dog in the morning barks and wakes him up and says, 'I brought it for you', and the first dog has it for his dinner". Later Charles got out a bull and put it all by itself, then said "the mummy farmer comes to make a sheep pen in the corner".

My general note made a week later runs "Definitely freer in movements and expression. Everything done in sessions is done with great eagerness".

This set of three Worlds made a series of their own which are discussed more fully later on. They demonstrate very well the difficulty of recording Worlds in which a story is told, owning to the constant changes in the placing of the objects.

Session 23 was occupied with a Mosaic and a drawing of a family of four (like his) going in a ship to America – "because they don't like living on the land"; a man in a spare ship tries to stop them. The following two sessions (24 and 25) were spent in colour-painting* and Poleidoblocs. At the end of it he ran a lorry and cannon about in the sand. On Session 26 he did a Mosaic and an interesting drawing† (see later for the reason why the obvious symbolic meaning of this drawing could not be touched upon).

World 9 *not illustrated* (27th session)

In this world a road running parallel to all the sides, except the further edge, is fenced in with the usual accompaniments, lamps, traffic signs, etc. At the further edge are a number of soldiers with guns, who are said to be "having a practice shooting match". A big tree stands near them, close to which a plane crashes; another plane takes off from the front "to see why the other has not come back". When asked whether anyone was hurt in the crashed plane, Charles said he was not quite sure and "telephoned" for an ambulance.

Discussion. This is a kind of transition World where the themes of Worlds 2 and 3 reappear with the new element of "soldiers learning to shoot"; a crash occurs, but it is uncertain if anyone is hurt and the idea of possible damage to people evokes in Charles immediately the idea of assistance; but it only arises in response to a query.

Dreams. About this time Charles had a dream "that he was on a horse and it was about to bolt".

World 10   Figure 27 (28th session)

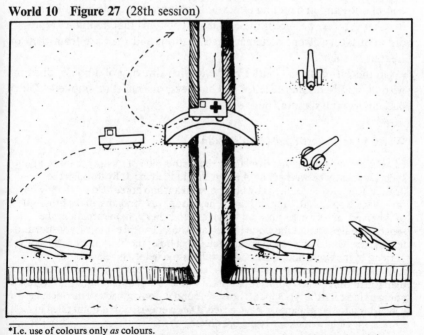

---

*I.e. use of colours only *as* colours.
†A house with three upstairs windows and one downstairs and a door, thick smoke coming out of chimney. On left a tall tree some way away, a cut-down tree just by the house with a man standing on the stump – a "gardener" to the left side having just planted a small tree.

This was made two days later.

Charles constructed a T-shaped river bisecting the centre of the tray, and then running along the near edge. In the centre he put a bridge across the river and upon it an ambulance. War is vaguely said to be going on somewhere. In the near right half of the tray two planes were put, said to be "taking off" – one a bomber, and beyond them two guns. On the left side, a plane put at the nearer corner was said to be bringing more men. Near the bridge was an open army lorry; the marks made by it and the ambulance are somewhat reminiscent of World 9.

Discussion. The bridge over the centre of a river (or the idea of a to and fro movement over the centre of the river) have appeared in Worlds 4 and 5; an indirect idea of war, plane-crashes and an ambulance come from World 9, and crashes from Worlds 2 and 3. In World 10 the instrument of repair of damage, the ambulance, is now placed squarely on the centre of the bridge; vague war weapons are about, and along the front runs a river.

We have already seen this interchanging of train and river in the same place in the tray in Mary's Worlds; its occurrence here in Charles' illustrates the mode in which our interpretation of Worlds (and at the same time validation of interpretation of Worlds) has been built up. When identical "object/place synonyms" such as these two, have occurred many scores of times in Worlds of children of different ages, temperaments, I.Q.'s and complaints, and in handling by several different therapists at the I.C.P. and in other centres, we accept these as true synonyms that do in fact represent different facets of one statement or situation, and they are from then on treated as such.

On the 29th session Charles made another drawing of a house, this time with two tall trees on the left, two chimneys, one emitting smoke – a black path and a man standing beside it.

World 11 *not illustrated* (30th session)

Charles scooped out a long river along the further side of the tray, banked up the sand very neatly between it and the edge and looked carefully through the drawer, found two mounted cowboys; one on a white horse held up the cowboy on a black horse, said "stop or I fire", the reason was "Indians on the other side of the river" and Charles now put these in, 5 together and one separate; the separate Indian shot at the white horseman who did not see him, he got shot and fell off; the white horse ran away and fell into a hole; the black horse, which was a friend of the white horse, came to see if he could help. The black horseman rode back (to the right) to tell what had happened; he came back with another man (on another black horse) to the place where the man was shot, said "I am going to look for that shot man's horse", found it, took it back to its rider; he rode round to the Indians to make peace. The river was at that point filled in toward the right to make crossing possible.

Discussion. In the series of Worlds to date we have seen Charles, as it were, walking round the idea of deliberate hostility and aggressiveness of one individual to another. He can allow himself to conceive of it in wild animals (crocodiles and later lions), of man as a big game hunter, or in a very general way concerned with human beings vaguely said to be "at war".

He has now come to a point when he is nearly ready to allow himself to conceive of it in human beings and needs a codified symbol for its presentation. This lies ready to hand in the conventional theme of Indians and cowboys.

On the following session (31) he ventured a little further and drew "an angry person", i.e., a figure crying on a chair because a man "just went and broke his toy".

World 12   Figure 28 (32nd session)

A river was dug out vertically in the centre of the tray with two "arms" branching off to the left, leaving a tongue of land projecting from the left-hand side and a small piece of land at the left top corner. The right-hand side was a solid mass of sand with steep banks along the river which was crossed by a bridge in the centre of the tray. Against the right-hand edge Charles put a tied-up white man with an Indian beside him who was said to be "a bad Indian". As Charles made the World he told the following story about it. "The Sheriff had crossed the bridge to ask the Indian if the white man can be released". One of the Sheriff's men on horseback was placed just crossing the bridge and on the left-hand side an Indian's horse was tied to a post, "waiting for his master". Charles explained that "the Indian comes, mounts, and rides to hold up the two whites. The white horseman sees this, turns quickly, gallops toward the further shore and jumps

89

across the arm of the river. A second Indian appears on the right who is a friend of the white horseman and who shoots the Indian horseman who falls into the river". Meantime Charles put an Indian chief on the right. "The Sheriff runs away over the bridge, and the Indian chief shoots the Sheriff".

Having made a sort of general tentative trial of the possibilities of Indian versus cowboy in World 11, Charles now made use of this theme to continue his series.

Discussion. The ground plan of this World resembles that of World 1 in reverse, with the addition of a bridge from the tongue of land to the opposite side. Cowboy–Indian symbols are again used, but the loyalties and enmities are confused. For the first time the ideas of good and bad appear. Charles is very confused between them (this confusion to some extent mirroring a similar confusion in a percentage of "Westerns" shown on T.V. and films). The figures and the incidents in the story are conventional and only partly originate with Charles; it is doubtful if they present any part of his individual problem except for this confusion between good and bad. The layout, however, is in his pattern and repeats the basic ideas of the two sides separated by water with a bridge in the centre.

In session 33 Charles made a drawing of a man on a horse capturing a bandit on a horse. The school reported that Charles flies into a rage whenever crossed, and on session 34 Charles, agreeing with this report, made a drawing of three such incidents.

The term ended one week later and the Christmas holidays intervened.

As usual on the first session (35) of the new term Charles made a Mosaic following it with a drawing of the same kind as the last ones; on session 36 he did a Newspaper Game and on sessions 37 Kaleidoblocs.* On the following session he started on an elaborate World of a new shape.

World 13   Figure 29 (38th session)

Charles made a sunken pond in the centre of a circular fenced-in field and put in this field 6 cows and a horse, one cow drinking from the pond; he found a stile and put it leading out of the field. A circular road was made surrounding this, then disappearing at the left-hand nearer corner. In the centre of the further long side he put a road sign, and in front of this a car, an ambulance and a man leading a bull; in the centre of the nearer side a gipsy caravan was placed facing to the right and a horse beyond it; it is stationary, he said, "because the horse has been taken out"; facing this caravan he put a lorry and said, "the lorry stopped because there is not enough room to get past the caravan"; to the right

*See Appendix.

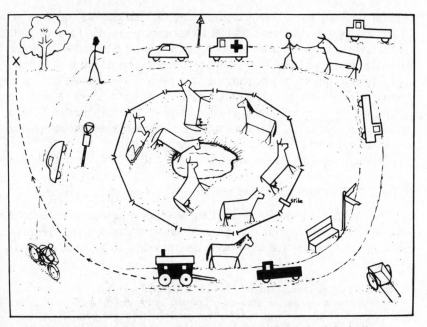

of this were a bench and a signpost, and between the signpost and the bull, another lorry. On the left part of the road was a policeman holding up the traffic; further down was a car, and beside it a road sign. In the four corners, the following objects were placed, starting from the left-hand nearer corner: a motorcycle combination, a tree, a lorry and an old barrow. Charles told the following story about this scene. "The man on the motorbike used to help the caravan people; he now helped the caravan to move up to the tree to the left so that the lorry can get through. The old barrow has been dumped because nobody wants it; before, a man sold vegetables from it to the people in the caravan; he has stopped doing it now".

Discussion. The form of this World, with the exception of the break of the road to the left, is that of a mandala. This is the most coherent design so far made, and in it items from his incoherent traffic Worlds move around a centre. A number of the elements of this World we have already met, such as: circular field and pond (World 4); field with cows and the bull (World 8); policeman (World 3); cars and lorry (Worlds 2, 3, 4 and 8); bench (World 4); ambulance (World 10). New features are the caravan, the motorcycle, and the old barrow dumped because nobody wanted it. Charles' interest was focused on the horse, the lorry and the caravan.

Since a certain degree of stability had been expressed in this World, in the following session (39) the question of ideas about birth and babies was ventured upon. It is difficult to assess whether this was correct or a mistake.

Just before the next session (40) Charles had a violent attack of rage and was brought by several of the older boys to the Play hut. This was a most useful opportunity to begin explanations to Charles. We therefore sat together most of the session while I explained about E. To begin with Charles held his head down and was completely withdrawn. When I said however that it was awful to feel like that, there came a faint nod, and this gave me an opportunity of showing acceptance and of demonstrating to him a method we use in these situations of throwing "conkers" against the hut door, as a way of discharging fury without causing damage. Charles accepted this with vigour but in complete silence and spent the last part of the session hurling "conkers" at the door of the hut.

During session 41 we continued with talk, and Charles made a Mosaic.

World 14 *not illustrated* (42nd session)

This was a moving-about story. Charles set out the scene, then became wholly absorbed, moving the objects about with accuracy and ingenuity, making up speeches for the actors, and showing an unusual ability to shape a story.

A covered wagon was carrying silver, it had a driver, 2 men inside and a guard on a white horse outside on account of Indians. A bandit knew about the silver, jumped on his horse and with pistols in his hands halted the wagon. The Indians following the wagon didn't know this; one of the men in the back jumped out and stood at the back, saw the Indians and shouted "Indians coming"; the driver jumped down in front facing the bandits, the guard (on the white horse) shot and the bandit fell off his horse; the guard turned round to help the other man with the Indians; 3 Indians came creeping up, the white man shot and the two front Indians fell, the driver jumped back; the bandit's horse was moved out of the way and the wagon drove off. (The scenery was then rearranged and a pond put in with the Indians round the corner.) The wagon didn't know the Indians were there and drove right into them, passed the pond, turned round backwards into the pond, an Indian fired and wounded one of the wagon men who got the bandit's horse and went to find the wagon, saw it in the pond, jumped into the shallow part to guard the wagon. Another wagon man shot two Indians, but another Indian crept up toward the guard's horse which kicked him away (the sense of space got confused here, because although certain of the white men are really with the wagon they get rides *to* the wagon). Charles gave the following description of his actions: "He says to them 'jump on my horse and I'll take you to the wagon', does so and they stay there till safe; an Indian comes to his senses and gets up, a wagon man shoots him and that's the end of that Indian; the wagon man rides back into town and they are safe. They give the silver to the people who ordered it and live happily ever after".

Discussion. This is an important World as there appears in it for the first time the "covered wagon carrying treasure". The themes of cowboys v. Indians and cowboys v. bandits are combined in it (although the men are called "wagon men"and not actually cowboys). As in the drawings of session 33, this ends happily.

The following 9 sessions were mainly occupied with discussion of the working of the body, leading up to reproduction. Charles had never seen a small baby or an animal with young; he knew that kittens came out of their mothers and said that "babies come from God".

At the end of session 43 Charles made a Pin Picture set of drawings about a witch capturing a fairy intending to do her a mischief and the fairy escaping.*

At the end of session 46 he made a pattern of gummed paper shapes resembling his first Mosaics, and at the end of session 49 Charles made two Pin Picture drawings of a boy angry with his mother; when asked what the boy would *really* like to do to his mother, Charles answered "get her down on the floor and pummel her as hard as he could". On sessions 52 and 53 he drew a series of the boy being angry with his mother because she objects to his doing various ordinary things† and one cheerful series about a Christmas stocking.

About this time the school reported that Charles was now very keen on his sessions, asking when I was coming, turning up immediately on my arrival and cooperating well. We agreed that there was a tiger inside him that leaped up the moment anyone stopped him doing something he wanted to. Nevertheless just before the time for the 54th session Charles was found in his bedroom, all the clothes pulled off his bed and piled on the foot with Charles lying face down under the bed in the further corner. When touched he said he would run away; he would bite his own fingers off; bite holes in his clothes ... Reassurance, acceptance and comforting brought a sudden roar "I want my bath" and Charles departed to the bathroom while the other boys made his bed.

Only one more World was made this term.

World 15 *not illustrated* (55th session)

After Charles had made a ground plan of river and roads, he kept running lorries around, making motor noises, so that the position of the roads continually altered. The main plan, however, was a river starting from the left further corner and dug out along the further edge; this then turned at right angles and made an S-curve across the tray and flowed in the opposite direction leftwards along the nearer edge of the tray; a road starting in the middle of the left short edge was made parallel with the straight reaches of the river and ran across the tray to the loop of the river which was crossed by a bridge, and turning at the other side of the bridge to run out at the further edge; another road forked from this and ended at the nearer loop of the river; a lorry was put here which "has taken the wrong fork and come to a standstill at the river".

Discussion. Charles ended this term by summing up his experience of himself in relation to the outside world by identifying himself with the lorry in this country scene of road and river, whose progress is blocked through having taken a wrong fork; the position of this lorry, Charles

---

*Unfortunately my notes do not state whether the idea for this came from him or from me.
†Going out with his best clothes on – giving him a pillow to sleep on – making a noise.

agreed, was like him in a temper. Three days later (session 56) he made a drawing of "a happy day".*

The general opinion in the school concerning Charles at this point was that while "trouble" continued to blow up between him and the other children, Charles was definitely brighter and more in contact with the community.

Here the Easter holidays intervened.

Mrs. Robinson reported that Charles "had been awful" in the holidays, although in some ways more mature; a particularly bad outburst had occurred in a teashop where Charles had been with his mother and sister. But when the summer term started, Charles was talking much more freely and even singing at times. Taking advantage of this greater approachability on the first session of the term (57), I took up with him directly the question of outbursts of the kind reported by his mother and discussed with him various ways of dealing with these impulses. In this and the next session (58) the sink was used for fights between Charles and myself with boats, interspersed with bouts of hammering on tins. The usual beginning-of-term Mosaic was made.

World 16 *not illustrated* (59th session)

This was almost a duplicate of the bandit story of World 14 and done with great gusto.

Discussion of bodies and the differences between boys and girls occupied sessions 60 – 62. One drawing on session 60 is of a boy being angry "because his parents want him to go to bed when he doesn't want to".

During this early part of term the local authorities explained that owing to misconceptions on the part of Mrs. Robinson of what Charles said to her during the holidays, they did not feel they could support any discussion on my part of sexual themes.

World 17 *not illustrated* (63rd session)

Charles made an airport and put in it two aeroplanes and a lorry on one side of the tray. A third plane was made to crash beside it; another lorry was made to go through the gate to the airport; the two planes then circled, looking at what has happened and landed by the crashed plane; a house was put in the airport "belonging to the man who looks after it"; other lorries and a car were taken out and moved about – one lorry was carrying milk churns, one had sand, one was

---

*Two trees in the background, one with a thick trunk, one thin, an adult standing and two children sitting on the ground.

empty – these were parked by the plane on the ground facing each other; the milk churns were delivered to the house.

Discussion. This World marks a definite step forward since although a plane crash occurred, elements of "caring for" objects were included; a house, hitherto only used in connection with the idea of a farm, appeared, and also the lorry containing milk churns.

The school now reported that Charles was becoming difficult in class, and there had been some outbreaks of verbal aggression against his mother. With encouragement from the headmaster, ways of coping with impulses towards violence which Charles and I had discussed in sessions, were made use of; Charles on one occasion hammered tins for 2 hours.

On session 64 this incident and several others of conflict with the children were discussed with Charles. I pointed out to him that he had probably felt smothered by his mother and Mary as a child, to which he agreed. Charles also made a Mosaic.

Mrs. Robinson called at half term at the school. The headmaster reported that she treated Charles like a small child and he sat with his thumb in his mouth and behaved like a 5-year old. His sister and her boy friend called in at the school to show his new car and took Charles out in it. The expedition proved a success; Charles showed a definite improvement following it.

World 18   Figure 30 (65th session)

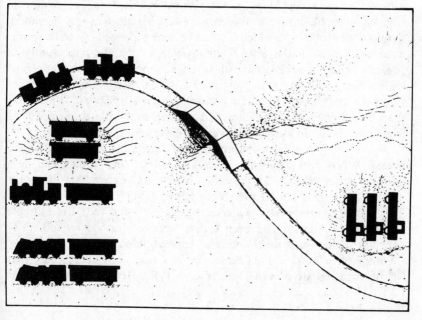

Charles dug out a curving "railway" from left to right with a bridge over a dip in the sand, and put 2 engines by the left edge on the rail; an engine with a carriage and 2 sets of trains were stationary on the left-hand side with 2 single trucks between them and the railway; in a declivity on the right he placed three "unwanted" lorries.

Discussion. It is characteristic of the way in which children use the different types of going-along-ness that Charles made a World mainly composed of trains, which he conceived of as being "active", before they became stationary on the left-hand side of the tray. The 3 "unwanted" lorries repeat the "unwanted" barrow in World 13.

Discussion was continued on the next two sessions (66 and 67); Charles was affectionate to the Teddy bear of another child; referring to the friction with the other children he said that if anyone took a stick away from him he felt they were taking a part of himself. This was taken up and explained in general terms.

On session 68 Charles splashed brown, black and yellow paint on large sheets of paper, his tongue moving round and round all the time.

World 19 *not illustrated* (69th session)

This World was quite incoherent and impossible either to report or record, since changes were continually made. The following were the elements used: a round pond, a caravan made to make tracks, soldiers and cannon, aeroplanes, fences, army lorry, trees, and a field with horses; each category being put in in fours.

Discussion. The confusion in this World reflected the confusion in Charles' inner life now that the pressure of E within him was beginning to find symbols through which it could become expressed. Since there was an improvement in the general atmosphere I took the opportunity in sessions 70 and 71 to examine with Charles the present situation in regard to his use of his cognitive powers. His actual performance in school subjects was still very poor. In session 72 he made his first "objective" drawing of types of aeroplanes and also an odd little drawing of "a frightened child". In session 73 we did a Newspaper Game.

On session 74 we discussed an incident when Charles had run away because a boy had called him quite a harmless name. Charles made a drawing of himself as a king receiving tribute, and agreed that this is the way he felt he should be treated. A curious mixed-up period followed, and from some points of view Charles was much improved; for example another boy whom he had been teasing knocked him down and really hurt him; Charles was upset and cried but had no outburst.

On the other hand just before session 75 the school staff reported that Charles had recently "been impossible in P.T.* He wants to join in, is

---

*Physical Training.

miserable if told not to, says, 'I want to play too' and then either simply *cannot*, for example, bring himself to throw a ball, or just interferes with the others". During the session we discussed this and Charles agreed that this feeling was the opposite of the driving force of his temper outbursts. The session ended with a World.

World 20   Figure 31 (75th session)

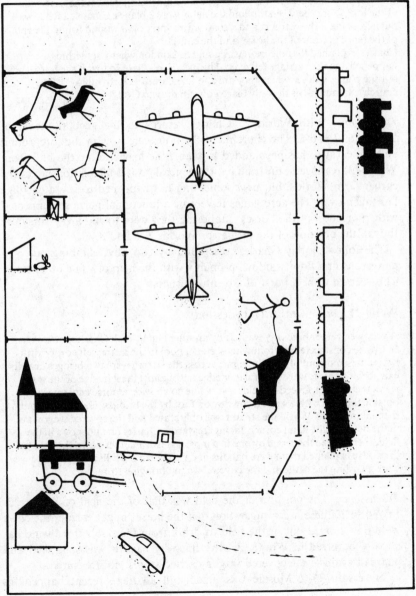

Charles put fences across one short end of the tray and down the side, cutting off a narrow L-shaped space. Outside and running parallel with the long side he put a train and beside the engine a second engine, said to be a "loose engine"; the last carriage of the train had fallen over on its side. On the left further side he put two fences joining the main fence to the edge, enclosing a small field; in this were 3 small horses and one large horse, said to be a mare and foal, the others "just ponies". A second field was added later extending down from this; in it he put a hutch and rabbits. Further along a church was set and a farm house and between these a caravan; a man leading a bull was placed at the inner side of the long fence; between this and the fields were 2 planes. Finally, a fence was put across the railway track, and a road with a lorry on it wound round the end of the fence in front of the house and the church.

Charles explained that the train was going to London when "something happened and the carriage fell over. The planes are there so that if the horses get out the planes will see where they are and telephone the farm house". "The church", he added "is the only place you can pray to God".

Discussion. With World 20 Charles returns to the general theme of Worlds 6, 7 and 8. The church and the house are now in the foreground and the caravan has been added to them; the man leading the bull from World 13) reappears; the train has the general positional relationship of the earlier farm Worlds, but now something has happened to it – a carriage has fallen over. The aeroplanes have now a functional purpose connected with protection of the horses, supposing they were to run away; they are thus in the position of the farmer of Worlds 7, 6 and 8.

The following day Charles was found by two boys climbing out of a dangerous first floor window, probably with the help of some other boys. This seemed to be a burst of adventurousness.

World 21 *not illustrated* (76th session)

A very wet, rather bare tray was left by another child which Charles took over. In this he constructed the following scene: a pool in the nearer left corner with a stream issuing out of it to the right; across the stream were two bridges near its exit; behind this towards the further edge and against the left edge of the tray was a rectangular fenced-in field; a very fine cowboy on a horse kept guard outside the field with a second cowboy on foot by the bridges. Half way through the making of the World the stream was obliterated and the covered wagon put in the nearer right-hand corner, facing forwards. Charles first put cows in the field, then moved them one by one in a most realistic manner down the field to drink. He explained there were bandits and rustlers in the hills; the cowboys were guarding the cattle and the covered wagon bringing stores.

Discussion. The position of the field was that of the field of World 20. In World 20 there was a suggestion that the horses might escape; the cows were now moved out of the field to drink from the pool; this theme has already occurred in World 13. An attack by bandits was suggested and guarded against; the covered wagon carried stores, not treasure.

In session 77 a Mosaic was made and all these recent happenings discussed, Charles showing himself very much more aware of his actions and reactions and more able to reflect upon them.

World 22 *not illustrated* (78th session)

This scene presented motor cars racing along a country road. So much action took place that only a general description can be given.

Starting at the left edge near the front two parallel lines of fences outlined a road which curved to the right and ended in the further right-hand corner, while the fences continued along the further edge to the left. A pool was made midway between the further and nearer edges, near the left-hand edge; a stream issues from it crossing the tray diagonally to the right further corner where a windmill was placed; two bridges cross the stream, one carrying the cars from the road and one leading to the hospital. A village hospital was placed by the left-hand edge. Five racing cars were close together on the road with an ambulance first placed behind them; along the nearer edge, facing right, a train was placed with a policeman standing beside it; a second engine was put beside the train "in case the first breaks down". Road signs were put at sensible places, and a kennel with a dog beside it, who was said to be "sitting in the sun".
Charles explained that a car had crashed and a man was hurt; the ambulance was taking him to the village hospital; the policeman was keeping people away from the races.

Discussion. Racing appears for the first time, though three stationary racing-cars appeared in World 4. Crashes had frequently happened in earlier Worlds, but this is the first World in which an ambulance takes a wounded man to a hospital. The train along the front has appeared in previous Worlds, and the pool and the stream repeat those of World 21; but the windmill is a new feature. Charles seems to put an emphasis upon the bridges. The policeman, between the race and the train, is said to be "keeping people away from the race", although no people were put in. This is a very masculine World, and to psychoanalysts much of its symbolism will be familar. Discussion of this World brought out Charles' rivalry with his sister and his unwillingness to admit it.

The headmaster reported that Charles had recently written a charming and affectionate letter home.

The summer holidays now intervened. In order to protect the family from outbursts such as had happened in the Easter holidays, Charles spent three-quarters of these holidays at the school.

At the beginning of the Autumn term Charles was much more spontaneously conversational. He made a Mosaic on his first session (79) and discussed the holidays. On the next session (80) an important connection appeared between two types of power phantasy. He moved aeroplanes about with loud noises and drew and talked of Egyptians whipping slaves, owning that to do so was a pleasurable idea.

On the third session in the term Charles made a World.

World 23 *not illustrated* (81st session)

A river ran along the long right-hand side of the tray for four-fifths of its length; then it made a right-angled bend, to end in a square lake at the nearer left-hand corner; two bridges were put across the river. Five enemy soldiers and a cannon were placed on the rectangular ground on the nearer side of the river; British soldiers and army trucks and a spotter with glasses faced them on the opposite bank; Charles said the idea was to stop the enemy crossing the bridges. A plane, said to be bringing supplies, was made to come in from far away, and crashed from a faulty engine; the men and supplies were got out and another plane came in bringing more. A railway was then put in along the left-hand side, leading to the left bridge and over it; this carried passengers and troops. An ambulance was put by the further edge of the left bank of the river. Having set his stage, Charles worked out various incidents in this battle.

Discussion. The emphasis on bridges which was implicit in World 22, now becomes explicit. The idea of the bringing in of supplies, expressed in World 21 by the covered wagon, appears here in relation to an aeroplane. Charles' tolerance for the idea of conflict has considerably improved. This is the first time that "we" and "they" have appeared. The river motif of so many previous Worlds is again a central feature in this one. For the first time a train is thought of as actually in movement.

In session 82 we discussed the sort of toys he would create for himself in a "magic toyshop': these were all to do with movement – rocking horses, trains, etc.

World 24 *not illustrated* (83rd session)

This World started with a lorry carrying a small car, put in the centre of the tray; next, a lorry carrying milk churns was put facing inwards in the left-hand nearer corner; a river was cut out crossing the tray from further to nearer edge on the right-hand side, and a bridge across it was placed at a point where the lorry in the centre could drive over it. Fences were now put in on either side of this lorry and the milk lorry, and extended on the other side of the river to make a road. Between the milk lorry and the first lorry was a covered lorry, said to be "carrying goods from the farm". The fences had a gap by the milk lorry, which made an entrance to an airfield running all along the nearer side of the tray. Five planes were constantly taking off and landing with appropriate noises; at the very end a small car moved out from the airfield through the gate beside the milk churns.

Discussion. The theme of the river running across the short side of the tray with a bridge across the centre of it has appeared often before; here it appears in a new guise: three lorries are about to drive over it. For the first time there appears a lorry carrying a small car which reappears often later. The-vehicle-carrying-goods has now become an organic part of this picture, and the lorry-with-milk-churns is a normal component of the scene. Psychoanalysts will notice again familiar sexual symbolism (a mother/baby lorry, the maternal qualities of the other two lorries, the planes going up and down, etc.).

World 25   Figure 32 (84th session)

At the beginning of this session Charles saw some wild animals left by another child and said "I think I would like to do something in Africa".

The World presented a realistic jungle scene, very well carried out. A drinking pool occupies the further right-hand corner; a small island with a palm stands in the middle of it. Some camera men came in a lorry to take films of the animals; they wanted protection so two soldiers came in a second lorry; these were placed behind a curving hedge at the nearer edge. The mother elephant and her two babies got to the water first; the daddy hippo and two small hippos followed; the old elephant in the centre was "cross" and liked going about alone. Towards the further edge were 3 small giraffes, the mother some distance away facing towards the old elephant; a lion was going towards the pool between the giraffes and the hippo. "The lion", Charles said, "knows the giraffe and the hippo have a very strong kick, so he is being careful". A gorilla to the left, holding on to a tree, was said "to like to go and drink in peace and so he is grumbling". A zebra, a tortoise and a snake occupy the rest of the space on the left, and a monkey was put between the hedge and the big elephant; nothing was said about any of these.

Discussion. If this World is compared with Charles' previous "jungle" Worlds, the progress he has made becomes clear. This is a coherent picture, and several aspects of his family are presented. The gorilla and the old elephant probably stand for his father in one aspect, the father hippo in another; the mother elephant represents the protecting mother, the mother giraffe the "mother with a strong kick". The lion probably stands for the E he has so much difficulty in controlling. The emphasis is once again on drinking. The relation between the animals and men is that of observer and observed. Danger exists potentially from animals to men, but not from men to animals. A considerable change for the better was appearing also in Charles' general behaviour.

World 26 *not illustrated* (85th session)

This was said to be "Christmas day in heavy snow". A stream with a bridge across it was put almost in the same position as in World 24. A train running in a curve and along the further edge was going to cross the bridge but ran into a snow drift just before it got there; the engine and some carriages got burried in snow. An aeroplane trying to bring supplies to people in the train got into difficulties and came down and the snow covered it, leaving only one wing out; a new plane saw this wing and came down and started digging the people out. An ambulance had heard the crash and came with one covered and one open lorry to see what could be done; they got the people out and put them in the ambulance while they dug the rest of the plane out. The people were then taken to hospital by plane.

Discussion. The central point here is the stopping of a train-carrying-people by a natural obstacle, and this marks considerable progress in symbolisation of Charles' actual experience. As has been pointed out, Charles wanted to share and to play with the other children but the impulse gets blocked interiorly. The people-in-the-the-train are cold and need rescuing and the whole emphasis of the World is upon the work of rescue.

World 27   Figure 33 (86th session)

This World was said by Charles to be a direct continuation of the last one although the only connecting link was Charles' selection of aeroplanes to begin the making of this World.

A wide centre strip across the tray formed an airfield, fenced in on either side, with an entrance and an exit; outside on the right was a road with two standing P.C's warning people when the planes are going to take off, and one policeman on a motorcycle; two lorries each carrying a plane moved into the airfield and deposited the planes side by side on the ground, beside them the lorry carrying a little car; in the centre of the scene were a milk van with milk churns and a man beside it; road signs were placed at each side of the entrance; a private car was just entering. Against the left-hand edge of the tray a field was fenced off with 2 horses and 2 foals. Just by the exit to the field was another fenced field which contained at one time a horse and foals, at another time a lorry. The two lorries moved about. All the incidents were realistically carried out.

Discussion. This is an interesting development of Charles' type of

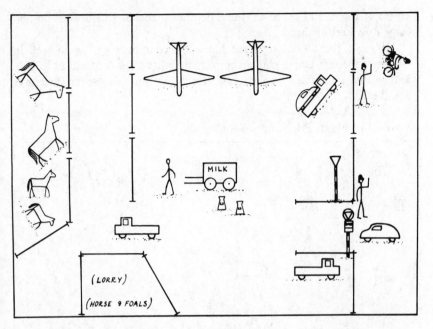

(LORRY)

(HORSE & FOALS)

symbolism: two powerful engines "from above" are deposited on the ground side by side and the lorry-carrying-a-small-car beside them, a grouping which is certainly suggestive of parents and a child. This possibility is strengthened by the milk cart and churns in the middle of the scene. On the left are two "adult" horses and their young as in Charles' family, and an identification in space of horses-with-their-young with a motor vehicle. Police prevent unauthorised entry.

At the end of this week one of Charles' rare attacks of asthma appeared and at session 87 he was seen in bed. In our view asthma is intimately related to blocking of E and this attack was therefore treated according to our general rule, by the study with him, both during the attack and immediately afterwards (sessions 88 and 89) of his ideas concerning force. He made two sets of drawings, one of a boy left alone in a house, throwing stones at a window, turning on the taps of the bath, basin, etc.; the other, in response to a suggestion from me that he draw "a powerful live thing" he drew wind blowing a windmill round and then a house down and branches off a tree. When he recovered the school reported the appearance of impishness, rolls of paper being put down the W.C., etc.

Riding lessions were now arranged for him; he fell off frequently, but took it in good part.

At times during these sessions he took to pouring dry sand through a funnel and a sieve with evident enjoyment. Session 90 was spent with a toy train, and session 91, happening to fall on Guy Fawkes day gave an opportunity to discuss fireworks; Charles felt both attracted to them and afraid of them, and asked to draw, he drew a rocket which went up and came down on his head.

Although the school reported his work as improving, he showed in elementary constructive play a complete inability to look ahead or to plan and needed a great deal of encouragement to get quite simple constructions completed.

World 28   Figure 34 (92nd session)

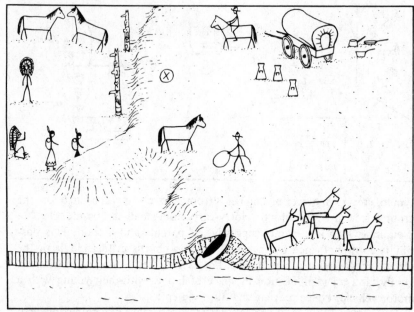

A river runs along the front edge; a landing place was made in the middle and a canoe drawn upon it. The right half of the tray was occupied by cowboys and their cattle, the left by Indians. The objects were arranged as follows: on the right is a covered wagon, with 3 milk churns and cooking pots on the ground beside it; between the wagon and the front edge are the white men's cattle; in the centre a white man was about to lasso a packhorse which had strayed; a cowboy on horseback stands beside the wagon. At the left further corner are two Indian horses without riders, a standing Indian, a seated Indian, a squaw and a baby (hidden by a fold in the land); later a second squaw was added and the standing Indian moved to face the wagon; 2 totem poles, a large one for the centre of ceremonial dances and one small one for tying people to, were placed against the fold in the land.

Discussion.   Here Charles reverts to the cowboy/Indian theme to express two forces essentially in conflict with one another, but between which active conflict is at present absent. The maternal element appears in relation to each, symbolised by the milk churns on the cowboys' side and by the papoose of the Indian squaw. It is interesting that Charles recognises

104

both aspects of the totem pole. The river runs along the front in the same position as the river of World 10 and the train in earlier Worlds.

World 29   Figure 35 (93rd session)

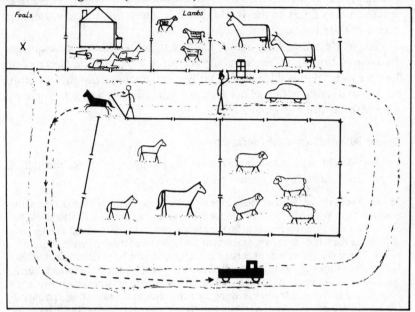

This World was made in response to a suggestion from me that Charles might make a peaceful World: he carried it out with concentrated attention.

A farmhouse was placed against the further edge, with a wheelbarrow and 2 dogs lying in front, and a water butt by the house; this was fenced in, and the fencing extended to the left edge of the tray to make a small field and to the right to form two fields. In the centre of the tray Charles made a large rectangular enclosure, divided into two fields; he got out a lorry, a car, and a telephone box, a policeman and a farmer, sheep, lambs, cows, horses and foals. He then told the following story, moving the objects about appropriately.

The sheep and the lambs were out in the right-hand centre field. Charles said, "All the lambs try to get out, but they cannot because the sheep dog is watching them". He then put the horses and foals in the left half of the centre field, saying: "The farmer opens the gate to let out the foals who have to go away from their mothers; a car is coming along; the policeman stops it to let the foals out; one mare tries to get out, but the farmer pushes her back; one foal gets out and runs round the fields; the farmer gets into the lorry to catch him and puts him with the other foals in the field to the left of the house'. Two cows were next put inside the right-hand field at the further edge, with a telephone box outside, and the lambs in the small field next to the house. The whole World was very neatly made.

Discussion.   There is a certain resemblance in layout between this World and World 13 and in content between this and World 7. Now, however, it is the young – the foal and the lambs – who try to get out; and once again the farmer goes in the lorry to catch the run-away animal. The other authority figure, the policeman, is also occupied in protection of the young. These two reflect Charles' experience at the school. There is no female human figure in the World, but it is interesting that the telephone box is outside the field of the cows.

This World marked the end of another stage in Charles' development. Its construction and Charles' comment made it possible to discuss with him his own "removal" from his mother to the school and the reason for it. A few days later the school reported that Charles was much more at ease with the other children.

World 30 *not illustrated* (94th session)

This World was made in response to a suggestion from me that he might do "something he would really like to happen".

In this World a river with a bridge over it runs across the tray in almost the same position as in World 24, with a boat on the river and a canoe on the bank by the side. There are three lorries, one on the bridge, one towards the further edge of the tray at the left of the river, and one at the right-hand nearer corner, but no roads. Three grounded planes occupy the left half of the tray. Charles made the following comment: "This is a naval place; the river starts a bit before here and goes down to the sea; a naval launch (the boat on the river) operates between the airport and London; the lorry is going over the bridge; the launch is starting off for London to get information about the planes; the canoe takes the boxes from the plane to the shopping centre, and is paddled by two men".

Discussion. As a means of checking the content and form of Worlds, the suggestions asked above were given to Charles in regard to these two Worlds; but as will be seen, they have practically no effect upon the form and content of the Worlds he made. World 29, both in its layout and its content, carries on Charles' normal development. The content of World 30 could hardly have been "what Charles would really like to happen" although it forms a basis for a later World representing a scene by the side of a river, which does express this. The layout is compounded of elements which have already occurred several times with an added coordination between most of the elements.

During this week an incident occurred while the children were watching a T.V. programme; Charles got up against the fact of rules and hit a girl left in charge of the children. The general "loosening up" which had taken place in him, however, made it possible to discuss this with him on a reality basis (sessions 95 and 96) and to get him, somewhat grudgingly, to begin to see the value of rules.

Session 97 was spent by Charles in drawing angry scenes between boys and (98) in drawing scenes of blasting operations upwards from a flat surface and of the men taking refuge in a hut.

106

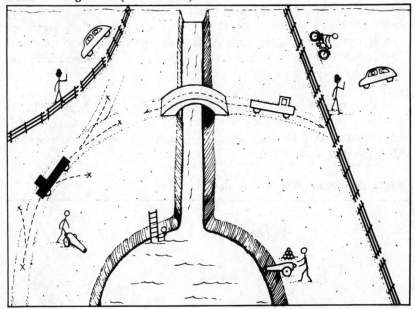

Charles now broke entirely new ground. He cut a deep river directly across the centre of the tray, ending in a semi-circular lake by the nearer edge; a bridge was placed across the river in the centre. The right and left-hand corners were then fenced off, and a policeman put outside the gates at each side. "Important work" was said to be gong on. On the right bank of the lake was a cannon with a pile of ammunition beside it, "in case this runs out"; a little further back on the left bank was a second cannon. A man was put by each of the guns. A very long ladder was placed near the junction of the river with the lake, against the steep banks of the latter. Two lorries were put in carrying ammunition and moved about making roads. Outside the right-hand fence was a car facing towards the fence and a motorcyclist; outside the left-hand fence was another car. At first there was a man on the bridge but he was later taken away.

Charles gave the following account of the World. "*The work*": "The men are using the guns because they want to find out how deep the lake is; the ladder is for divers and frogmen going down into the lake". In the car (outside the right-hand fence) "are people who have to go to town from the country; the policeman prevents them stopping there because it is dangerous while the work is going on; the motorcyclist is there to see no one tries to bash down the fence. There is a person in the car (in the left-hand fence) who has just come for a picnic".

Discussion.   This is the kind of world which has contributed to the theory of the proto-system outlined in the Introduction. The basic layout is almost entirely formal and so to speak stabilises and formalises the river and bridge of Worlds 4, 10, 12, 15, 23, 24 and 30. The lake is in the same position as the small bay with canoe in World 28; the two fenced-off corners enable a sharp contrast to be made between the people who use a car to go to town and work and the people who use a car to go for a pleasure picnic. The lorries going vaguely to and fro in the middle have appeared in several worlds. The new element is the *action* that takes place in a vertical plane, i.e., the firing of the guns into the lake and the diving of frogmen into the lake "to see how deep it is". It is the first time that Charles has used the idea of "depth".

At the next session (100) discussing the question of force, I asked Charles to draw a picture of a strong force that happened on its own and which was not dangerous. He drew a house with a domestic fire inside, trees and wind. He then made a World.

World 32   Figure 37 (100th session)

This belongs to the wild animals series.

Charles cut out a semi-circular drinking pool at the centre of the near edge of the tray, put a crocodile on the right side and a hippopotamus on the left side, both drinking. In the centre he put an elephant mother with two babies behind her and a giraffe mother with 2 babies behind her. A standing lion was near the further edge with a lying lioness beside it and to the left a zebra; all these were facing left. To the right was a monkey, "teasing the lions". A small giraffe was placed in the centre of the tray with a rhinoceros to the right. Charles then put together two small trains and placed them in a semi-circle, with the engines towards the centre behind the drinking pool, and a "spare" engine at each side. He finished the World by putting a male elephant in the right-hand corner and moving the crocodile across to the left.

Charles gave the following account of the World: "One small giraffe has wandered off and he doesn't know he is going into danger; the rhinoceros is a friend of the giraffe's family and thinks he ought to help the small one; the zebra thinks he had better walk away, because he spoke to the lion and he knows the lion wants a dinner; the hippopotamus is coming in for a bath and he is good tempered if no one annoys him; the elephant father is trumpeting to scare the people in the train; each train has a spare engine which is going to take over if anything goes wrong; the drivers of the trains are annoyed because there are too many animals about; the crocodile doesn't like all these animals going to his pool: he thinks he is more powerful than the male elephant, but he isn't; he crawls down in front of the male elephant who comes and treads on his tail; the crocodile crawls into the water and up the other bank and hides in a crack in the ground".

Discussion. In this World the symbolism is on two planes. The animals embody the sort of attitude and reactions that Charles has observed in himself and in other people at the school; the monkey, the zebra, the small giraffe and possibly the crocodile standing for himself. The trains are on another plane; they would appear to represent the feeling of force in himself which would like to get on but which is annoyed by there being "too many people about". The lack of integration in the scene regarded objectively of these two types of symbols presents very nicely Charles' feeling of the lack of integration between the force he feels in himself and his growing power of observing the interactions between himself and other people. Taking the individual symbols, Charles' comments on this World give us a clue to the significance of the monkey and the zebra in World 25, as in that World the father elephant is separate from the elephant family. The layout is interesting in that the drinking pool has now become central and repeats the lake of the previous world, the semi-circle of the trains being the inverse of the semi-circle of the lake.

World 33   Figure 38 (101st session). See page 110.

A fence with two gaps was placed parallel to the right-hand short edge of the tray, curved round and ran parallel to the front edge of the tray; this was said to delimit a railway yard with a road running outside it and was called "a station"; two passenger trains facing in opposite directions were put inside the station, the further one about to move through a gap in the fencing; between the two trains were 3 stationary trucks, the middle one carrying a beehive; between the further train and the tray-edge was an "old milk wagon". The space between the nearer train and the nearer fence was thought of as representing the station yard; two cars and a lorry carrying a rabbit hutch were parked here. Outside, on the road, Charles first put a number of racing cars, then removed them, and put there instead a Halt-sign and a car "going to the station".

Discussion. This is the first time Charles has been able to mobilise trains into coherent functional significance (apart from World 23). He did not, however, notice that the train going towards the left could not in fact have arrived where it was, unless it had been made up in the station, as there was no opening in the fence behind it. He manoeuvred the cars in and out

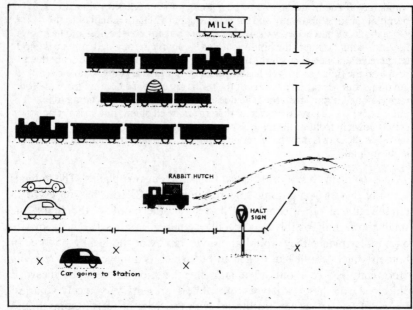

of the station most competently, leaving coherent tracks. The arrangement of the isolated items in relation to the two trains is interesting in that each stationary item includes a certain feminine element: the milk wagon, the beehive and the rabbit hutch. The lines of traffic have thus an alternate feminine and masculine significance which is reinforced by the engine of one train going through the opening in the fence.

The Christmas holidays intervened here.

Mrs. Robinson reported that the Christmas holidays had been satisfactory. There had been no upsets, and Charles had got on with other children and had been helpful and considerate at home; at the circus he sang with the other children. Charles was beginning to feel himself and to know his identity.

On the first session of the Spring term Charles began, as usual, by making a Mosaic, and followed with a World.

World 34 *not illustrated* (102nd session)

This was an "action" World and could not be drawn. Charles made a square enclosure in which he put two mares and three foals. A covered wagon then drove in from the right and was halted in the centre beside the further edge of the tray. He then took the fences away saying that the cowboys had come to fetch their horses; two cowboys sitting and playing musical instruments were put by the wagon and were said to be "sleeping and playing in the sun". He then dug a ditch along the left-hand shorter edge and put in it a two-gun bandit on a horse and a man with a lasso; this man wanted the mare; the bandits shot one cowboy dead; the owner of the mare then crept up behind the bandit on the horse and shot him; the cowboys got the mare and drove off.

Discussion. Compared with his other "bandit" Worlds this was clearcut and simple, and expressed the idea that two males were in competition for a single female, in this instance, a horse.

At the second session of the term (103) I went over with Charles what we had done and pointed out that what we had now to do was to think about the shaping of the E. I suggested he should draw what he would do if, when out with a friend, something unexpected happened. He drew various incidents concerned with falling over a cliff.

The school reported a number of incidents in the classroom and the playground, when Charles had tried to throw things at other people. In discussing these with me he put into words for the first time "I wanted to be a nuisance". Charles also reported that he had had a dream that his mother did not come for half term.

In the next two sessions Charles played out the attitude of wanting to be a nuisance in a series of two delightful Worlds about circus animals.

World 35 *not illustrated* (104th session)

Charles went to the cabinet and took out a number of objects with great care and put them on the table beside him. He then started setting his scene, putting in and moving about his animals and people as he told it. He put his whole self into the story and you could see, the animals were alive as he moved them. This was a story about an elephant and two small ones. "The elephants", said Charles, "belong to the circus, but in this town there was not enough room for them with the other animals so . . . (while talking he had set out a triangular enclosure in the centre of the tray and made a road going past the long side) they were put in this field". Charles ran a big black car up to the gate of the enclosure – this was the "head of the circus" arriving – two policemen regulated traffic of two other cars and two labourers were in the field. Between them all the big elephants and the two little ones were driven into the field and the gates shut. The cars now drove away and the two policemen were left standing "on guard" by the fencing. "Now", said Charles, "it is night – the big elephant, the mother elephant, and one of the baby elephants have gone to sleep. The other little elephant tries to knock over a part of the fence but cannot do so, so he goes to sleep too". Later in the night, when both babies are asleep however the mother elephant takes over. This elephant wakes, knocks down a part of the fence and gets out, hits the policeman on the head (Charles forgets about the other policeman) with "his" trunk and the policemen falls down and the elephant goes off down the road – she "wants to be troublesome".
A horse now appears in the scene. (Charles rapidly makes a second field to the right of and joined to the first one and puts a horse in it). He continues "the horse has never seen an elephant. The elephant stops when she sees the horse and pushes down a part of the fencing round the horse and goes on out of the picture

111

to the right. The horse now gets out of the field and runs away to the left where he comes upon the policeman who was knocked down by the elephant". Charles here introduces a dramatic change of atmosphere, he says, "This man was not a real policeman, the real policeman were all too busy so this man came in to help" – the horse runs up to him – and sees he is master. Charles continued, "The man wakes up, finds the horse there and tells him to wait: he sees the elephant running away and runs to the circus to tell them about the elephant". (At this point it began to show that the same combination of "circus" and "zoo" as had appeared in Mary's Worlds was happening here too – "circus" and "zoo" are fused in Charles' interior picture). He continues, "He tells the boss man of the zoo of the elephant's escape and some men come back with him.

"It is now early morning. A man sees the elephant on the road and runs away to tell people, but the elephant knocks him out; meantime the people have come from the circus and have put the horse inside the enclosure to look after the baby elephants with a man on guard; the other men go after the elephant and get in front of it" (dramatically acted out) "and shoo it back; the other man from the circus helping". They get the elephant back into the enclosure; "the elephant does not like this, but thinks it was worth it to get out".

Discussion. In this delightful story acted out with great vigour and absorption, Charles personified vividly himself "being a nuisance". When this wish was explored it was possible to get Charles to see that what was now annoying him was that other people in his community were getting on cheerfully either with work or play; and that he was unable to do either.

World 36   Figure 39 (105th session)

This was also an "action" World, the ground plan of which is illustrated here:

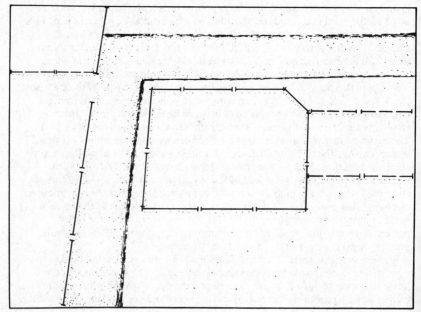

A circus lion was driven into the paddock in the centre of the tray by circus men, and an elephant put in to guard him; the circus men then closed the gate and doubled it with an extra fence. "One night", Charles went on, "when the elephant had gone to sleep, the lion was still awake. A little boy came along; he was quite naughty and thought it would be nice to open the door so he quickly undid the latch and opened it and then went back to his bed. The lion saw it was open and trotted out and found a second fence and turned round it; he then turned back and jumped the gate, pushed it to, and was free. In the field by the left nearer side were some ponies and horses. The lion thought, 'I think I'll kill and eat one of those'; but in the next field, at the far left corner, was a bull, guarded by a dog on an old sleigh; the lion jumped into the ponies' field and they jumped into the bull's field. The bull thought it would be nice to have someone to charge, so he made a run at the fence and bashed it down, got into the field and the bull and the lion had a fight; the bull knocked the lion over and stood over him.

The bull was a friend of the horses. Early in the morning the lion was snarling to try to get the bull off, but the bull was not scared; a car came along and the driver saw what had happened, stopped his car and said, 'I'll go and tell the farmer about this'; he turned and raced off to the farmer at the farmhouse, gathered some men and away they went to the bull and the lion.

Now the elephant had woken up and said, 'Oh the naughty lion has escaped', and trumpeted, which nearly deafened the man in the car – and the lion snarled even louder. The men climbed over the fence (the bull only attacks animals, not people). A dog now came racing after them, jumped into the field with the men and started barking at the bull. Another dog came too; the bull got off the lion; the lion didn't see the people and thought he had a chance to spring, but the bull got ahead to bar the way. The elephant thought, 'I will have something to do there', and knocked down part of the fence and got over the other; the dog got scared and hid behind the men. The elephant knelt down; the lion turned round and they shooed him off; the men opened the gate and with the elephant behind and the farmer shouting and waving sticks and a lighted branch they drove the lion back into his cage; the elephant came too. One man went and got the bull back to his proper field and the dog went back to guard the bull. Then they decided to get another elephant from the circus to join in guarding the lion".

Discussion. Charles greatly enjoyed doing this World; it was very dramatic and vivid, he played all the parts himself, making the appropriate noises. At the same time it typified the kind of situation to which Charles reacted with aggression as was shown in the incident described below.

The school had recently reported they now knew the pattern of Charles' outbursts of temper; they come when concentration on something is suddenly broken into, and also in response to teasing.

During the weekend following this a series of incidents happened which – because they illustrate so well both the interaction between the school and therapy and the method of therapy – are given below in detail.

These incidents happened on the Friday and Saturday; they were not reported to me by the school, but were recounted to me by Charles during his Saturday afternoon session and checked up later with the school. The sequence of events as they emerged piecemeal during the session and were re-arranged in order later, was as follows.

On Friday morning in school meeting Charles hit a girl who put out her tongue at him; after meeting the headmaster brought him down to the hut. Charles then drew a very detailed drawing called "wartime" of fighter planes and helicopter "patrolling" over a closed line of loaded army lorries all going the same way. On Saturday morning in school in a grammar lesson Charles recounted as follows. "We were doing adjectives and I got muddled up; the teacher said, 'A woodchopper chopped down 5 trees' and we were to put an adjective in; I said, 'chopped' and got stuck and shouted at him; it came off all of a sudden. I didn't know why I shouted at him; I got 15 adjectives right". The teacher sent Charles out of the class and the headmaster took him down to the hut. Charles then made the following World and left it for discussion at the afternoon session.

World 37 *not illustrated* (106th session)

This was a battle between Indians and English soldiers, conducted along the length of the tray. At the further side hills were made and the Indians disposed among them, infiltrating along the long right-hand edge. The English soldiers were very well placed; a group round the tents was realistically centred on an officer with field glasses. An interesting feature of this World was that on a hill against the further edge an Indian chief was placed, who "was a pacific chief who did not want to be drawn into the battle".

Discussion. This is the first war scene of the deployment of two opposing forces. It was very well laid out, the Indians' side being dramatically arranged with cover behind hills; the position of individual Indians obviously carefully thought out; the soldiers were much more schematised, arranged in groups of four on flat ground with very little individuality to them. It is obvious from the arrangement that Charles identified with the Indians, but at the same time expressed in the pacific Indian chief his equally real wish not to be at war with his companions.

This World was waiting at the beginning of session 106, and Charles was very impressed with the fact that this was the first World in which he had set out two opposing enemies. After discussing the World Charles was able to discuss with me the circumstances of the war-time drawing, and then to give me the account, quoted above, of that morning's upset (grammar lesson).

I then asked Charles if he had dreamed, and he reported as follows.

"G (teacher) went out of the classroom, telling a big boy to be in charge. No one obeyed, all shouted and screamed; a girl said, 'G is coming'; all quieted down".

I took this on two levels, asking first what – supposing this very possible scene had happened in reality – would have happened had they not quieted down, and Charles replied they would have been sent over to the headmaster and would have missed T.V. at the weekend. I then asked him to go back into the dream and say what he thought he would have *dreamed* had happened, supposing the noise had gone on when G resumed. Charles said, "G would probably have chopped my head off and my arm". I then asked him to draw "chopping down trees"; Charles made a very careful coloured drawing* of 5 trees and a woodchopper; 2 trees are standing and have leaves, one very big one is half chopped and leaning against a fourth small tree; a fifth big tree has been cut down, lying on the ground some distance from the stump. When asked why the man was chopping the trees down, Charles gave the rational answer, "to use for fire wood for the winter".

Charles arrived at session 107 looking well but frowning when asked to think. We talked about what one can and cannot "know" about oneself, Charles taking part and being interested; going back to the events of last week he stated quite clearly that when he runs away, goes into rages, etc., he does not know he is doing it until he finds he is. I demonstrated in the World tray a river getting only a part of itself over a mill dam, explaining that what we want to accomplish is to get nearly the whole of his force manageable, pointing out that some remains always in reserve; he was then asked to draw a force being constructive, *not* using water; he thought for a bit, then made a drawing and said it was a drill going down into the earth to get oil; it was worked by a cable going into a house where men worked it.

On session 108 Charles reported himself as having heard in class the teacher's sentence "He thought a great deal" as "He fought in the battle", and in the ensuing disturbance Charles had knocked the paraffin oil stove over. As a calming technique I got him to do a Mosaic and a Newspaper Game.

World 38 *not illustrated* (109th session)

Charles dug out a space in the tray roughly in the shape of a club, which he said was water; between the end of this and the further tray-edge he placed a caravan and three lorries; a canoe and a boat were drawn up on the shore; the sand was made to slope down from this end; on the flat part on the further side of the stream were two cannons, and opposite these, on the nearer side, a boat with a man in it, a man on shore and two men on horseback. About this World Charles gave the following account.

"It is a little river which branches off the river Thames; it is a smugglers' hide-out and they tie the boats up here. They go in the boat to London by day and lay up there. In America their pals put valuable jewels in cigarette boxes; the smugglers meet the Americans and the Americans put these boxes aboard their boat and they go off at night with the boxes, and if there are too many they put them in the canoe and tie it to the end of the boat. The hide-out is camouflaged by bushes; there is an old boathouse, the back of which opens and they sail in through the back. They live in the caravan. The lorries take the boxes to an old barn where they are stacked up; one lorry is unloaded, and one loading canoe drawn up on land, and the boat by shore. The guns are kept ready so that if police come they fire at them. The man by the shore is a scout and the launch is

---

*The castration content of this drawing is obvious; the reason why it was not taken up with Charles will be found in the summing-up pages.

the smugglers, used for, when, if they spot danger, they whistle and they run down to the boat and get away in the launch".

Discussion. This is a new theme which represents also a new stage. Charles is now envisaging a community of antisocial people, which has a certain organisation; a definite development is taking place in his power of thinking out a situation. A good development here is that the smugglers "have friends in America". Charles cannot yet conceive of the possibility of "friends" nearer by, but the whole World is not entirely hostile. The hide-out is up a river: i.e., the river of division is here the place of protection.

The occasion of the following World (39) illustrated well a characteristic of this technique of treatment. Owing to an emergency in relation to another child at the moment of Charles' session, I was called away and a colleague, a member of staff of the I.C.P. who was also working at the school, took the session for me. Charles was so completely absorbed in the making of his World that he accepted her without question, used her as a helper to find the things he wanted, and threw himself wholly into the work. Another characteristic, both of Charles and of other children working with this technique, also came out strongly and was commented on by my colleague, which was the detailed care and determination with which Charles sought in the cabinet drawers for exactly the objects he needed.

World 39 *not illustrated* (110th session)

Charles made a rectangular enclosure against the further edge with a pool of water at the centre of the edge, and a haystack in the corner. Into this field he puts 5 sheep and 3 lambs. He then dug out a roughly triangular pool against the centre of the nearer edge with steep banks, and placed 4 cows in the water, 3 other cows drinking at the pool to the left and 1 lying down, a man and 2 dogs beside. Between the field and the pool he made a road curving from the further to the nearer edge (the mirror-opposite of the river in World 30). Starting from the right the following traffic was placed on this road: a covered lorry, a cannon, a motorcycle-combination, and at the far end by the sheep field the lorry with the milk churns; one private car facing in the opposite direction. The cannon was afterwards moved and a lorry carrying a rabbit hut was put in its place. A policeman and a road sign were placed in the centre of the picture.
Charles described the World as follows: "The man on the left is looking after the cows; both dogs belong to him; the policeman is holding up the traffic to protect the cows. The milk lorry is going to the farm to which the sheep and lambs belong. The rabbit hut is new and is being taken to the farm because the door of the old one of off its hinges and the rabbits may get out. The private car is coming away from the farm".

Discussion. In this World the objects (masculine in type) from his incoherent Worlds move between two scenes of animals with young, with water for their drinking, and with human beings looking after them.

The clarity of this presentation made it possible for me, when I saw Charles at the following session (111), to start a discussion of his series of Worlds in relation to the theme of mother and child. At the same time Charles was able to talk spontaneously about his experiences with the other children, saying for example "I was being noisy; I got into a temper; I was cross".

During the following week very cold weather prevented all outdoor constructive and expressive activities; some of the children had developed mumps and the staff were overworked. The epileptoid character of Charles' attacks began to change into straightforward "aggressiveness"; the school report runs: "Charles pushes the other children, interferes with them, loses his temper without cause and rushesu pstairs". At the same time the fertility of invention shown in his Worlds began to appear in his ordinary life. In discussing this with Matron she confirmed that she had noticed for some time on walks "that Charles' head is full of stories of all sorts, he is always living within some story he is making up".

The drive of E within Charles therefore is beginning to find ways of reaching expression and its pressure upon him is becoming tempered by imaginative activity of a cognitive kind but this did not appear in school work because his slowness in writing made it impossible for him to get anything out. Later in the session I asked Charles to draw a scene in which a child means well with an action but the adults are infuriated. He was able only to think of playing with a bill poster's brush.

During the following week Charles had an outburst of temper and was sent down to my Play hut by the Headmaster. He made a drawing of a rocket, and set to work for a considerable time and made a most detailed and carefully worked out World of a wayside cafe (World 40). Here his longing for nourishment and for protection were expressed skilfully combined with his strong sense of object reality.

World 40   Figure 40 (112th session). See page 118.

A road was marked out along the further edge of the tray by fences with two openings; a parallel road, fenced in the same way, ran along the nearer side of the tray with one opening; the centre part of the tray was divided into three parts. On the left was a field containing a drinking trough, 2 mares and 2 foals; in the field to the right he dug out a pond and put one cow in it, with 3 cows and a calf standing round it; a line of 3 cows were looking over the fence to the road. The centre of the tray was occupied by a "workman's cafe", 3 tables with four chairs each situated round the cafe building; 2 loaded lorries were driving in, and one lorry was parked with a child's school-desk on it. On the road along the further edge of the tray was a milk van; the milkman himself standing inside the fence; against the further edge toward the right is a road sign and on its right again a man on a motorcycle. On the left of the road which runs along the nearer edge a shepherd and his dog were driving 7 sheep and 2 lambs; to the right of this a policeman was holding up a car and a lorry carrying a small car.
Charles said that the lorries were going into the cafe because the drivers wanted

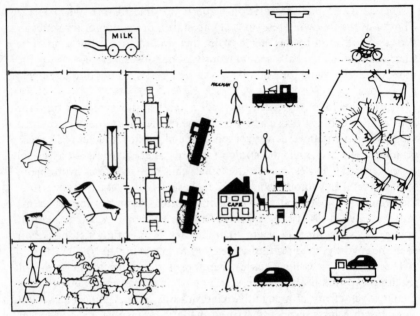

to "have something"; one driver is already standing in the yard. The lorry with the desk is to show that "goods" is being moved by this lorry. The milkman was delivering milk to the cafe; the policeman was holding up the traffic to let the sheep get past safely.

Discussion. This is an entirely "real" World; it is well observed and very neatly carried out. The emphasis upon drinking that has appeared in so many of his Worlds is here socialised in terms of a place of refreshment for human beings as well as in drinking water for the animals. All the animals are safe; the young with their mothers, and the sheep are under the care both of the shepherd and his dog, and of the policeman.

These recent Worlds made possible for the first time detailed discussion with Charles (session 113) of his daily life and relation with children and staff in which he, having first found his way to generalised expression in his Worlds, became able to put his experiences and feelings into words, as "I was waving a broom about – I saw T's thumb – I thought it would be a nice thing to hit – I tried to stop myself and couldn't and hit him". One of Charles' rare dreams occurred here "I was a groom – grooming horses – one got away. I tied it up and it must have broken its rope. I felt cross because it was my own horse".

World 41 *not illustrated* (was made during the week)

This was a World of a covered wagon with treasure being ambushed in a valley by bandits and getting away, an even number of men on either side being killed.

Discussion. Charles now developed mumps and was seen in bed (session 114); World 41 had been drawn and was discussed with him. This was the first World in which Charles identified himself equally with both sides of the conflict, enjoying the ingenious disposition of the bandits as well as the courage and resource of the man with the wagon who eventually got it away.

By this time Charles came so much more into contact both with his own experience and with the school community that he was able to notice what actually occurred between him and the other children and to make good verbal reports to me about these incidents; that is to say, the confusion and state of semi-consciousness have disappeared, and although he was not able to control himself as yet, Charles was in contact with himself and reported to me his conscious efforts at self-control. That made it possible to turn our attention to his school work. The teaching staff reported that Charles' arithmetic was so bad that even the sequence of ordinal numbers was not secure (he was now $9\frac{1}{2}$ years old).

Session 115 was spent exploring numbers; Charles did not really know the difference between odd and even and was unsure of the meaning of "ten" and "unit". In session 116 work was done with Poleidoblocs G and it became clear that Charles did not look at objects or think about things that are of a fixed shape; he thought about everything as flowing and being the way he wanted it to be; this was explained to him and he agreed.

As our talk went on it became clear that these mechanisms and inner procedures had been dominant all along in Charles, but only now – 22 months after the beginning of treatment and around the 116th half-hourly session – was his interior organisation sufficiently firm for him to be able to observe what was going on in himself and to realise something of what his attitudes were. It may be that, from some points of view this can be regarded as slow progress but it must be remembered that at the beginning and for quite a long period afterwards Charles was entirely inaccessible to ordinary contact and that the ban from the Authorities on all discussion of sexual themes considerably slowed-up work. At session 117 Charles' ability to be aware of his own feeling was discussed with him and I suggested he might do some drawings of a boy in a rage; his first was of a boy having a dream of his mother being attacked which puts him in a rage because he cannot go home and save her; the other two drawings were about a boy with a knife, but the content was vague.

In the middle of the week the headmaster suggested, after a confused incident with the other children, that Charles cool off in my Play hut and he made the river-World 42.

World 42 *not illustrated* (118th session)

A wide river with naturally curving banks was dug out across the tray from further to nearer edge to the right. On the right bank was a wharf with a boat drawn up against it; on the left bank was a town arranged as follows: two houses and a telephone box are set against the left-hand edge with people in front; between the houses is a road and another road runs in front of the houses; on this road were put 4 cars and a policeman holding up the traffic; against the further edge were set two houses and a church, a ladder with a man on it was leaning against the church; a lorry was placed facing the river. Opposite the wharf on the right was a wharf on the left of the river with a boat drawn up by it containing a beehive and a luggage carrier. Between this wharf and the road were 2 lorries, a well-arranged group of people, and 3 more men standing by the lorries. An ambulance stood near the wharf. Further up the river were 2 boats.

Charles gave the following description of this World. "It is a town on the river Thames" (Charles' town is by the Thames); "the boats take goods up to London; it is Saturday and a busy day; everybody comes down to the river, because it is sunny, to watch the boats and have a picnic". Charles then pointed out certain of the people as follows: "A woman has come from a farm to get eggs; a shepherd has come to collect some sheep with a man to help him; the group of people have come for a holiday; of the two lorry drivers one drives the lorry, the second takes over from him when he is tired; the ambulance is there in case anybody falls in the river; the beehive and luggage carrier are just about to be put on a lorry; the man on the ladder by the church is seeing if there are any loose slates on the church roof; the motor launch is there if any robbers start attacking their boats, to throw things off them".

Discussion. This is the first time in Worlds or drawings that overt pleasure has appeared. The scene was well observed and well executed, and in describing it, Charles indentified himself in turn with the various people he mentioned, actively enjoying with them their sunny Saturday by the river. The one element of unreality is the protection against robbers.

It was not until we discussed this World that I realised that Charles' home was within reach of the river and that the Thames played an important part in his home life and experience. After the making of this World, the river-across-the-tray appeared only once more, a long time later. Then it occurred with an almost exactly similar layout, even including the beehive and the luggage carrier; the only difference was that the tea garden (the cafe of World 40) was on the left bank of the river; there was no hint of danger or violent action, and the lorries (and a train) were hard at work carting sand.

Session 119. Charles had a dream "I was with the cowboys to round up cattle and a rock fell down and startled my horse and it ran away and I was scared and woke". Explanation was given about E. Charles spent the session covering a large sheet of paper with red and blue paint in a primitive pattern. Next session (122) Charles reported a dream in which Boadicea led armies against Caesar's armies and Boadicea won! He agreed in talk that in his family it was his mother who took all the decisions and that his father hardly counted. Just about this time my notes say "great change in Charles; he is much more forthcoming, talks spontaneously now in short sentences and with much vigour", and it became at last possible to discuss his whole family with him, including Mr. Robinson's first family. Charles then made a drawing of a mother tiger in a cave; the (tiger) father got killed; the mother got a new mate; a boy cub outside the cave put his head in; the new mate growled at him.

Session 121. Charles was looking well and did a Mosaic. Its greater accuracy suggested to me that it might be worthwhile checking back at arithmetic; here there was a slight improvement and it was possible to point out to Charles that as he was getting a greater ability to "see" the shape of his own feelings, so he became also more able to see the shape of outside things and to think clearly about school subjects. Charles took this up at once, and referring to last time's drawing of the tigers recounted a memory of a morning when "he had gone into his parents' room to get into their bed and his father had shooed him away and *his mother had said nothing*".

World 43   Figure 41 (122nd session)

This was a valley in the hills; the right-hand nearer corner was filled in with an enclosure in which were 3 mares, 5 foals and a drinking trough. In the further right-hand corner 2 other mares were placed standing by a hedge; these were riding horses. In the left centre, in a gap in some hills a road issued from a valley into a flat camping place on which were placed a tent and a fire with cooking pots around; the cowboys' covered wagon had turned off the road and driven into the camping place; one cowboy was sitting on a log playing a guitar; another was riding towards him; 3 other cowboys were standing on guard with pistols behind the hill, facing the road; at the further centre edge was a sledge. On the left side of the valley a procession of bisons was moving along; above them, near the further edge a mother bear and a baby bear were sitting behind the ridge. Charles explained, "It is the end of the day; the cowboys are going to camp; the men with the pistols are on guard in case any attack should come; but the bisons go on their way without noticing".

Discussion.   This World marked a turning point in Charles' development. He was able to contemplate the idea of possible danger without simultaneously conceiving of attack. The cowboys with their fire, their food and their music are at peace and their horses are safe although the procession of bisons pass nearby them. We discussed Charles' earlier relation to people and how he could not imagine that things that happened were not directed against himself, and he told of a time when his sister had stood upon his soldiers on the floor. When I acted out grownups shooing children away, Charles laughed and became for the first time a merry boy.

The Easter holidays followed. The reports were excellent, and apparently nobody had any complaints to make or even criticisms of Charles throughout the holidays. Mary was now the difficulty as far as the parents were concerned; she was said to be aggressive, bossy, dominating, nasty to Charles and troublesome with her boy friends. Charles appeared to take it quite well.

General Review of Charles' Worlds

Having now outlined the course of Charles' treatment we propose to analyse the modes of expression he develops in his Worlds and the symbols he uses.

Before we can do this we need to be able to pass the whole series of 43 Worlds in review.

In *Table 2* the material is presented in tabular form. This enables the relation to be studied between the type of symbol used by Charles and the coherence or incoherence of the World in which it occurs. From this table it will be seen that over twice as many Worlds are coherent as incoherent. Since in four of the Worlds classified as Incoherent, islands of coherence appear and in one, classified as Coherent, there are elements of incoherence, these five Worlds have been grouped in a central column entitled "Composite Worlds". In this table the symbols are grouped according to their relation to each other and to the layout of the World.

The interaction between coherent and incoherent Worlds supplied some of the material from which the theory of E and the proto-system set out in this book, have been derived. If the sequence between coherent and incoherent Worlds be studied it appears as if each coherent World focuses, as it were, some part of the E which activated the makings of incoherent Worlds.

To gain a satisfactory grasp of the symbolic nature of Charles' or any

Table 2

	Coherent Worlds	Composite Worlds	Incoherent Worlds
Wild Animals			
In wild setting	1–5–25	(32)	32
In relation to circus	35–36		
Country Scenes			
Farms	6–7–8–29	(20)	20
Other rural scenes	13–15–39	(4)	3–4
Country cafe	40		
Fighting Scenes			
Soldiers (war real or implied)	23–37		9–10–19
"Western" setting	(11–12–14–16–21 28–34–41–43)		
Transport and Movement			
Planes and Cars	24	(24–27)	2–17–27
Railway	26–33		18
Racing Cars	22		
River (as transport)	30–38		
Proto-system			31
Urban Scene			
A town on the River Thames	42		
Total	**31 Coh. Worlds**	**(5)**	**12 Incoh. Worlds**

child's Worlds they need to be considered along five axes: in relation to time, movement, coherence and incoherence, type of symbol used, patterning and design.

In the analysis of William Carter a sixth axis will be found necessary, that which may be called internal and external space. To the experienced eye this is present also in Charles' Worlds but it is difficult to demonstrate until it has first been seen in a series of Worlds in which it is more easily recognisable.

We will now consider these axes in turn.

Time

In a series of Worlds the factor of Time appears in two ways: in the way in which World follows World, and in the relation of time to the individual World.

a. Sequence of Worlds

In the first 33 Worlds that Charles made, coherent and incoherent Worlds occur in groups – one type alternating with the other. The Worlds following No. 33 are all coherent. Something the same occurs in respect of the symbols used, Worlds using one type of symbol tending also to occur in groups as with, for example, the farm Worlds 6-7-8 and the circus ones of 35-36.

b. Time structure within a World

All of Charles' Worlds "take place" in the present time. In none of them does he use the device, so constantly employed by other kinds of children, of placing some of his scenes in historic or prehistoric time, or by mixing prehistoric animals or historic human beings with present-day ones.

Apart from the question of the use of "historical" time, Worlds can be entirely static or entirely moving or sometimes partly one and partly the other. None of Charles' Worlds are static.

The concept of Time is of certain events in a structure of story or scene occurring before or after other events *to which they are related*. The point at which Time enters most into a World is in those which tell a story, which starts at the beginning of the layout of the World and is carried through in continuous narration to the end. *Group a* Worlds 11-12-14-16-26-35-36-41 are of this nature.

In relation to a time sequence two other types of Worlds can occur; one in which a number of separated incidents, each a small episode of story nature, occur which, though separated in fact have a common background and a relation to each other; and Worlds in which no actual

124

movement of objects takes place but their arrangement is such that a central core of movement has been or is about to take place. *Group b* Worlds 1-5-6-7-8-20-21-25-29-32-34 belong to the first type, and *Group c* Worlds 13-15-22-23-24-28-30-33-37-38-40-42-43 to the second. The remaining Worlds are so incoherent in nature that no concepts occur in them which could include an idea of Time.

Study of these three groups throws light upon Charles' "inner" experience.

Group a. The first four of these and the last one (41) present coherent stories of Wild West adventure. Charles took part in all of them, moving the men and animals about, and taking each of the parts in turn. The themes were of battles with Red Indians and bandits and the attacks of bandits on the covered-wagon-carrying-treasure. Worlds 35 and 36 also carried continuous stories, this time of circus wild animals (and in 36 a bull) getting out of control, running away, and being brought again under human control.

All these themes are taken either from Charles' experience of film or T.V. scenarios or are reconstructions of his own running away impulses in circus animal terms. In the only use of possible real life objects (26) – a train carrying passengers – the time sequence is one of rescue from disaster.

The Worlds of *Group b* are of a different type. Four of them (1-5-25-32) are concerned with wild animals, all – except World 32 which has an incoherent element – in a coherent setting. These four Worlds contain small pieces of stories occurring simultaneously and all concerned with interpersonal relations of a family type. Worlds 6-7-8 similarly contain intermittently recounted incidents of relationships expressed in human beings and their relations to farm animals and farm animals to each other. A somewhat similar concept of sequence in incidents occurs in Worlds 20 and 29 within a farm setting. In World 21 a short series of incidents occur concerned with cowboys' care for their cattle. World 34, which is also a Western theme, introduces a new element, that of the rivalry between "bandits" and cowboys for possession of a mare.

World 13 is a kind of border-line World between this and the next group as though, in the main, it is just a "laid out" scene, a series of incidents concerning the caravan and a helping man bring it partly into Group b. One other World (23) is difficult to place as although a number of incidents occur one *after* the other, they are too confused in meaning to be sorted out into a straight time sequence.

The Worlds of *Group c* are of two types, either straightforward scenes carefully laid out such as 15 (landscape), 24 (road beside airfield), 33 (Railway station), 37 (moment in battle), 40 (a roadside cafe), 42 (Thames on a Saturday), 43 (cowboy camp and bisons) in which it is true that actions of various sorts are said to have taken place or to be about to, yet

125

there is no sequence or story; or Worlds 22 (a crash in a road race), 28 (cowboys, their cattle and peaceful Indians), 30 (a naval depot by a river), 38 (smugglers hide-out on a river) where a certain series of movements occur implying passage of time but which are not, as in Group a, a connected story taking up the whole session.

It would seem clear therefore that conscious passage of time is only felt by Charles in relation to violent, and to some extent hostile movement or to clearing up the damage caused by blockage of orderly movement.

Movement

Time in our normal attitude to it is measured by movement, and in much that has been said in the previous session, movement as well as Time is involved. Charles, in marked contrast to William Carter, was very active with his Worlds. His Incoherent Worlds consisted almost entirely of movement. He occasionally, as in those of Group b (of the previous section) put sentences and sentiments into the mouths of objects he did not move, but for the most part he moved the World objects about the tray as he talked of them.

This quality of Worlds, that the objects in them can be moved about at will and that this movement can be made in all directions, fast and slow, vigorously and gently, pressing lightly or deeply into the surface – is a very important element in the World Technique. Neither in drawing nor in modelling is this possible though the lightness or heaviness of lines in drawing offers some of the same possibilities. It is the possibility of identifying with the movement of the objects used which assists in expressing and "fixing" the E. It is a characteristic of Charles' relation to the objects he uses that the movements he made with them were realistic, in contradistinction to many children who make objects move about and fly through the air which are quite incapable of doing so.

When Charles does not actually move the objects of his World, the layout of the World and what he says about them, as for example in the racing car World (22) or the naval base (30) or the smugglers (38), implies movement on the part of objects and people in the World. It was only much later in his treatment that Charles made Worlds in which the significance lay in the position or relationship of objects to each other and not in any movement of them.

Coherent and Incoherent Worlds

Charles' position on admission to the school and at the beginning of treatment was of a boy driven by interior forces which impelled him to two kinds of wild behaviour – verbal outbursts against his mother, and outbursts of a physical nature which, as far as external observation can tell, did not arise from direct or recognisable stimuli from his actual real situation. The question we have to consider is "what is the relation between this situation and his work with Worlds?". It is in the answer to this question that, I feel, a clue is hidden to both the nature and the treatment of this condition.

A basic characteristic of Charles' reaction to the World material is the very sharp contrast between his coherent and his incoherent Worlds. One of the puzzling, and at the same time most valuable and illuminating aspects of Charles' case, is the contrast presented by the poverty of his school work, the emptiness of his contacts with his fellows and with the adults in the school, and the vigour, definiteness and imaginative content of his coherent Worlds. The answer to this puzzle is concerned with the whole question of focus and of the means of expression that are available for children of what is going on within them.

Small children have only movement, noises and various simple actions with objects at their disposal. In psychoanalytic study and treatment, particularly of the Kleinian school, the significance that is given to these modes of expression is that which derives from the appearance of comparable modes in retrospective work with adults. This attribution depends upon a concept of a continuity of significance throughout the passage of time and also upon a belief that the factors found to be fundamentally operative in adult analysis have, in fact, been the factors fundamentally and causally at work in infancy and childhood. Since, however, it has been our endeavour throughout our work to look at the behaviour of children both within and without the treatment session from a fresh standpoint (not ignoring the material brought to light by other schools of thought but keeping them in the background of the mind for comparison and checking), the question of what *exactly* a child does with the opportunities and the material provided for him by the World apparatus, and how this compares with his behaviour outside the treatment session, becomes the main focus of our enquiry.

The eagerness with which Charles took to the World apparatus and the completeness of his concentration upon his work with it had to be seen to be believed. His first World was made on his fourth session and the essential fact about it is that it is a completely coherent production. It is this ability of a child like Charles, inaccessible along all other routes, to produce a scene in which the parts are coherently related to each other and which has a beginning, a middle, and an end, which is most remarkable. The objects he uses are realistically conceived in strong contrast to William Carter's reaction to his objects, and the actions he makes them do and the comments he makes upon them are those possible to real versions of these wild animals in a jungle setting. At this time Charles was $7\frac{3}{4}$; his reading powers were limited, the family possessed no T.V. set, his period in the school had been short; although he will have been to a zoo, the

127

number of wild animal films he may have seen will have been very limited; so this World must be regarded as an imaginative adaptation to his own needs of very limited actual experience. In this World he expresses little but the statement of the existence of mother-and-child, of mates, of hostility between men and some animals and animals among themselves and of an ambivalent attitude to water; it contains danger (crocodiles) but is also pleasant to wallow in (hippos). When a child, however ill or inaccessible he is, makes a first World of this degree of imagination and coherent presentation, the prognosis for him is favourable.

Striking as the coherence of this World is, the contrast between this and the next (made at the next session) is even more so. It is difficult to convey in words a clear impression of the making of an incoherent World. The essence of the thesis set out in this book is that in children like Charles a high charge of E has been unable to find any mode of coherent expression and has, in consequence, tended to explode through channels of the most primitive type. The exact nature of this second World carries us a step further in the understanding of the nature of Charles' condition. In his first World Charles selected a number of creatures whose size, strength, and wildness puts them right outside the possibility of domestication or control by humans and presented them as acting, as it were, at a distance. The result was a planned and a coherent presentation. In his second World Charles sought out and selected machines which were part of his reality environment, that he knew could be controlled by man and that he knew to be possessed of – to him – unlimited force, mobility and direction. In this World these powerful machines drove about, up and down, and along the level with minimal organisation and no goal. Charles threw himself violently into their movements and identified with them in intense absorption. What is not in this World is as interesting and revealing as what is. There is no previous planning, no coherent layout, no consistent relation of individual objects to each other.* There is, however, a clear perception of difference in the types of machine; aeroplanes are collected together, there is a rudimentary reality realisation of an airfield (although the landing and taking off of planes is not confined to it); lorries move along the ground† – the human figures who are introduced are such as could in reality appear in relation to such machines.

The contrast between the violent extravagance of action and noise shown by Charles in the time he was occupied with these toy machines and this sense of reality in regard to them provides a surprising contrast to the lack of adaptation to reality shown in his outbursts of violent action or equally violent retreat in a reality setting. This contrast raises one of the many problems that sprout like mushrooms in a field around the reaction

---

*cf. with the absence of this in William Carter's Worlds.
†Many children of this age under treatment confuse planes and cars in action, making cars circle about the air in the manner of planes.

of children to the World Technique. It is as if Charles were able to focus his E upon objects which he could choose and manipulate and so completely understand (within the terms of the play), but that this comprehension of and ability to focus upon people or objects in his real external environment was lacking.

When he had, as it were, got into the rhythm of treatment, Charles repeated in World 3 the general form of World 2 – but this time cars took the place of planes on the left of the tray. This brought his layout into line with what we had by now learned of his general type of play at home when he monopolised the floor space of the living room and got very much in the way of the rest of the family by running a collection of toy cars to and fro on the floor of the room. He foreshadowed his later development of Worlds in the construction of a field on the right and the selection of cows from the cabinet which, however, were not actually put in the field. Although Charles' absorption in this World was as complete as in World 2, a certain awareness was shown of controlling powers in the reality world by the inclusion of policemen figures; the cars in the picture, however, took no notice of these figures and "crashed" in consequence.

Having, as it were, discharged some of the unmanageable force of E within him in Worlds 2 and 3, he became able to make a step forward.

The next World (4), set the pattern for the later development of his Worlds. This is a crucial and important construction because in it he demonstrated an awareness of the existence of what proved later to be two idioms of expression, divided by a river which flowed across the tray. This is therefore not exactly an Incoherent World, but a Composite one, the animals appearing on the left and neatly fenced in, while various types of engine are placed separately on the right. No planes appeared in this World and the racing cars placed against the further edge appeared only once more – when they were the central feature of World 22. The phone box which forms so persistent a feature of Mary's Worlds appeared here as an isolated feature, and the train which became a constant feature of Charles' later Worlds, makes its first appearance.

Already Charles had made considerable progress in devising modes of expression of E. He now directed his attention towards the thinking out and manipulation of objects in relation to other objects in the tray with *rudimentary purpose* and content. There was a bridge now between the two sides and the milk van and the empty lorry passed each other on this bridge. There were no people in this World. Having combined the two types of World in one Charles felt free to swing to the other aspect of his work of expression and to continue a discussion of the family situation. In Jungle World 5 he presented for the one and only time in this series both a father whose attention and care is focused on his daughter and a father who is protective to his son.

The construction of this World is interesting as here this factual boy achieves the same sort of expression as is common in dreams and in modern art; that is the simultaneous presentation of two aspects of a single subject – father and children – by the use of different symbols. The "coherence" however of this World, both in design and content, is much less than that of World 1.

The left-hand side of World 4 provides a bridge to Worlds 6-7-8. These three illustrate another aspect of the relation between the child and the Worlds he makes; this is what might be called the "mirror effect" comparable to reversal of the letters in "mirror written" words, with the difference that there is no "right" order in the arrangement of Worlds. For instance the "farmyard" is on the left of the scene in World 6 but on the right in Worlds 7 and 8. The other feature in these three is the fact so commonly found in series of dreams and drawings made either by adults or children of the gradual appearance (in the third World) of detailed story fragments concerning the farm animals which were possibily implicit in Charles' first presentation of the farm but of which he was not then sufficiently "aware" for their representation.

These three Worlds present a tangled skein of observations, feelings, queries, hopes and desires, the expression of which Charles worked out through the medium of human beings and farm animals in a setting much nearer both to external reality and to his own experience than the previous Worlds. They demonstrate one way in which different elements, coming from several different aspects of personality, can interweave with one another and appear simultaneously, if material in which it is possible for them to be expressed is present.

Three weeks intervened between this and the next two Worlds which were incoherent.

In World 9 the formless movements of Worlds 2 and 3 have, as it were, crystallised into curved fencing and roads set around the shape of the tray, and explosives coming out of guns with which soldiers are "practising". Charles' absorption in the up/down motions of aeroplanes, their noises, and crashes of planes upon the ground, came in here without any relation to the semi-coherent scene of practising soldiers. World 10 is discussed in more detail in the section on design – its function here is to "fix" the scaffolding of forms in the T-shaped river with a bridge across the upright arm. The rifles in World 9 made a transition to the direct expression of destructiveness in World 10. The planes which crashed here turned into bombers which instead of crashing themselves upon the ground dropped explosive bombs.

This "war" item in World 10 makes a transition again to a fully fledged "fighting" picture in World 11 and this theme continued in World 12, leading on to a group of coherent statements.

In World 11 the whole scene changes. Charles does not make a story of his own, as in the wild animal and farm scenes, but borrows from his experience of "Western" films and stories. He is, however, not at home with these, the coherence of the story is tenuous and the significant actors in it are horses.

World 12, from the constructional point of view, is interesting as the general layout of the river resembles fairly closely that of World 5. Here too a powerful man is placed in the centre, as it were, of the river, not a "father" but a sheriff, and not in a boat *on* the river but on a bridge crossing the river. The action here is in several directions and the World contains the single instance in this series of Worlds of a human being falling *into* the river.

Between Worlds 12 and 13 a holiday period intervened.

World 13 is of a new type. The carrying out of circular movement demands and implies a far greater control of muscle and nerve than movement in a straight line. This World presents a different kind of coherence from that of the former ones. It is not a coherence of factual content as in the farm or jungle scenes, but of symbolic presentation. The pond which appeared by the edge of the tray in World 4 is now the centre of the scene: cows and a horse surround it and drink from it. Charles as an infant was a lazy feeder and was weaned at 2 months – the relation of mother and infant is here in the centre of the picture: the form of the scene is a mandala and the coherence is that which belongs to a mandala.

It is clear that the E which had been driving Charles hither and thither to actions completely out of relation with his actual situation is beginning to become organised, though as yet in a rudimentary manner. With World 14 a quite new form of coherence emerges, that of a coherent story played out in dramatic movement of figures on the tray rather than of a moment in a scene which could be presented as a whole. Charles' power of invention was sufficiently good to be able to carry a whole and exciting incident developing in a credible fashion with only one lapse from consistent sequence.

Two months passed between Worlds 14 and 15, and in this time Charles' realisation and his awareness of his own position had significantly increased. World 15 is the first presentation that he has made of a scene which is in general terms realistic. The pattern of the river in this World repeats Worlds 5 and 10 to some extent, but the significance of the World is that in it Charles has found a mode of expression which states in clear terms that this E within him is blocked by an obstacle which he would have been able to surmount had he not "taken the wrong turning".

World 16 repeats World 14.

This repetition of a statement already achieved was followed by three experimental incoherent Worlds. World 17 contained many features of Worlds 2 and 3; only one plane crashes instead of many and this is made the focus of the scene; lorries go to it, but although in World 10 an ambulance had appeared stationary on the bridge, Charles had not yet arrived at the idea of active rescue from disaster. The feminine aspect (house and milk churn) is now of equal importance with the planes as part of the scene.

Worlds 4-6-7-8 had all included a train, but this was a schematic train that did not go anywhere. In World 18 for the first time Charles experimented with the idea of actual trains; his power of organisation, however, when applied to the management of any movement with a *purpose*, broke down completely, and World 18 is incoherent. World 19 was chaotic; it illustrated very well the extreme difficulty experienced by a child in Charles' condition when attempting to achieve coherent expression of more than one aspect of his interior experience.

A month elapsed between World 19 and World 20. World 20 is particularly interesting as it enables us to analyse out various modes of expression of cognate themes and to gain an idea of the kind of combinations of them in which they were experienced by Charles. There are three types of animals here – mares, foal and ponies, rabbits and a bull. The grouping of these on the scene is by their symbolic rather than their reality significance. The position of the mare, foal and ponies, and the rabbits repeats their general positions in World 8. These are animals which "get out" and this possibility of their getting out is the central theme of the picture. The aeroplanes are now geared to this possibility, they become the "watching eye" of the farmer. The bull, on the other hand, moves alongside the train suggesting a symbolic identity with it. It is led by a man: there is no implied relationship between the bull and anything else in the picture; a fence placed across the further end of the World would soon block the progress of the man and bull and there is no enclosure in which they could be put.

In Worlds 6, 7 and 8 the train placed across the front of the scene was referred to by Charles only in terms of noise; in World 18 trains were conceived of as being able to move; in World 20 for the first time a single train is seen by Charles as a moving object with a definite goal – "the train was going to London". Charles' feelings in regard to escape and to danger are well exemplified in the right and left side arrangements of the picture and these are a development of the arrangement in World 4: the fields on the left with "schematic" animals have become fields with animals to which some simple defined characteristics have been given: the miscellaneous engines of the right have become the train which has a certain amount of story. In an interesting way, however, action and passivity in relation to the two sides of the picture have changed, the animals are, or may be, active, it is the train "to which something has happened". It is in relation to the train also that a "spare" is provided.

Another aspect of this World, as drawn, is the light it throws upon the relation between a child's statement in a World and the effect upon it of interpretation. At first the World contained the horses' field and horses, the fencing, train, church and farmhouse. After this was discussed with Charles and its linking up with earlier Worlds pointed out, the bull was put in, a foal added to the horses, the positions of the horses changed, and the rabbits put in and the caravan was added near the building. Much later in treatment it came out that the family had twice gone for a holiday in a caravan. It is in this way that the making of a World, and its discussion with the therapist becomes a kind of conversation composed of verbal and material symbols.

In World 20 a dominant theme had been that of protection of weak animals from the consequences of their own actions by strong men; these ideas were presented in a fantastic manner. Two days later Charles was able to embody them in a Wild West setting in a coherent and realistic manner, good men protecting cows from possible attack from bad men (World 21). In World 22, made a week later at the end of the school year, Charles brought into explicit statement a concept that he had been working up to since World 10, that of an ambulance and a hospital which rescue human victims of a crash. This scene to some extent repeated the country layout of World 15 with a road along which cars race instead of a river; the river which is also present in the form of a small stream arising from a pool is crossed by the road between the ambulance and the hospital and flows diagonally across the tray to exit by a windmill, the only time this symbol is used by Charles. It is interesting that a train once more goes in front of the scene.

In the period up to the making of World 23 Charles had embodied the unruly E within him in the force with which cars and lorries moved along the road and planes across the sky, identifying himself with them and enjoying a sense of power and destruction when he made them crash into one another or upon the earth. This was a kind of indiscriminate force smashing its way about. In his attitude to trains, as has already been pointed out, they were present in his Worlds and it was their noise which caught his attention; but he had not as yet been able to conceive of that orderliness and controlled direction of movement which a train embodies.

When this feeling of force within him began to be more defined, focused and combined with rudimentary ideas of human realtionships, the current conventional stories of Indians and cowboys, cattle, treasure, and bandits provided a vehicle with which he could experiment without the expressions of force and excitement he invented coming too near to his own experience.

In World 9, which came between the farm and the "Western stories", he had begun tentatively to experiment with the idea of real life aggression between human beings and had composed an incoherent World of "soldiers practising". A plane also crashed and this produced for the first time the *idea* of an ambulance in response to a question from me. The following World 10 carried the process a step further in the combination of two cannons with aeroplanes, in an incoherent World. Here a schematic river ran across the World, and the ambulance appeared in fact, identified with the bridge-across-the-river. The whole was seen by Charles against a background of "a war going on somewhere".

Nine Worlds later, in World 19, which we have been discussing, all these ideas were mixed up together. In the following four Worlds Charles sorted these out, dealing first in Worlds 20, 21 and 22 with the aspect of relationship between human beings and between men and animals. By the time he came to make World 23 he had made sufficient progress in becoming aware of, and being able to tolerate and to some extent to focus the force within him, to construct a World in which two opposing real life forces – "we" and "the enemy" became explicitly expressed. The river appeared in the World also. An ambulance, plane, lorries and soldiers express the "we" of the picture; men and a cannon "the enemy". Two bridges spanned the river and formed the focus of the picture – at one point Charles said, "the idea is to prevent the enemy crossing the bridges"; at another he made a train – conceived of for the first time as a forceful vital element in the scene – cross the bridge, carrying both "troops and passengers". The planes in this picture were "helping" planes, bringing supplies not soldiers.

Up to this point trains had been to Charles only moving objects or implied noise; in this World he conceived them as carrying people within them and the vagueness of his concept of "war" is shown by the fact that this train, presented as being in the middle of a battle, contained also "passengers".

In the series of 43 Worlds we are considering Charles made only one other "war" World (37), a detailed presentation of a moment in the course of a battle between soldiers and Indians. Only men took part in this scene; neither ambulance, nor cannon, planes nor lorries appeared.

In World 24 Charles invented a new type of symbolism; three transport vehicles follow one another on a road, the first carrying a small car, the second a covered lorry carrying goods, the third a lorry carrying milk churns. The significance of these is discussed in the section "Milk".

Planes which were made to take off and land safely on an airfield beside the road, were connected, in idea, with these three vehicles by "a small car going through the gate". If it is allowed at all that mechanical vehicles in their type, position and manipulation can symbolise facts of human experience, then it is inescapable that this grouping of objects presents as yet in a distant and unrealised way, a concept of intercourse between the male and the female with the ideas of pregnancy and lactation. The road goes toward a bridge over a river and this river was deliberately made to curve, a mode of presentation used by Charles for rivers included in "real life" scenes.

In World 25 the progress that Charles had made in his concept of the relations between men and animals is shown. It suggests an expression of his experience of relations between human beings and of aspects of himself within himself.

World 25 is a wild animal scene focused about the idea of drinking. The human beings in it are not hunters, as in World 1, nor do they form a separate (and unlikely) element having no connection with the animals, as in World 5. Here human beings are interested in wild animals; they have come to photograph them. At the same time the photographers are aware of the potential aggressiveness wild animals may show towards humans and have brought soldiers with them to protect them.

The significance of the drinking pool in this and World 32 is difficult to assess since boys in Charles' position will inevitably have seen films which contain similar jungle scenes, but the interesting part about this World is the manner of its execution. The formality of the illustration of this World gives only a slight idea of the World itself which was constructed with a grace and imagination in striking contrast to the force and crudity of Charles' usual movements. The layout showed a power of composition most unexpected in a boy of Charles' background and personality to date and there was both observation and humour in his treatment of the animals. He used the different kinds of animals in an ingenious way to suggest different types of relationship, the father elephant for instance who takes his two children to drink at the pool while the old male elephant is "cross because he likes being alone". The gorilla "grumbles because he likes to drink in peace" and the lion, watching the young giraffe is cautious "because he knows of the mother giraffe's strong kick".

This World was followed by Charles' first fully developed reality scene (World 26), the train blocked by snow just before crossing a bridge. Here planes, covered lorry and ambulance were all "helping" figures and the actions both of the snow (sand) covering the train and the first aeroplane, and the digging out of the (presumed) people in the train was acted out with full detail and good invention. This scene repeated the essential situation of World 15 where the car was blocked by the river; that blockage arose from a mistake of the driver of the car, with no one helping; this blockage was brought about by a natural force with all his other machines mobilised to help.

World 27 combined the fields on the left side of World 4 with the airfield and lorry-carrying-small-car of World 24, in an incoherent World with islands of coherence, in the centre of which he placed the milk van and milk churns. The fields contained mother animals and young and once again a vehicle was just about to pass through the gate. Charles was feeling his way about ideas of milk and motherhood, not only in themselves but in relation to a symbolic use of aeroplanes.

After an illness he pursued these themes in the following coherent World (28) of cowboys and Indians in peaceful association. The cowboys were outspanned, with the milk churns at the side of their wagon and cooking pots behind it and in this World, for the first and only time, a human mother-and-baby appeared in the form of two squaws with their infants. In this World, also for the first time, the idea of ceremonial dance was introduced and paralleled with the dance of triumph around a victim. The river took the same inarticulate place in this picture as the trains in the early farm Worlds (6-7-8). The drawn up canoe *implied* movement upon it, but implied it only.

World 29 is an important one. It deals with a theme which had appeared briefly in the earlier farm Worlds 6 and 7, that of animals which have been put in enclosures forcibly breaking out. In Worlds 6 and 7 it was a horse which breaks out, the farmer goes with a lorry and brings him back. In World 20 the aeroplanes are "there in case the horses get out". In World 29 the action was wholly focused on the idea of "running away", getting out from enclosures, but this time it was the young that do so. First the lambs try and are defeated by the sheep dog, then the story shifts to the mare and her foals. The scene depicted the moment in farm life when the young are taken from their mothers; the mare tries to escape and is blocked by the farmer, one foal however does succeed in getting away, runs right round the central fields and the farmer, as in Worlds 6 and 7, goes after him with a lorry. The two kinds of young were finally parked in fields each side of the house. There is a remarkable coherence in this layout and the story as compared with Worlds 6, 7 and 8.

Having reached a temporary resting place I suggested to Charles on the next session that he make "something he would like to happen". The response was surprising. Charles turned his river for the first time into a means of transport, put a boat upon it and worked out a story in which a naval launch works in a rather confused way with planes on an airfield (World 30). In the fact that it was the first time that a river was an actor in the scene, it forms an introduction to World 31 made three weeks later.

World 31 is the only one of the type which appeared so frequently in William Carter's Worlds and which is part of the evidence which has given rise to the theory of the proto-system. Its layout is discussed more fully in the section on Design. Its importance here is the addition of a dimension of depth to the lake which corresponds to the dimension of height above the earth in which the aeroplanes move. This is the single World of the series which embodies an intellectual question "how deep is the lake"? Charles conceived of this question as so important that police keep people who are having a picnic and also people who are going to work, away from interfering with it. The cannon was the instrument used for the solution of the intellectual problem. It is noteworthy that this is the only World in which Charles dealt with the idea of depth and that in a very rudimentary way. Cannons shoot their balls into the depths of the lake and frogmen move up and down a ladder into and up from the lake. The work is safe, there is no danger in it, it is serious and the police cooperate with the men

136

undertaking it.

This World presents some important problems which are crucial to the understanding of what children do with the World tools and their significance. A number of people appeared in the scene, but on two planes of meaning: the police and the people in cars belong to everyday life; the lorries, said to be carrying cannon balls, move to and fro over the bridge as in World 4 but the river and the lake were purely symbolic. The formal angular layout of the river is that of incoherent World 10 with the "extension", to use a term borrowed from philosophy, in a vertical instead of a horizontal plane. Worlds of this nature, it is contended, are projections into material of something for which there exist no descriptive terms and which can only be described as the dim awareness of a neutral E within him – an E whose "depth" Charles is curious to know.

To investigate this a little further I began the next session by asking him to make a drawing of a force that was not caused. Charles responded by making a drawing of wind around a house with shut doors and following this by World 32. This was a Jungle World repeating the animals of World 25, the drinking pool taking the place of the lake of World 31, with the same circular lines of the lake inverted into a crescent made by two trains. As the police and the car parties of World 31 were "real" but formaly disposed and the river/lake schematic, here the animals are real and the train schematic. The details of the layout offer a clue to the meaning. It falls into three parts: the group of animals within the crescent of the trains: the trains and the animals between them: the three animals on the pool side of the trains. Between the engines of the two trains and moving at right angles to them, the giraffe and elephant mothers and their two children move toward the drinking pool. A spare engine flanked each train "in case anything should go wrong" – i.e., if the force of the trains fail – within the crescent of the trains a little giraffe wandered away into danger, where at the back the zebra is walking away from lions "who want a dinner" and were further irritated by the teasing of a monkey. The mother giraffe was oblivious of the danger to the small one and only the rhinoceros saw it and contemplated helping. Two massive animals, the father elephant and a hippopotamus were between the trains and the pool, the hippo "wanting to bathe and good tempered unless anyone annoys him" and the elephant "trumpeting to scare the people in the trains". The third animal, the crocodile, like the driver of the trains "doesn't like all these animals going to his pool" and in rivalry with the elephant gets the worst of it and crawls across the pool to hide.

Later in his stay at the school Charles' provocative teasing of the other boys became a major feature of his relationships. He did not know where these impulses came from and felt they arose within him without his willing them. This World is the beginning of this theme. It is an expression of the confusion within him of the unfocused E he cannot control, which one side of him feels brings him into acute danger but which is somehow (he feels) mixed up with the family and a fear of all drive failing within him (as in the spells of withdrawal). In the previous Jungle World (25) the lion felt the mother giraffe would defend her young, in this the mother is indifferent. In this World human beings are neither hostile, nor observant and interested, they are only ciphers, "people within the train"; so far no idea of a *relationship* between people and these wild animals has appeared.

The railway station in World 33 marked achievement of a further stage of development. Charles experimented with several types of vehicles and arrangements of trucks within the station before settling to the one drawn. As in the Jungle World (32) this scene embodies two aspects of Charles' personality. The conception of the trains, the arrangement of the fencing (except for the absence of an opening in it behind the nearer train, already commented on), the placing of the car "going to the station" and the Halt sign all show an increased reality. The "old milk wagon" on the other hand, the beehive and rabbit hutch are symbols linking this World with others in which they have been used, as the first placing of racing cars outside the station (later removed) in a somewhat similar situation to those in World 22, links it with that World.

Although the holidays following this were outwardly successful, yet periods at home tended to stimulate interior disturbances, and the first World (34) made after Charles' return from the Christmas holidays depicted a struggle between cowboys and bandits to steal a mare. Disturbances between Charles and his fellows at school were discussed with him and in Worlds 35 and 36 he depicted his side of these incidents. These develop the earlier "running away" stories by stating the interior experience of the runaway. In World 36 the lion's point of view, which has been hinted at the jungle scenes, is also made more explicit. Projected into and focused on these World figures, the impulses and emotions within Charles were becoming more accessible to his awareness.

This greater ability to express the unmanageable E within him and the aggressive impulses to which it gives rise, and at the same time the increasing power of observation and control of concepts within himself was well shown in World 37 (Soldier/Indian battle). The creation of these three Worlds (35-36-37) and the discussion of them had had something of the effect of good digging of a patch of ground whose surface had become hardened and caked over with a rigid crust: the nutrition latent in the earth beneath the crust was becoming available for working.

Now Indians are "savage"; soldiers are people trained to destroy others; circus animals are creatures who, to a certain extent, have to be given in to; bandits are "bad": in World 38 Charles presented a group of human beings who are rebellious against authority, and adventurous and predatory but for whom, because of their daring, it is legitimate for a boy to have sympathy – that is smugglers.

The general layout of the smugglers' hide-out was a mirror image of that of the "Naval place" of World 30. Here too "boxes" were loaded on boats and taken up and down to London; only this story was elaborated into far greater detail than the naval story and is much more coherent. This story contains more original invention than any of his other "near-reality" stories so far: the rigidity of Charles' mental processes were beginning to loosen up. In World 39 Charles made a step forward in expressing organisation of different aspects of his ideas and emotions; both types of farm animals, cows and sheep, were introduced into the World, each having their own drinking pool. Hitherto the ideas of sheep as mothers of lambs and sheep-and-lambs-drinking have been separate; Charles emphasised this aspect by putting the lorry with milk churns beside the field of the sheep. In contrast to this field, in the other a man with dogs to help him is taking care of the cows, and the policeman also stands aside "to protect the cows". This is the same care for the protection of cattle that Charles had previously expressed with cowboys (World 21). The road that runs curving between these two fields contained originally a cannon, which may be the cannon by the lake in World 31. This possibility is supported by the fact that it is the lorry-with-the-rabbit-hutch which was put on the road in its stead and the emphasis in regard to the rabbit hutch was on its door and "getting out".

It had been clear from the beginning that Charles' arrest of emotional development, intense egocentricity and complete inability to relate to the human beings around him was bound up with his relation to his mother. This relation was so little defined, so amorphous and confused that nothing could be done to aid him in this respect because of this confusion and amorphousness. Through the progress made since then, Charles was able in World 40 to create an imaginary real life scene which focused and expressed his needs and desires. Horses and cows with their young have food and protection each side of a central space where enjoyable food is provided for human beings. In front sheep and lambs are cared for by a shepherd and his dogs and protected by a policeman who stops the traffic for their sake; as they go past him they will pass also the lorry carrying the tiny car. It is interesting that the lorry within the cafe enclosure carried a school desk and that the milk van man stood beside this.

A few days later Charles developed mumps, and working with him while he was in bed it was possible to help him to bring a number of aggressive phantasies to expression. Expression of these considerably relieved the anxiety which had been mounting in him through the pressure of unexpended E, and the interior fears aroused by it came to expression in another Bandit World (41) in which a covered wagon carrying treasure was ambushed and an equal number of "good" and "bad" men killed: it was done by Charles during the week and left for me to see.

From a theoretical point of view World 42 is of intense interest. It was very well constructed, not only for Charles but exceptionally so for any child of his age. The arrangement of the boats on the river, the wharf and lorries collecting from it, the groups of people on holiday, the traffic on the road and the houses showed quite exceptional power of observation and capacity to set out imaginatively the essentials of a real life experience. It is the contrast between this and his school performance which needs elucidating; no teacher, meeting Charles in school could possibly have guessed at these abilities.

As we have found all along, the sexual aspect of Charles' ideas and emotions came only dimly to expression. It is possible that the man on a ladder "seeing if there are any slates loose" on the roof of the church bore for him the psychoanalytic interpretation. The designing and the discussing of this World showed that a profound change in the disposition of E had taken place in Charles. E was no longer blocked in expression in him to a point where an explosion became the only means of releasing the resulting tension, but was beginning to find its way into normal channels in his personality. In the final World of this series Charles returned once more to a "Western" setting. He was capable now of setting out a coherent scene involving potential danger against which adequate precautions have been taken which did not arouse anxiety, but only if this situation is set in people and circumstances far from his own. A lot had been accomplished but very much still waited to be done.

To sum up therefore – in Coherent Worlds the symbols used have been worked into a kind of temporary integration with each other in a background of story. In Incoherent Worlds the force of E within Charles, seeking expression, takes up symbol after symbol for its momentary power to carry and express part of the thoughts and feelings at work in him, but the symbols do *not* achieve integration with each other. In Composite Worlds both integration and non-integration are present together.

Charles' Use of Symbols

The word "symbol" is a dangerous word to use, as it carries so many connotations; dangerous, that is, to understanding between writer and reader. The sense in which it is used here must therefore be made clear. Worlds are essentially groups of objects which the child arranges, manipulates and reacts to from sources within himself. They are to him "real": they are an expression of his inner world in objects from the outer world. They are not in any sense literal, and the varying contexts in which the same objects are used, show that it is by no means the meaning which adults attach to the object that the child accepts but the significance that the object assumes in the scene in which the child puts it.

Since the same collection of objects is available for all children, the same sand, water and tray, the objects a child chooses and the structures he makes in the tray have to him a special relevance; they are cognate in some way to himself and his experience; they become, in his use of them, not his actual experience but symbols of aspects of his experience.

It is in this sense that the word symbol is used in this book.

There are, in this sense, three modes of symbolism available in the World apparatus –

A) the manipulation of sand, water and amorphous objects in relation to the tray

B) the varying objects used and their disposition in the tray

C) the factor of overall design.

We will now consider these in turn in relation to Charles' series of Worlds.

A) Manipulation of sand in the tray

What any child does with a World apparatus can only be fully understood if seen against a background of what other children do, and there are certain common aspects of World making which need to be considered first in relation to Charles' Worlds, because they do *not* occur in his World series, either those discussed in this book or at any other time during his treatment.

These aspects are:–

1) Mounds, moats, tunnels and caves. Most children, at some time or other make mounds or a mound, tunnel through it or down it* under one pretext or another and/or make caves and tunnels in different parts of the tray.

2) Islands. The creation of an island and the events which take place on it, form an important stage in most children's World series. In Charles' only one tiny island occurs, quite unimportant, more a rock carrying a palm than an island, in the drinking pool of the third jungle scene (25).

3) Presentation of depth. In only one World (31) did Charles present the idea of a depth below the surface of the sand. Cannon balls were fired *into* this lake and frogmen went up and down but nothing *happened* at the bottom of the lake. In the same way, no people live inside a mountain, under the sea or at the bottom of mines or within deep caves.

Charles' mind moved firmly among the reality structures of his real world, even though he often uses them unrealistically. In this he shows a vivid and marked contrast to William's use of the same materials.

B) Charles' choice and use of symbols

The central characteristic of Charles' illness was the bursting out in

---

*cf. the volcano in Mary's series.

speech and action of uncontrollable force unrelated to other parts of his personality.

This force expressed itself mainly in a negative way. The first aspect we need to study therefore is the relation of this interior situation to his choice and use of symbols.

i. Symbols and actions expressive of violent neutral force

This came to expression mainly in his incoherent Worlds. Charles selected for his expression of massive force those internal combustion engines with which his real life experience had made him familiar.* He identified with them, put into his use of them all the actual force of which he was capable and accompanied this with appropriate noises. Vehicles did now and again crash in his incoherent Worlds, but for the main part the domination of this force over man was expressed in the crash upon earth of aeroplanes. When making this happen he drove the plane down upon the sand with all the force he had. Although the concept of water constantly appeared in his Worlds, he never used real water, and the idea of using water destructively, which is so common a feature of other children's Worlds† did not occur to him. It is just possible that heat, which is an inseparable part of the functioning of engines, was part of his interior feeling about them and water may have appeared to him cold. It is also possible that the fear of mechanical toys which was reported of him by his home environment at the beginning, may have been associated with this. Clockwork toys move on their own; the small cars to which Charles was devoted, have to be moved about by the child playing with them and are therefore under his control. When Charles ran his cars and lorries about on the sand he made deep marks with them and often devoted very careful attention to studying them. Force, therefore, to Charles moved in lines fast and violently and changed the face of the ground on which it moved. The question as to whether this force can rightly be called aggressive, seems decided by the fact that, in Charles' case, it had no goal: sheer straightforward aggression against definite objects or persons does not appear. It is in this sense that this type of symbolisation is termed "neutral" force; it was the movement of force in itself that Charles here wished to express, not movement against an object. As has been pointed out in the section on Time, there was no pattern or sequence in the manipulation of individual objects in these Worlds, and time did not enter in.

It is interesting in this connection that Charles did not create a train crash. In the two Worlds in which troubles occurred with trains (20 and 26) the train was passive, things happened to it, it did not *do* anything. This

---

*Although common this is by no means the invariable form of objects in which the idea of immense force is embodied by children.
†cf. in Mary's series and in William Carter's.

question of the use of trains by Charles is so interesting that it is considered separately.

ii. Stories

When, after the 29th session, some shape began to emerge in Charles' relation to the force within him, he began to make continuous stories. In all he made eight of these. Two (11-12) were about cowboys in their relation to Indians; three (14-16-41) of white men guarding and carrying treasure being attacked by Indians and bandits; one of a train and its passengers being blocked by snow and the passengers rescued (26); and two of the behaviour of circus animals outside the circus (35 and 36). There is a definite progression in these. In World 11 Charles was feeling his way toward a story in which violent actions happen, carried out by humans in a human world. The conventional figures of the World of "Western" films, T.V., pictures and comics offered a ready-made medium for him to use, but at the 30th session he could not quite get there; he set out the scene but it was between the horses on which the cowboys rode that most of the action took place and at the end peace was made with the Indians. In World 12 he could let himself go a step further; the familiar figures of the sheriff and of the man captured by Indians and tied to a stake were available for use, and the fact that some Indians did as a fact of history (as well as of conventional story) become friends with white men, offered him a possibility of bringing to expression without too much self-revelation or imaginative effort on his part, the bewildering changes of attitude between children and adults and vice versa, that he had experienced.

By the 42nd and 59th session Charles had become very much centralised and more sure of himself and a new element had come in – the concept of treasure which men value, desire and fight for. Here again the Western stories of the covered wagon which carried gold for the banks, was ready to hand, and Charles manipulated it successfully, identifying with the characters as he had done with the planes and cars of the earlier Worlds, only this time making a significant step forward from his sheriff World in that he could now identify with the "bad" as well as the "good" figures of the story and carry out violent aggressive actions for each. The same applies to World 41.

This acting out of directed violence in pictorial stories of an accepted and current type acted as a vehicle for the focusing within Charles of his inner E, so that he became more "tiresome" in his outer life than before but with his "bad" actions to some extent focused and conscious, though still impulsive and arising without deliberate intention.

The story which followed this series, that of World 26 at the 85th session, strongly emphasised the other side, that of the experience of the arrest of E by an irresistible force. Here Charles' suffering under his own inability to "join in", to move decorously and cheerfully in harmony with the others came to expression and with it his passionate compassion for himself. It is a truism of all analytical work that until one can weep for the sorrow of one's own child self, one cannot weep for the sorrow of any other: Charles was beginning to feel pain and a desperate urgency from the blockings of E in himself. The train, and also one of the planes that came to help, were buried in snow and only hard cooperative effort of many people saved and rescued the people. The idea of working to clear the snow from the bridge and track and get the train going again across the bridge over the river did not occur to Charles. In this, this picture re-affirmed that of World 15 where the car was blocked by the river. This question of bridges and of the river in Charles' Worlds is of such importance that it is considered separately.

Two stories complete the set (35-36) made on the 104th and 105th sessions, showing a marked progress. Charles selected as symbols the wild animals which he had already found could be made to carry the expression of individual feelings and impulses and embodied in them the impulses he was coming to recognise as operating in himself. They were controlled in the end by the men in charge, as he has found himself controlled by the staff in the school, but they get out and have their fun first, and, as Charles remarked, "the elephant, when he is captured, feels it was worth it".

It is questionable whether Charles could have achieved what he did in the five first stories of this group had not the "Western" models lain close to his hand. In this they played the part for Charles that myth and ritual did for many earlier communities* in that they made possible for him a contact between his impulses and the small part of himself of which he was fully conscious. They focused the E within him and gave him a ready-made shape into which it could pass.

iii. The dramatisation of feelings and interactions between individuals

For Charles, as for many children, *wild animals* treated in an anthropomorphised way formed a bridge between himself and other human beings. The men and the one woman (farmer's wife, Worlds 6 and 7) were shadowy beings exhibiting only one or two characteristics. Jungle animals on the other hand were varied in character and spontaneous in reactions and Charles was able through them to represent a number of the things he had observed about human beings.

World 1 set the pattern. Charles selected his elephant mother and child (duplicating them in two Worlds), his big giraffe and two small ones, the lion and lioness, zebra and monkey that feature in the subsequent Worlds. Crocodiles were added in this and the next Jungle World (5) as the

---

*See *Myth and Ritual in the Ancient Near East*. E. O. James. Thames and Hudson. London 1958. and also *Homo Ludens*. J. Huizinga. Routledge & Kegan Paul. London 1949.

threatening figures, and a mother and baby hippopotamus were "in the water". In this World the animals were just "there", nothing of significance happened between them.

By World 5 Charles had become able to express a good deal more. A number of the same animals walk about the scene being, as far as one can judge, just animals. A baby giraffe walking by himself gets into a position where he is prevented from drinking by threat of a crocodile in front of him and is unaware of a lion behind. The elephants on the other hand present Charles' first indications of feelings in a family. It was characteristic of Charles that no communication took place between father and mother and that all the baby did was to move from one to the other.

The man-in-the-boat is the single example in this series of a man playing a family rôle and the only appearance also of a human "daughter". Charles was at this stage too inarticulate to make it possible to pursue this any further.

In the next jungle scene (25) Charles' ability to use his animal symbols had considerably developed. The small giraffe that wanted to drink now became the pivot of the scene and Charles used three sorts of animals to represent his family: the mother elephant and two young get first to the water to drink followed by the father hippo and his two young; the giraffe family on the other hand present another facet, the mother was away from the children (three this time) and the lion the danger, but here both giraffe and hippopotamus are on guard. Two animals were said to be "cross", an old male elephant and a gorilla, but no other interrelations between the animals appeared. In the fourth Jungle World (32) the theme which had been running through the whole series, that of a young animal leaving his parents and wandering into danger, appeared again. This time the adult giraffe was thought of as having a friend who helps with the protection of the young. The provocativeness to others, which was beginning to be such a feature of Charles' behaviour in regard to the children at the school, was put here into the figure of the father elephant and the monkey (Charles seems unable to imagine a female being provocative). The lion and lioness threaten, the crocodile is boastful and the zebra shows prudence. It is definitely a more differentiated picture.

Charles made use of *farm animals* in five Worlds (6-7-8-20-29) with a very small number of human beings in rôles of protection and organisation of them.

The first farm World repeated the running away theme of the jungle scenes and contained in addition only the idea that the runaway might get into danger and need saving from himself. This theme reappeared in the second farm World, a horse being the runaway in both. A rudimentary relationship between husband and wife was the centre of this World, the farmer's wife asking her husband for instructions, and the farmer giving the horse a mare companion "because he is lonely". Charles used these two to embody an idea of marriage and pregnancy. In the third farm World the danger to the-one-who-goes-out, which had been feared in the other Worlds, actually happened in this and the cow was knocked over by the car. Charles now expanded the protection theme by the addition of sheep/lambs and sheep dogs. As the male elephant had been provocative in the Jungle Worlds, the ram was "troublesome" here: Charles' action made clear his identification with the ram. What is interesting is that although in the jungle scenes Charles several times presented some animals as threatening death to others, it was a dog with rabbits who actually carried out the threat. This exemplifies again Charles' strong sense of reality: dogs killing rabbits is within his actual experience, lions killing giraffes is not. This World gave also the first example of a generous action – the first dog brought his killed rabbit to the second.

The fourth farm animals World (20) added little to what had already been stated. The bull which had been, as it were, just mentioned in World 8, was in World 20 identified by position with the stationary train. The aggressive and violent 'planes of the earlier Worlds became, in this, part of the powers that protect animals from themselves. In the final farm World of this series (29) Charles focused almost entirely upon the running-away theme but combined this with a necessary separation of young from their mothers; a policeman in this World was an additional looking-after symbol.

The Western idea of farm animals, the cowboys' "cattle" appeared in one World with action and a partial story, World 21. Here Charles once again used a ready-made Western theme to present the essence, as it were, of the protective aspect of adults towards their animal charges. A Western story again, in World 34, made it possible for Charles to depict battle between "good" and "bad" men for the possession of a female embodied in a mare.

iv. Worlds without stories

(Worlds 13-15-22-23-24-27-28-30-33-37-38-39-40-42-43)

In these Worlds Charles took a collection of objects and arranged them in a scene. In some, as in World 13, a very small piece of story was included but this referred to only part of the picture and was in no case central to its plan.

From the point of view of the theory of E and of the study of the integration within a personality of the different functions which E is energising, the group of Worlds without stories is the most interesting of the four groups.

The arrangement of these in subject matter and *mise en scène* is as follows.

146

English Countryside	6	(13–15–22–24–27–39)
"Westerns"	2	(28–43)
"War"	2	(23–37)
River	3	(30–38–42)
Railway Station	1	(33)
Road Cafe	1	(40)

All these scenes were constructed with intense concentration and focusing of attention. Considering that the making of each and its discussion had to be fitted into 30 minutes, this is a fact of major interest in a boy reported by school teachers to be slow in thought and movement. The intensity of focus and swiftness of execution makes, indeed, one of the main puzzles from the point of view of the psychology of cognition, concerning the diagnosis and description both of this type of boy and of his condition. Here the element of time appears in another dimension: with his stories, not only enacting them but moving with "clock time" as he did so, the events in the story he was working out running with the minutes as the clock in the hut ticked them away. In this group of Worlds, on the other hand, some swift concentration of thought took place as Charles paused, at the outset, to look at the tray and then at the cabinet. As he made few corrections or alterations, it would appear that within this pause the "time" needed for selecting each set of objects in turn from the cabinet and putting them out, telescoped for him into a single interior perception. This kind of immediate perception (or conception should one say) as a whole of a statement for the objectification of which consecutive "clock time" minutes are needed, is characteristic of the proto-system structure. We would expect therefore the subject matter of this group of Worlds to differ from the other two, and when we study them we find that this is the case. Charles' "landscapes" or Worlds in which any features of an ordinary English landscape are included have hitherto either been composite or incoherent (4-9-10-18-19) or "farm" scenes (6-7-8-20-29) in that in most of the scenes, events either have just happened or are about to happen and Charles had been able in a high degree to collect together the salient features of a scene he wishes to present and to combine them effectively.

Of the "Countryside Worlds" only two, 15 and 22, are such as *might* be found in a countryside. Two (13 and 39) depict a road carrying a specially assorted set of vehicles in relation to a field or fields containing ponds in which farm animals drink. In the remaining two (24-27) an airfield occupies the central space. What then, we must ask ourselves, is Charles "saying" in these Worlds?

Worlds 15 and 22 (that of the single car blocked by the river, and that of the line of cars racing along a curved road in which one car has crashed, the ambulance taking the man to the hospital) are statements about strong and rapid movement. In one it is altogether blocked – in the other disaster has overtaken a speeding vehicle. To make clear that it is E with which this World is concerned, Charles put a train along the front edge of this second World with "a spare engine in case the other breaks down". These then present two aspects of speed: either it is blocked or it is dangerous (though in this one repair of disaster is included). The next pair of Worlds combined traffic and protected farm animals.

The layout of World 13 is frankly unlikely. This is a mandala shape with the animals' drinking pool in the centre. The traffic here goes both ways and includes an ambulance in front of a man-with-a-bull: movement in this direction was free but in the other it was blocked by a stationary horse caravan. Time comes in here in the sense that a now-abandoned barrow in the past supplied vegetables to the caravan; a puzzling item. By this blocking caravan is a seat and a signpost emphasising the "sitting" aspect of the caravan and the stile leading out of the pool field. One of Charles' rare trees filled a further corner. This was the first pond-from-which-cows-drink and is in the nature of an experimental World. All that is clear is that its meaning is something to do with male (bull) and female (cows), living-in-intimate-quarters (caravan); a block to movement and a hint of danger (ambulance).

World 39 is more explicit: the road curved between two fields with animals drinking and in the further, as has already been pointed out, the fact that the sheep field contains mothers-and-young is emphasised by the milk lorry beside it. There was no ambulance on this road and the cannon placed at first was removed, the unlikely item of a lorry-carrying-a-rabbit hutch being put in its place. In the remaining pair of this group (24-27) Charles made the same use of unusual possibilities of traffic combined with civil air planes. In the first this presentation was "occult" as it were, in the second (27) the fact that factors concerning maleness and femaleness are involved is made clearer by the milk van and lorry-carrying-small-car within the airfield beside two grounded planes, and together with the combination of these with two fields containing horses and young. It seems to me legitimate, therefore, to take it that these six apparent countryside scenes are not this at all but are struggles to present dormant ideas and feelings about sexual factors and events.

The two Western Worlds (28-43) differ from the ones already studied in that they are peaceful and that the maternal element is prominent both with the cowboys and with the Indians. In the last World (43) the Indians have disappeared and only a possible danger remains in the row of bison absorbed in their own affairs. Bison are immensely powerful animals and in this World Charles seems to state that force need not form either a danger or a threat. These two Worlds would seem to belong, the one to the male/female group, and the other to the "force" group.

Of the two "war" Worlds, World 23 is considered in the section on bridges and World 37 is a straightforward boys' "war-game" World very well executed. The river Worlds (30-38-42) are those in which the river acts as a highway, up and down which men move boats, and are considered in the section on rivers. The Station World is the climax of a line of Worlds concerned with trains and is considered under "trains". There remains to be studied in this group only the roadside cafe.

Here a fact is important which only came to light much later. Mrs. Robinson's one friend keeps a cafe not far from the Robinson's, and Mrs. Robinson works in it. This World makes it look as if the idea of a cafe and mother working in it (the milk van) incorporated for Charles the concepts of mother-and-himself-protection, nourishment, and enjoyment, not in a stable well founded "home", but as one might meet it "along the roadside".

To sum up: it looks as if planes and cars, manipulated individually by himself, expressed the pressure of E within him in its inchoate form: that Western figures and idioms carried for him the aggressive and forceful aspects of E: that wild-animals-in-a-jungle made it possible for him to express those fragments of interpersonal relations within the family that he was able to become aware of, while with circus wild animals he could objectify his driving impulse toward teasing and toward running away. The group that remained, the static Worlds, carried his struggle to express ideas and feelings about maleness, the mother aspect of femaleness and rudimentary ideas of coitus, World 37 remaining as the one example of the ordinary play of a boy of his age.

Special Symbols

Certain of the symbols used by Charles need to be considered in greater detail as their use runs through the groupings we have been considering and plays an important part in the development of his self-realisation and of his control and direction of E. These are:– river and bridges, trains, and symbols of maternity.

River and Bridges. A river occurs in seventeen Worlds (1-4-5-10-11-12-15-21-22-23-24-26-28-30-31-38-42): in three it arises from a pool (21-22-23), and in one, the proto-system World 31, it flows into a lake. The key, as it were, to Charles' feeling about a river-in-itself is given in Worlds 4 and 10. In World 4 it is the dividing factor between two of his main types of symbolism – cars, lorries, train and farm animals with young. In World 10 (ambulance on bridge) the river is the central feature but carries no significance in the manifest content of the scene. It appears in this manner once again only in the proto-system World 31. Charles was not able to say anything about these rivers; they were an essential part of his conception but a part which could not be expressed in any other way.

This sense of a river being a barrier or a limiting fact which cut across the movement embodied in the "sense" of the scene, and which therefore "had" to be crossed, appeared in six Worlds (12-15-22-23-24-26) and it is interesting that these six Worlds include one example of each of his types of coherent scenes as follows. In World 12 the sheriff rode across the river to rescue the tied-up man; in World 15 the car was blocked at the river's edge because it had taken the road fork away from the bridge; in World 22 the racing cars must cross the river; in World 23 the troop train had to cross the river separating the two warring forces; in World 24 the three symbolic vehicles were approaching the river which, but for the bridge, barred their road; in World 26 snow had buried the train as it approached the river flowing at right angles to its rails. In two of these, therefore, the force moving horizontally failed to cross and in two succeeded in crossing the river; in the remaining two (22-24) the river was still some way off from the moving vehicles. One other World exists (11) in which the river was first a line of division between enemies (cowboys and Indians) but was filled in when these became friends.

In a number of the "river" Worlds, the river flowed both across the short dimension of the tray and along the front or back edge.* In one (World 28) it flowed along the front edge only. This is a cowboy/Indian scene, peaceful, and imbued with ideas of maternity. As a scene it forms a bridge World between the group we have just considered in which the river itself operates only as a barrier and has no character of its own, and those in which the river is either the home of animals or carries boats on its surface, as an Indian canoe is drawn up on the centre of the further bank of World 28.

No idea of fish appeared in Charles' Worlds; submarines also do not form part of his ideas and symbols, and it is in connection with jungle animals that the river holds dangerous elements. This is in keeping with the study we have already made of his types of symbolism. It is in connection with the family and emotions arising in family relationships that Charles is directly aware of danger. In Worlds 1 and 5 crocodiles live in the river. These will be met with again in the jungle drinking pool World (32) but here there is no river.

Only in four Worlds (5-30-38-42) was the river conceived of as a means of transport. The first of these (World 5) is the single instance in which the river carried human beings in a rowing boat (the idea is potential in the canoe of World 28 but not worked out) and here it represents the interpolation of one type of symbolism in a World consistently conceived in another type. It is only much later on, when Charles had achieved a considerable degree of management of E, that the river-as-transport appeared. Here the two cognate themes appeared of the river as legitimately the means of transport "to and from London" of naval vessels (30) and illegitimately of smugglers' vessels (38). Finally Charles achieved a temporary mastery of the idea of the river as a force, in his presentation of "a Saturday afternoon by the Thames" (42).

One World remains (World 21) which for purposes of accurate classification has to be included in this list, as a stream was in fact made to issue from the pool (though filled in in the later stages of the World) but although two bridges were put over it, it fulfilled no function in the story of the scene.

When we come to consider *bridges* the significance of the river becomes considerably clearer. Bridges, as such, have a different significance for adults and children. To an adult a bridge is essentially a structure designed to carry movement, whether of people, vehicles, or trains from one side of an obstacle to the other. Without a road or track leading to and from the bridge, a bridge has, to adults, no meaning. With children the situation is different. Bridges occur frequently in Worlds made by children and only in a certain proportion of them are they the bearers of movement. Several bridges can occur in a single World and they can be, and often are, put directly upon the surface of the sand, well in the middle of the tray, without any connection with the idea of movement. In others they are made use of as features of a structural scene. In these they perform the same functions as they have in real life, people, animals, or transport go either over or under them, or they canalise present possibilities of being places to look down from, to jump or fall or throw things from.

In Charles' Worlds all the bridges which appear are functional in the sense that they connect two separated strips of land; in *no* case does any form of transport go *under** a bridge; in every instance the bridge is level with the ground on either side.

Bridges appear in twelve of Charles' 43 Worlds. In eleven of these, they cross a single river (4-10-12-15-21-22-23-24-26-30-31); in one only (18) a bridge was placed across a dip in the sand as part of a railway. In ten Worlds the bridge was designed for road vehicles, in two only was it to carry trains.

In six Worlds the bridge was placed in the centre of the tray (4-10-12-18-30-31), and in three slightly to the right-hand side (15-24-26); in two, two bridges are placed close together at the near edge of the tray (21-23), and in one, two bridges crossed the same river at a distance from each other (22). It is when we consider the bridges in connection with the river that we get a closer grasp of their significance.

It is in World 4 that the bridge first appeared. This is the World where Charles was first able to put two of his types of symbols together and the bridge linked them in a double manner – it actually joined one side of the river to the other and in *idea* the symbol of the left side (lorry) moved

---

*cf. the opposite fact in the Worlds of Mary Smith.

across the bridge from left to right and the symbol of the right side (milk lorry) crossed from right to left.

In the next World (10) bridge and ambulance were identified in a World of possible (mechanical) danger: this might appear to say that linking between different aspects of the self is a restorative function which repairs the dangers consequent upon unfocused force. In both these Worlds therefore the bridge is symbolical.

On its next appearance (12) the bridge fits in with what we have already worked out as Charles' use of "Western symbols". A "saving" man rather than an ambulance crosses the bridge to rescue a comrade; here a bridge is a necessary means of help for reaching a victim. In World 15 Charles had progressed toward seeing a bridge as a necessary element in a real life scene of movement if, that is, the car decides to take it. Eight Worlds later a series of three Worlds occurred in each of which there are two bridges. The first of these follows Charles' usual line of development, in being a "Western" World. The bridges here have no significance and the significance of the World lies in the pool where the cattle drink; both river and bridges carry shadows of meaning only. As with Worlds 14 and 15 he managed to follow a Western World with a reality one, here also he follows World 21 with a reality scene of cars racing on a road. In World 22 the possible significance of the *two* bridges appear; one was for the cars to race over, the other connected the ambulance and the hospital. Having, as it were, gained confidence in this "reality" development of the "repairing" concept, Charles was able to move in World 23 to the idea of one bridge carrying an aggressively charged power symbol (a train carrying troops and passengers). The content of this World is confused as it did not emerge at all clearly to which side these troops belonged. In Worlds 24 and 26 the bridge, on a river on the right of the tray, is provided but not used. In 30 ("naval place") the only other instance (other than World 10) occurs of something being actually *on* the bridge, this time a lorry with only vague relation with the actual scene. The following World is the last instance of a bridge over the river, i.e., the bridge of the proto-system World where it is again a schematic element as in World 4.

One World falls out of this survey, that where a bridge was used across a dip in the sand (18); this, an incoherent World of trains, possibly reproduced a frequent incident in England of railways being carried over contours in the landscape.

If we turn out attention to the sand surface on each side of the bridge a significant fact emerges. In our usual idea of a bridge, the existence of roads or rail on each side of the bridge is taken for granted. In only one World (15) did Charles make a road with no traffic crossing the river over a bridge and curving toward the further edge of the tray. Of the seven single bridge Worlds (4-10-12-15-24-30-31) in only one (12) that-which-is-crossing has a direct objective for doing so.

In Worlds 4 and 31, where the purpose of the bridge was to permit an object situated on each bank to cross the bridge there was a small piece of road either side. In World 30 there is a small indication of a road on one side of the bridge. In World 24, where a road leads realistically up to a bridge, there is nothing at all at the other side, and the same applies to the railway bridge in World 26.

It would seem, therefore, that bridges in this sense do present Charles' actual situation; he is arrested at one side of "something-which-has-to-be-crossed" and cannot see his future. He can conceive, however, of the possibility of a means of crossing, and in this conception the bridge and the ambulance are identified. He can use a bridge as part of a power story; he can see that a bridge takes other people over the river when he has taken the wrong turning; he can see that two contrasting parts of himself might cross and re-cross the bridge in a not-resolved dissociation, but when he puts reality symbols coming up to a bridge in order to cross it, he cannot conceive of a road at the other side.

Trains. A symbol, separate in itself, but as important as that of the river, is the train. Trains occurred in eleven Worlds (4-6-7-8-18-20-22-23-26-32-33). In four of these (4-22-23-26) a river also appeared: in seven (6-7-8-18-20-32-33) there was no river.

Study of the mode of use of the train illuminates Charles' attitude to powerful force.

There are four stages. In the four Worlds of stage I (4-6-7-8) the train was either put in an incoherent scene as World 4 without any mention of it, or as in the Farm Worlds of 6-7-8, placed in the same position in each, "running" along the front of the tray with no connection with the scene and thought of as "noise". In the three Worlds of stage II (18-20-22) progress in differentiation had been made. In World 18 trains were shunted along in an unrealistic way but with realistic noises, and emphasis laid upon "unwanted" carriages and trucks. In World 20 the train, although stationary and in an unrealistic position, had a destination. It is this train to which something had happened and a carriage had fallen over; it also had a spare engine in case of need. In World 22 Charles had gone back to the stage I use of trains, only without the element of noise – a train was put in running along the front of the tray, nothing was said about it but its function was implied, as a spare engine was supplied in case of breakdown. There are again three Worlds in stage III (23-26-32). In these Worlds trains are thought of as containing passengers, and it is interesting that Charles did not at any time use goods trains in his Worlds. In the first two Worlds of this group the emphasis was definitely on the passengers; they are aggressive in World 23, and had suffered disaster and need rescuing in 26. In World 32 the emphasis shifted to the drivers of the trains. The trains themselves were completely unrealistic, and in another dimension to the rest of the scene. Unrealistic as they are, however, Charles displayed more interest in them, as trains, than previously. Stage IV contains one World only (33). Here trains stood in a station; the scene illustrates the ability of this material to express several types of meaning simultaneously – the trains are trains but at the same time the trucks between the two carry a symbolic significance of a different kind.

In order to understand the part played by trains in Charles' expressions we need to consider for a moment small boys' views of trains. Charles had small cars at home to play with but no trains, and to most small boys trains are not machines as they appear to the adult, but powerful, almost magical forces. It is essential therefore to consider the trains and the river together.

The thesis which underlies this study of Charles is that his maladjustment and his disturbance arose through the non-differentiation of an inherently powerful charge of E. Both river and train therefore in their early stages represented for Charles this force. Gradually as both differentiation and control developed, so these symbols changed from purely schematic indications of a power not integrated with the scene in which they occurred, to semi-realistic and finally near-realistic presentations of both river and train as carrying out their normal functions in real life. Parallel with the conventional symbolic meaning attached to trains, the idea of potential breakdown and actual damage (World 20)* persists with the trains but does not appear in relation to the river.

It would seem therefore that a river and a train are complementary symbols – a river at first expressing for Charles something which separates (World 1), a barrier which is to be got over, with an initial significance (which does not return), that it may carry danger (crocodiles in 1 and 5), and with which only later the idea of conscious and deliberate movement (boats) is combined. Trains on the other hand are, from their second appearance, "a going-along-ness" and in 23 and 32 an instrument of realistic or symbolic force.

Ponds and Maternity symbols. Ten of Charles' Worlds contained ponds (4-13-14-19-21-22-25-32-39-40) and two lakes (23-31). Two of these in the middle of the series (21-22) were the source of the river or stream and in two (23-31) the river flowed into a lake. Six of these ponds were drinking places for animals, three of farm animals, one of cowboys' cattle and two of jungle animals: the other six were unconnected with the idea of drinking.

The significance of the pond is perhaps suggested by the first World (4) in which it occurs. This was the first introduction of farm animals, and in it a group of sheep and lambs were fenced in by themselves. At a short distance a pond was also fenced in, by itself. From the later connection between animals drinking and maternity symbols it looks as if Charles could not at this stage allow himself to combine the two. When he did so, three months later (World 13), he made a circular fenced-in field of cows

---

*Probably associated with "castration" fear.

and one horse, around a circular drinking pond, the centre of a "mandala" shaped World. The Western story-World (14) following this contained a curious incident, a pond into which the treasure-carrying-wagon backed and had to be guarded and rescued. The next World with a pond came in an incoherent fighting World (19) and seems to have no significance, tracks made by the same caravan as used in World 13 being the only link with a former World. World 21, the scene where cowboys guard and care for their cattle and "bad men" are indicated, was the first realistic World where animals drink. It is interesting that here there are no young and the guardian is male. The next two ponds (or lakes) have significance only as the source of the river and it is not until Charles returned to his jungle presentations (25) that a drinking pond became the central motive power of the scene (though not central in position). Between this World and the second jungle drinking scene occurred the lake of the proto-system World (31) where the idea of depth in the lake becomes central. In the last jungle scene (32) the drinking pond formed the hub of the whole concept. In Worlds 39 and 40 at the end of this series, ponds as the feminine element came to clear expression.

If we now turn to symbols implying maternity, *milk* takes a prominent place. Milk churns with or without an open lorry to carry them, or the cart marked "milk" outside and the white-coated man who accompanies it, occurred in nine Worlds (4-6-17-24-27-28-33-39-40). Three of these Worlds contained also a pond; these three are significant. World 4 as it were started the thought off and the milk lorry went over the bridge from the side of the engines to that of the pond. In World 39 ideas of maternity, femininity and masculinity came to clearest symbolic expression, and World 40 (the roadside cafe) put them into a realistic setting.

Five of the remaining six Worlds with milk churns (6-17-24-27-33) contained no animals although in two (24-27) what we have suggested is a maternity symbol, the lorry carrying a small car, beehive, or hutch, also figured. The one remaining World (28) is the single one in which human mothers-and-baby (2 squaws), appeared with milk churns standing by cowboys at rest.

The two Worlds in which the river flowed into a lake are similar in theme and very different from these others. Here the masculine element predominates. In World 23 a train, very male in its outer form, thrusts forward over a bridge into enemy territory: and yet carries within itself passengers as well as troops. In World 31 a very "male" cannon fires into a lake, and men go up and down within it. The sexual nature of this symbolism will be clear to all experienced psychiatrists, as is the unexpected and unusual identification of this with "work", and work so important that the ordinary affairs of life must be kept away from it.

Right through these 43 Worlds, as we have attempted to show, runs a thread of expression of the mother/child relationship, but it is only a thread, coming to fuller expression very much later.

Fire. It is particularly striking that, in contrast to William Carter's Worlds, fire did not appear in Charles' except once in the concept of an aeroplane catching on fire after a crash. He neither used fire as a part of a camp scene nor the fire engine in relation to his transport scenes.

C) Design

A final axis needs to be considered, that of the element of design in these Worlds.

Charles was a boy who, at the time of his admission to the school, was unable to use or to understand abstract concepts. Nevertheless in his Worlds certain abstract arrangements appeared, taking the form of a series of formal designs reminiscent of the abstract paintings of modern art.

Workers in the field of Analytical Psychology are familiar with the appearance of formal designs in the paintings of their patients, irrespective of interest in or training in the arts. Such design formations in our experience of Worlds appear not infrequently with the most unlikely children and Charles falls into this class. We do not yet know from what aspect of the psyche these arise.

The first World to exhibit this characteristic is the Incoherent World 10. The river runs along the front of the tray and cuts the area of sand in two by an arm directly in the centre and at right angles, like an inverted T. Exactly in the centre of this again is the ambulance/bridge.

This T-shaped river and central item echoed World 5 with the centrally placed boat and occupants, an additional arm being added along the further edge. These two in turn echoed the design of World 4 with the difference that the river there was obliquely instead of vertically arranged. In World 12 the central bridge and the vertical river remain, but the design of the rest of the World is a mirror image of World 1 plus the H arrangement of the river from World 5.

Worlds 28, 31 and 32 form another series. In World 28 a river runs along the front of the tray; in the exact centre of this river was a small semi-circular bay upon which an Indian canoe was beached. World 31 is perhaps the most instructive of the series. The vertical river with the central bridge of World 10 was repeated here, but instead of running into a T-piece, it meets a semi-circular lake in the place of the little bay of World 28. Cutting off the further corners to right and left are oblique fences, each shutting off a small scene: two cannons fire obliquely into the lake.*

The nearer part of World 32 repeats the arrangement of World 31; there is a semi-circular pool in the centre at the nearer edge of the tray; but

---

*It is possible that the vertical river and the circular pool are a development of river and detached pool of World 4.

this is a drinking pool for animals, and a crocodile and a hippopotamus occupy the same positions on either side of this pool as the cannons in World 31. A group of animals takes the pace of the vertical river, and the semi-circular curve of marks on the sand of the lorries driving from the sides of the pool over the centre bridge of World 31 are turned the reverse way for two trains in World 32, which form a semi-circle facing each other, each with a spare engine.

To sum up: it would seem from this series of Worlds, those of William Carter and of many other children, that the putting of symbols into formal patterns is an integral part of the process of achieving control and direction of E and of organisation of the personality. (The occurrence and the value of the special form of patterning known as the Mandala has long been known and studied.)

Summary of Charles' Treatment

It is not for a moment suggested that Charles offers a model treatment of a child; mistakes were made and important clues missed, as becomes apparent in most psycho-therapeutic treatments when they are subjected to detailed investigation. Charles Robinson has been selected for report for quite different reasons and it is essential that these be understood. The choice arose from the following considerations:–

A major difficulty in the appraisal of psycho-therapeutic work is the impossibility of arranging controls. This problem was discussed in detail in 1958 by Miss Anna Freud in an address to the Psychiatric Section of the Royal Society of Medicine, London, in a paper on the work being done in her own Child Therapy Centre. As Miss Freud pointed out then, while the creation of external controls is impossible, interior controls can be devised, and it is from this point of view that the case of Charles Robinson is valuable, since the circumstances of treatment here were such that by force of external fact certain possibilities, deliberately sought in most forms of psychotherapy, were impossible. These were as follows:

Charles' mother was a severely neurotic individual, Charles' father an inadequate character, but anything other than the most superficial contact with them was impossible.

The embargo imposed by the County Authorities upon any discussion of sex blocked approach to and use of some of the most powerful dynamics of psychotherapy.

The limitation of time to bi-weekly half-hour sessions, even in time of acute stress, further limited the scope of therapy.

The fact that pressure of work upon the school staff and together with certain unavoidable irregularities in my own timetable made systematic reporting of Charles' behaviour in school and ordinary hours unachievable, also operated against a close weave of therapeutic texture.

Put together these circumstances added up to an almost unique opportunity to see whether work based upon the theory of E could, in itself, pull a child out of so serious a state of disturbance and it is mainly from this point of view that the study of this boy is offered.

As in all attempts to comprehend or discuss in words the structure and growth of a human personality, the main difficulty facing us in such an account is the complexity of that structure. What has been attempted in the foregoing account is to show how, from being the helpless victim of force within him which burst out through him in unmanageable violence, Charles became gradually able to master this force and to dispose it, as it were, along the abilities and aptitudes latent and potential within him and so to gain mastery over it. The passage of time during this period of treatment was considerable, bringing with it, as a powerful ally, the normal development of intellectual and personality differentiation proper to the years between 8 and 11. There was, added to this, the quite exceptional understanding and intuitional skill and commonsense of the Headmaster and the school staff.

Nevertheless, however much weight we give to these ameliorating circumstances, certain basic problems remain. To select three for discussion: firstly, how does it come about that a child who is so incompetent in school work can show the imaginative power and the detailed factual and executive logic shown by Charles in so many of his Worlds?

I put this question to Charles some two years after the close of the period reported on, and he thought carefully and silently for a while, then said, "because the things are there", referring to the World apparatus. This is a most suggestive answer bringing, as it does, to our minds the difference between the handling of concrete objects, where the success or failure of their disposal in conveying what the child intended can be seen and appraised by the child himself, as compared with the statement of ideas in words to be rated against the appraisal of the master. To objects children have a direct relation, to words an indirect one; to pencil, paint and paper a relation very really limited by skill, so that it is comprehensible that the use of discrete objects of definite and limited form should release the power of imagination and construction. This is a hypothetical conclusion only, and must remain so until tested out by detailed scientific enquiry. Charles has a practical mind and his later failure to secure a place for grammar school education is in correct line with this. From beginning to end of our connection with him there was no appearance of phantasy: all Charles' work remained firmly rooted in reality. Nevertheless his imaginative power was strong and his spontaneous power of attention to detail and care for the exact carrying out of what he intended, remarkable.

This point connects with the next problem to which his case is illustrative. How does it come about that children (and adolescents in whom this is a world-wide problem) become subject to such violent outbreaks of interior force, usually of a destructive nature and are, at the same time, so lazy and dis-inclined to undertake work involving physical effort?

Here the series of Charles' Worlds offer a clue, if regarded from the point of view of the theory of E. The concept of aggression is of a violent force, either with a conceived aim or *directed against an envisaged goal*. Charles' early Worlds made quite clear that there was no goal. It was force itself that was operating in him, force and enjoyment of noise: the destruction that was conceived as happening was incidental. This brings us to a most important element in the theory we are considering. At present actions of attack and destruction are construed as arising from the operation of an aggressive instinct: the inclusion of acts or objects of reconstitution being a manifestation of anxiety and desire to assuage the guilt of aggression through acts of reparation.

159

Study of Worlds made by children and adults has suggested to me an alternative interpretation. Human beings instinctively shrink from a threat of chaos: such a threat produces the deepest fear of all, that of disintegration, of losing contact with the self and in this sense of ceasing to "be". An experience of force rushing through one and doing things not willed or designed by the self is one of the most terrifying experiences possible: so terrifying that unconsciousness can supervene.*

The concrete mind of the child portrays this, as Charles did at the beginning, as the destruction of an object through force within it (the planes and cars). This appears in the guise not of guilt, but of a frightful and yet exultant "fact", the size of which, however, arouses further fear (of a different kind) and drives toward the inclusion in their pictures of symbols of repair, hospitals, ambulances, breakdown cars. For this reason also and to escape from the recurrence of this sequence of experiences, boys will commit small crimes within sight of a policeman *in order to be* "overpowered" and the disruptive force within them brought under external control.

The "laziness" in these boys which puzzles their surrounding adults, is a corollary of this situation. Since the source of the force-tearing-through-them at certain times is unknown to them, as is the pattern of its stimulation, they are out of contact with this source – that is their centre of action – and cannot manipulate it. When, then, it is not in action the personality feels drained of power and unable to will any action.

As the practical experiments of being able to mime this experience, and so to begin to rob it of its terrors, commences to take effect, some elementary power of control of dramatic *symbols* of the situation begin to appear. Success in the working out of these stimulates imagination. Through exercise of this imagination on objects which are suitable symbols to carry the significance of E, the *experience* of control and of willed disposition of this force, albeit in symbol, acts upon the actual situation in the child, much as psycho-drama does for the adult, and so real control of E begins.

We come therefore to the third question: what is it that makes this kind of a child run away or find a hiding place in the house, away from human contacts?

It seems to us that in all children of this kind something has interfered with the normal development of contact and response in infancy and early childhood, during the period when "human contact" means bodily care and handling from an adult. The failure of the normal process whereby E flows into and through the various systems† results in a charge of relatively undifferentiated E being experienced. This is frightening, but at the same time absence of contact is more frightening still. The child

---

*See modern work on epilepsy and the fear of E.C.T. felt by some patients.
†As explained in the Appendix.

longs for contact but the pictures that this situation within him calls up in his imagination are often too violent to be born – he flees from them and shuts himself in from contact of any kind – or he expresses his longing in the only way known to him – by violence. This was discussed at one time with Charles and obtained his full affirmation – this, he said, was how he felt.

The provision therefore of objects with family relationships inherent in their design (in this case animals) makes a stepping stone for such a boy, with which he can move *toward* experiment (again on a projective psycho-dramatic basis) of possible contacts or putative contacts between these. Bit by bit therefore Charles, progressively relieved from the intolerable pressure of primitive E within him, and of the fear of consequences from the outside world following its outbreaks, began to be able to conceive of relationships of different sorts and to work out in the way we have studied, the possibilities of directed force. This brings us again around to the first question, that of the contrast between his performance in Worlds and at school. It is not enough that a child should find a way to achieve an interaction between his will and decision and E, and should begin to find his way to normal human contacts; the channels to the use of his mind and his intellectual powers must also begin to open up.

For this to take place, it is essential that the symbols the child has at his disposal should be capable also of expressing his ideational tangles, his factual muddles, his phantasies, and his ambitions. Here the greatest variety is found. Experience of numbers of children has taught us that the World apparatus as described in Chapter 1, is capable of providing these facilities for every child, but what will be selected by any given child to express this side of his problem it is out of anyone's power to foretell. Charles showed his characteristic factual outlook in the ones he chose, William Carter his separation from all factual reality in the ones he did. What is used is unimportant, the essential is that that which is provided for the child proves effective in giving him the kind of symbols he needs, and children have an extraordinary ingenuity in finding their way to such.

To present the inter-connections of all that appears in a series of Worlds, even in a comparatively simple series such as these 43 of Charles Robinson, is an impossibility, since here we are faced with the same difficulty as confronts all writers about psycho-therapeutic treatment, that a description in words gives only a pale and cold reflection of a process which is in itself rich both in colour and content.

What has therefore been attempted in this presentation is, as it were, to cut this series of Worlds into sections and to present in these sections the processes represented in the series from different angles, from which it is hoped the reader may be able to construct some conception of the whole.

Mosaics*

During this period Charles made 17 Mosaics. They are strikingly different from his Worlds. The first one, an outlined oblong with a central strip of squares and triangles does not appear again until Mosaic 13. The intermediate patterns are of quite a different character; the first seven of these being loosely constructed vertical patterns on the left side of the tray, three being representational designs. The remaining four patterns take the oblong shape of the first with increasing control of the pieces.

Group A

Mosaics No. 2–3–4 have the same general shape – a loosely constructed upright intermediate design using all colours and shapes, placed on one side of the tray and extending from edge to edge.
No. 5 is a slab placed in the top right-hand corner.
No. 6 is a symmetrical vertical arrangement of 20 pieces of the same general shape as 2–3–4 but with a hollow central space.
No. 7 (made between Worlds 15 and 16) was his first Representational Design, called "a clown and a ball"; it was a loosely constructed symmetrical arrangement of the same general shape as No. 6 but much more orderly, using green scalenes in a rough circle at the bottom right corner.

Group B

Between Worlds 16 and 17 the type of pattern altered and became an upright oval with a single line of pieces joining the two ends of the oval, placed in the centre of the tray. This was followed by a design (9) similar to the earlier upright ones but placed in the middle of the tray and called "a plant in a pot".

Group C

Between Worlds 19 and 20 the shape changed to one to be followed for a long time. This is a horizontal oval with central pieces.
No. 11 used this shape to make "a kind of a tank".
No. 12 went back to the earlier upright shape greatly simplified and with a humorous touch.
No. 13 made between Worlds 30 and 31 is a large intermediate horizontal oval ring completely filled with symmetrically arranged pieces.
No. 14 repeats the upright type but with much greater competence.
Nos. 15–16–17 and a continuing number are rectangular oblongs made of triangular shapes and many colours, fitted with differing arrangements of other pieces inside the frame.

---

*See Appendix.

Comment

Charles' inability accurately to image shapes is well shown in his Mosaic designs. Only in a very few instances was there any attempt to fit pieces accurately together, and his designs are mostly of the intermediate type; yet, apart from the slab No. 5 they all have a general overall shape, either horizontal or vertical, with a definite attempt at symmetry.

William Carter

William Carter

We hope, in the extract from the case of Charles Robinson, to have demonstrated the process of treatment in a child in whom problems concerning the management of E dominated the picture. In the extract which follows here from the treatment of William Carter, a boy of parallel age and similar complaints, it is our aim to present a case in which the central feature was the dominance of the child's whole personality and reactions by a proto-system of abnormal content and structure.

Three reasons guided the selection of this extract. The first, that the strange nature of his Worlds supplies us with an indication of the immense, almost incalculable, variety that appears in Worlds made by children. The second, that in the Worlds of this seriously disturbed boy the essential characteristics of the proto-system are more clearly displayed than in any other series of Worlds in our collection. The third, that in his relation with the factual side of life, the distortion of perception and reasoning brought about by a persistent dominance of the proto-system after the age when it should have been corrected and absorbed into the background of consciousness, is more easily seen than in other children where its influence is more hidden and less accessible to study.

Almost every possible obstacle was encountered during the course of William's treatment. His home was more than an hour's journey from London; his father was absent on active service for long periods; his family belonged to that section of English society to whom anything psychological is a closed book and rather "odd", and in which education of the most conventional type is the centre of a boy's upbringing. William himself was delicate, and long periods of illnesses of the ordinary sort, common to children, interrupted treatment. His father was seen three times only during the whole period of treatment; the only contact with the family was with his mother, a gentle, ineffective person, subject to severe anxieties. For a short period the maternal grandmother came into the picture and brought William to his sessions. Mrs. Carter had always been afraid of her own mother (outwardly a kindly and interested grandmother) and unable to stand up to her. William was fond of her and seemed to have a good relationship with her. During William's second period of treatment the grandmother committed suicide, through an overdose of sleeping tablets, which was said to be due to depression and a fear of illness.

One of the most hampering difficulties arising from Mrs. Carter's disposition was the impossibility of obtaining from her either a clear history or a complete account of William's symptoms and behaviour. Important factors in his past experience and present behaviour kept coming to light at unexpected moments.

Treatment was carried on mainly by myself at the I.C.P. The maximum number of sessions achieved was 2 hours a week over short periods; for most of the time this was reduced to one hour a week, owing to refusal by the school at which he was at that time a boarder, to make more frequent attendances possible. His first course of treatment extended over a period of 1½ years, covering 47 attendances. The parents then decided to discontinue treatment.

During the following year William came up to the I.C.P. for two follow-up visits. After the second of these I strongly recommended that treatment should be resumed. This was agreed to and William started a second period of treatment, attending once a week. Of this second period of treatment, three months are included in the extract, covering 11 attendances. During this time he was seen by other members of the non-medical psychotherapeutic staff as well as by myself.

History

William Carter, age 7¾ years, I.Q. 123* on admittance, was the older of two siblings, the younger being a girl of 5. William was referred to the I.C.P. for treatment by the family doctor.

Symptoms. Nocturnal enuresis; acidosis; temper tantrums; multiple phobias (water-closets, robbers, crocodiles and snakes, aggression from adults); poor school work; thumbsucking at night; masturbation.

Family. William came of an upper middle class family; his home was in a residential small town near London. *William's father* was a naval officer, typical, tall, thin, good-looking, highly strung, but sensible: he came from a professional background, his family being noisy and jolly, given to exaggeration which they enjoyed. William's father alone reacted into the opposite pattern and became different from all of them; he was enuretic till the age of 11, occasionally subject to rages (like his son). He had one brother and four sisters, now all married.

William's mother came of a non-professional middle class family, with one sister (single). She was good-looking, attractive, externally calm, but of the extraverted type with no contact with or understanding of the inner life of people or children; worried about external matters. Her father was "good with children"; her mother stern and extraverted in type, yet "a good mother".

William's sister, about 3 years younger than he, occasionally wetted her bed; at first William attacked her, later became protective.

History. William was a much wanted child, born towards the end of the war. Labour normal; birth weight 6 lbs.; breastfed only 4 weeks (his mother developed a breast abscess), put on to bottle, cried a lot, scratched his head and face and sucked his thumb; bad teething troubles, grizzled; inert and timid baby; walking and talking late; appetite quite good, but poor in quantity; clean early but nearly always constipated. Circumcised as a baby; age 2 fell out of car when with his father; age 4 had "pink-eye" and septic throat, treated with penicillin injections; a child threw sand in his face and the infection recurred; age 7 in hospital for a week for tonsils and adenoids operation, very depressed. He had had none of the common children's illnesses before the beginning of treatment.

---

*Re-tested during treatment, see page 251.

There were several environmental changes during the first 6 years owing to his father being on active service, but no separation from his mother till he went to boarding school for a year at the age of 8 while the family was away in the North.

William started school at the age of 5 (2 terms in Malta), then his parents returned to England and he became a day-boy at a private school and remained so apart from the one year, mentioned above, when he was a boarder.

In appearance William was a well-grown boy for his age, of very spare build with small bones and thin musculature, a pointed face, pale skin and very light hair and eyes; physically a marked contrast to Charles' thick-set body and brooding face. He was tense and jerky in his movements and as soon as he became friendly and absorbed in play, dictated to his therapists. His mother had reported that he found it very difficult at home to play on his own and constantly wanted an adult to play with him and to help him in whatever he was doing.

Treatment

Consultation

At the Consultation session William was asked to make a *Mosaic*, and produced a square frame made of squares of blue, white and red, attached to the top of the tray and extending over threequarters of the space of the tray; within this empty frame he put four black squares, one in each corner, which he said were "corridors" and one green square, said to be "a door" placed just above the middle of the bottom row of squares.

The World cabinet and the sand tray were then shown to him and the material introduced in the usual way; but he failed to understand that the toys in the World cabinet were supposed to be used on the tray, and therefore worked with the sand only, responding to the possibility of using it both in depth and as a surface. Since it was not possible to make an accurate record of this first World, a stylised diagram is shown.

World 1   Figure 42 (Consultation session)

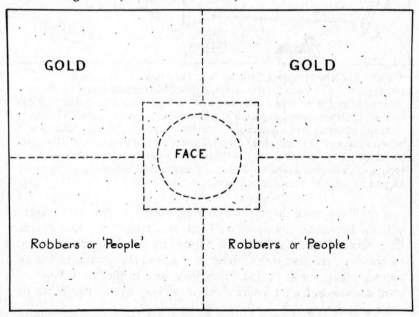

William started off by making rough mouldings and marks in the centre of the tray, which he said was "a face" in a square. He then drew crossing lines in the sand which divided the tray into four parts. Poking at these squares and talking about them, he conveyed a vague idea that there was gold hidden in the two further quadrants, and that somehow in the two nearer ones were people, sometimes called robbers, who were trying to steal the gold. It was all very vague.

On completion of this World, the use of the cabinet was again explained to William. This time he understood and started afresh.

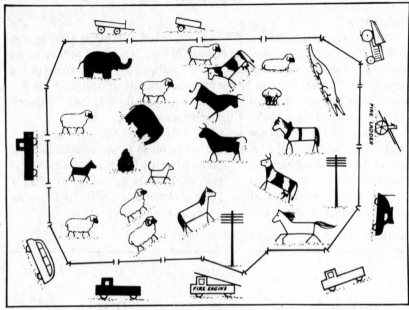

William smoothed the sand, took out fences and made a large, roughly rectangular enclosure in the tray, without gates, leaving a surrounding space thought of as a "road". In the enclosure he put four categories of objects: wild animals (2 elephants and a crocodile); farm animals (2 bulls, 2 cows, 3 horses, 7 sheep); domestic animals (2 dogs); miscellaneous objects (2 large telephone poles, a sheaf of corn and a bushy tree). These were fairly evenly spaced over the area facing all ways with the bull in the centre. Outside on the road he put 3 lorries, a fire-engine, a bus, a police car, a fire-ladder, 2 carts and a tip-up lorry, all going clockwise round the enclosure.

As William made these 2 Worlds very quickly, he was next presented with the Lowenfeld Kaleidoblocs. These he arranged in a long confused line, which he called "a train". He finished the session by making a series of *drawings;* the first was a house in a storm; the second, people on a journey with a sunset behind, "they have been to the North Pole"; the third consisted of what William called "talking trees"; the fourth of a house in a garden.

Discussion.   The work done by William Carter in his consultation session set the pattern for his later work. Within the hour he accomplished a Mosaic, two Worlds, an arrangement of Kaleidoblocs and four drawings. His movements were quick and active without pauses for thought. His Mosaic foreshadowed his later "houses" and showed one of the main characteristics of his productions; a three-dimensional quality: the black squares are not "windows" but an idea of length in a direction at right angles to the paper; they were "corridors".

World 1 repeated this three-dimensional quality. It is more a scaffolding of a statement than a statement in itself and comes nearer to a story than any other of his Worlds. The drawing of a face in the centre is the only time he used the sand in this way. The gold which was threatened came in again in World 6 but the idea of robbers (or bandits), so common in Charles' Worlds, did not appear again in William's Worlds.

World 2 is a key for a great many subsequent Worlds. The arrangement of fences marking out a roughly rectangular space, outside which circular movement takes place, occurred again and again as the ground plan of his Worlds. It is typical that motor traffic should be moving around the central enclosure, and associated with carts and a fire-escape ladder, a combination which frequently recurred. The combination of wild and tame animals in the same enclosure gives a clue to William's feeling about wild animals. He differentiated closely between actual wild and tame animals but at the same time, when asked, said he felt the wild ones to be "friendly".

Kaleidoblocs: As will be discussed later, William's use of trains is quite different from Charles' and it is only quite far on in his treatment that functioning trains appeared. This arrangement of blocks into a train was not repeated.

Drawings: Of the four drawings, two were of houses, one peaceful "in a garden", the other "a house in a storm". The subject of the second drawing did not appear again, but the "talking trees" gives the atmosphere of his "magic" Mosaics and Worlds.

World 3 Figure 44 (1st treatment session)

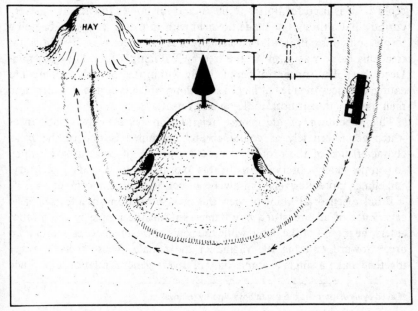

171

Owing to the vagueness of the execution of this World it is presented in the illustration in a semi-diagrammatic fashion.

William first said he was going to make "a circus", and traced a circular track in the sand. Then he smoothed this away and made, very carefully, a mound of sand in the centre of the tray; he then began to make a hole at each side of the mound; with my assistance this was made into a tunnel running right through the mound. He next found an open lorry and played about with it for a time; he tried to hitch a trailer on to it, but did not succeed and eventually gave it up; the lorry was then filled with sand and run in a semi-circular loop round the mound from the further right-hand corner to the further left-hand corner, where it was emptied; this was repeated several times till a heap of sand was collected by the far left-hand side, which was said to be "hay". He now made a square fenced-in field at the further edge of the tray, to the right, connecting it and the heap of "hay" by a path, and placed a Christmas tree in the field.
William explained there were a lot of people inside the mound; they slept there and ate there and sometimes they came out. He talked about the Christmas tree in an odd and quite unrealistic manner, saying "it was moved from the field to the top of the mound when the peoople in the mound came out".
Finally he moved the Christmas tree from the field to the top of the mound.

Discussion. This mound should be compared with World 11 of Mary's series. As explained previously, such a mound is a constantly recurring feature of children's Worlds and the tunnel through it made by William typifies similar tunnels through mounds made by children of all ages. The semi-circular road along which the lorry is run reflects dimly the concept of the circus with which he started and which appeared several times later on. The idea of hay is new; when William was asked what hay was he replied, "it is used for horses to lie on and for horses to eat". It was very curious that although he made the field with care and seemed to be going to put something in it, all that actually was put there was the Christmas tree (this name was given to the tree by William; it was, however, mid-December). The concept of people being within the mound, sleeping and eating, balances the idea of hay as something which is carted in a lorry and then used by horses both to lie on and to eat.

This repetition of an inverse relationship between two substances which act alternately as container and contained is one of the basic characteristics of the proto-system. It occurs in all cases at some time, sometimes easily observable as in this World and in World 11 of Mary, sometimes more elusively, but always of considerable importance.

From a sensorial point of view this inverse relationship affects a basic experience of all breast-fed boy babies, in that the nipple of the mother enters the mouth of the baby, while the penis of the boy carries within it an urge* toward entering the vagina of the female. These facts however together make a single example only of a very general relationship. Since

---

*Called by us in discussing this with boys' "pushy feelings".

although the experience of the girl baby and the adult woman is of penetration from outside, this proto-system characteristic nevertheless appears in girls also.

World 3 may therefore be summed up as follows: human beings sleep and eat within the mound; the hay outside the mound and in a similar heap within the lorry, has been, and later provides bedding for horses and food they eat.

One week later, at the beginning of his second treatment session, William came eagerly and settled down to make a *Mosaic*. It became an odd and inept construction, consisting of vertical lines of equilateral and isosceles triangles of indiscriminate colours (mostly red and white), which occupied the left-hand side of the tray. One of these columns was said to be "a Christmas tree" and the others were "fountains", "magic, which make the tree all wet and glittering".

Conversation. While William was making his Mosaic, "Picture Thinking" was discussed again; when it was finished, the similarity between fountains and urination was pointed out.

After this William made a World which falls into 3 stages.

World 4   Figure 45 (2nd session)

Stage I. The sand was patted flat as William wanted it to be "very flat and hard"; he then began to draw lines in the sand with his fingers; these "were to be water"; he pushed his finger down to expose the blue base of the tray which he liked very much; drawing his finger around he made a large oval; then, with circular movements, this oval was cut up into six shapes as represented in the drawing, the whole making a symmetrical pattern; the oval blocks of sand in the centre were said to be "pools" (he did not notice that you cannot have pools within water); the channels were said to be "where the water came out".

Stage II.   William now said that he wanted "rocks", and I produced some coloured plasticine; he punched and modelled some long pieces of green plasticine and stuck the bases against the blue base of the outer channel so that they stood up. Then he wanted some "lying rocks" and chose pink for these; he stuck them down in various places and said, "The fishes make their houses in these".

Stage III.   As he finished the last "rock" William said, "there are seals too in the water". The word "seal" seemed in some way to form a turning point. He asked for sharks, but was told there were none and that he would have to use crocodiles instead. William accepted this and went to the cabinet to find the seals; but as he took them out and turned with them in his hand to the tray, the sand "pools" ceased to represent pools to him and became land. He put the crocodiles in the outer ring of water and the seals on the right and also on the two centre islands of sand. He now wanted people. I opened the appropriate drawers and suggested an Eskimo (as belonging to seal country); William accepted it dubiously and selected for himself a cowboy with a rifle and a woman in riding clothes (which he called a man); he put these on different islands, saying they were shooting the seals. Next he made an oval mound on the bank in the further right-hand corner and said, "It is the people's boat". Two other unarmed men were "coming to take the seals". (No information was offered as to what they would do with them). A bridge was put across the right-hand stream, William reiterating, "but the banks must be high". When this was completed, he looked thoughtfully at a bundle of coloured thin slats, lying on the table, began picking some up and sticking them upright in the sand; he got flashes of worry that this was not "reasonable", but on being reassured went on until the tray was evenly filled with upright standing slats.

Discussion.   The true significance of this World only came out very much later. It is a good illustration of the nature of proto-system clusters.

A. *Spatial elements.*   The water "contains" water: it both flows and is still. The water also contains rocks and these are "houses" for fish. The mound shape of the previous World was repeated in the green rocks. The sand mound on the shore was thought of as hollow and as a boat for men.

B. *Patterning.*   The rough rectangle of World 2 now appears as an oval with further patterning within it. It was not clear whether William saw all the land islands as pools or only the centre ones; it would have disturbed him to have questioned him too closely.

C. *The concept of hollow and solid rods.*   Two men attempt to use long hollow rods for killing. Solid rods were distributed vertically all over the scene.

D. *Significance.*   The significance of this World clearly depends upon William's thoughts, feelings, and associations with the objects he used. The curious fact, however, is that seals never reappeared in his Worlds, and we have no knowledge of what he thought or felt about them or what they symbolised to him. Crocodiles were accepted in the place of sharks, and sharks are creatures which attack; but in the World they were not represented as attacking anything, nor did the hunter attack them. The shape of the pink rocks and the fact that they were "houses for fishes" may possibly be an echo of the fact that William's father was, during the war, captain of a submarine. The standing rods are a feature which occurs several times later and which was finally resolved into trees in World 46.

World 5 *not illustrated* (3rd session)

William made the next World with great enthusiasm. It was said to represent the layout of a children's model village near his home, but was very confused, objects such as a turnstile being placed without relevance to the scene in the centre of the World. It was not possible to record this World in detail since objects were continually being moved about; but the main features were a number of trains (actually existing in the "village"); something called "a bridge for trains" was made out of planks, but was placed where no train could go over it; and there were odd buildings such as "a barn", a "Pixie's house", a watchman's hut, benches, an empty farm cart without a horse, and a number of square pieces of wood placed in the sand to form a square pattern. The only human beings were a naked baby in a large pram wheeled by a Red-Ridinghood figure. At the end William looked out the same bundle of sticks he had used before and put eleven of them upright between the flat wooden squares; these, he said, were "fountains, to make trains glitter in the night". He added, there was "a glittering look about it all".

Conversation. William was not ready to talk about his fears as he recounted a *dream*: "some men hung their coats up, they fought with me". He said he was afraid of:

"Robbers coming in my bedroom window" –
"That the house is going to fall down" –
"I am going to roll out of bed" –
"If I sit on the lavatory I will go down it"
    (In the next session William added to this a fear of going down the bath hole) –
"I feel that spiders are going to crawl up the bath sides and that the bath is
    going to fall to pieces".

In regard to his mother he said, "I am afraid mummy is going to smack me; I get into terrible tempers and she is silly, a fool, is smelly, that I am going to put a lot of faeces on her face; I think she is going to kill me"; he finished by saying, "I don't want to wet". All these fears have a relation to space and also to movement and this point will be discussed further in the review of his Worlds.

Discussion. This time William made an attempt to represent a real scene belonging to his environment. The model village exists in reality, is near his home, and is a favourite excursion place for children. William had been taken to see it recently. The village did actually contain miniature trains; but William's picture of it was like a child's verbal report of an "outing" in that the features that had struck him particularly were the ones he had attempted to reproduce, but his "report" was lacking in any perception of their practical interrelation or significance.

On the next session, which was the last of the term, in order to get some idea of his relation to reading, writing and stories, we used the Newspaper Game* box for working out the titles of stories and talking about them. William was very proud of achieving 9 titles, none of them of particular interest.

Here the Christmas holidays intervened. William's parents reported that there had been no tantrums and that William's fear of going to the W.C. was rather less.

On the next session I had to be away and William was taken by a member of the psycho-therapeutic staff of the I.C.P. This made no difference to him and he started out busily with another World.

World 6   Figure 46 (5th session)

William chose a tray with mouldable sand and smoothed it very carefully with a roller. Out of the World cabinet he selected 4 big boats and put them in a row in the nearer right-hand corner along the right-hand shorter edge. He next took out 4 carts and placed them in a row at the right-hand far corner and, like the boats, along the right-hand shorter edge. He next fetched some wild animals and placed

*See Appendix.

them all over the rest of the tray; one small duck was near the carts. The therapist wondered what sort of animals they were and William said they were friendly. He then found a piece of wood (belonging to a building set) which with he made marks in the sand; first, one in front of each animal, saying it was for their food, then all over the rest of the tray, these were pools of drinking water. At the place marked with a cross he made a deeper hole in the sand, "which led down to a secret place where gold was kept"; "only the man belonging to the place knew about it, and sometimes he went down to make sure that it was still there". The man on the horse was in charge of the animals. The boats were there in case of a flood, when the animals would get on board and be rescued. No explanation was offered as to why the carts were there.

Discussion. This World combines the basic elements of Worlds 1 and 2 in that there are here many animals – mostly, it is true, wild ones, only the duck being tame – and an underground place "where gold is kept". There are no robbers and the animals were said to be friendly.

This World is a good example of the proto-system and as such merits examination. The objects which were placed in the tray take the place, as it were, of "headings" to themes which occupy his mind and feelings. There are five elements: (1) the twelve animals (including the keeper's horse) with the crocodile in the centre, two rhinoceroses facing inwards to him, two hippos diagonally across the tray, four bears, a camel and one solitary duck; these animals have one function, they are fed with food and water; (2) the carts about which we have no information; (3) the gold in the deep down hidden chamber and its human guardian; (4) the ships; (5) the idea of water. So long as William was thinking of the animals the idea of water was objictified in pools all over the tray. This water idea however soon "overflowed" and became threatening and the boats provided escape from it for the animals.

This session illustrates very well a cardinal principle of this form of therapy, which is that the attention of the child is so strongly caught and held by the Worlds that he is making that, provided the mode of handling is the same, a change of therapist, if essential for practical reasons, is accepted without hindrance to the progress of the work.

William's father was now moved to a station in a distant part of Britain and his wife joined him. William therefore went to school as a boarder and was reported to have settled down well.

Owing to external circumstances, at the next session William was taken by yet another therapist on the staff of the I.C.P. This therapist reported that he was quite at ease and started immediately on a World.

World 7   Figure 47 (6th session). See page 178.

With his finger William made an oval shape in the sand, then 2 oval shapes at either end; then he joined the lines and said "it was a river"; it looked like a river with islands and he made a 3rd island at the further end. When asked which way

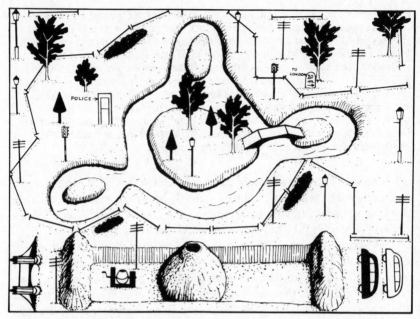

the water was going, he said: "both ways". At the nearer edge he made a round mound with a hole in the top, and said, "it was a farmhouse with a chimney". He scooped out the sand on either side and made 2 flat fields, and at the end of each field a ridge which he said was a fence. Having completed the sand-moulding part, he said he would put something else in. He then added the cement-mixer and said it was making roads, and started flattening the sand with a slat of wood which was "making a road". When he had done all this he moved the cement-mixer to the field and thought, "perhaps the farmhouse was where the road men lived".

He wanted bridges and used a slat until he noticed a real bridge in the drawer, then he joined a big island to one little one. At the same time he found the Tower Bridge and asked about it; then he put it on the left-hand side, for no apparent reason. He next added fences, putting them all the way round the river in an irregular line, so that sometimes they were close to the river and sometimes far away. He found a large lamp-post and thought this would be lovely and added more lamp-posts and telegraph posts, a police telephone box, traffic lights, and a milestone saying "To London"; finally he added trees and some hedges. At one point he also added buses in the right near corner, saying, "They are sometimes allowed out and sometimes not"; but he was vague about this, and when pressed said it was something to do with the animals. In fact his account of everything he did was vague.

Discussion. This World falls into the classification "fragmented". It is in two main parts which are independent of each other and the front segment divides again with several items. The making of the original shape of the waterways in this World had a general resemblance to the making of similar waterways in World 4. William's sense of reality has however progressed, so that there was no confusion here between pools and the river; nevertheless the water was said to flow both ways. The 3 small and the one large island were clear, definite and intended. The bridge from the central island to the right-hand one was in the same position in regard to the tray and the water as the bridge in World 4. The fencing around the river bears a general resemblance to that in World 2, except for the 3 separate fences placed by themselves near the further edge. The trees, lamp-posts, telegraph poles and traffic-signs have the same sort of irrelevance as the sticks in Worlds 4 and 5. The only item suggestive of human beings within the fencing was the Police telephone-box.

The second part that occupied the front of the tray is another proto-system concept. As in the previous one it consists of a number of separate concepts, and his last sentence in talking of it linked this part of this World to the last World. The first element in this concept is "a farmhouse and fields". The shape of the "farmhouse" repeated the mound of World 3 and was conceived of as being lived in, only this time the hole into it was vertical and to William appeared as a projection not a hole (a fact which often appears in proto-system constructions). The second element, coinciding spatially with the first, was "a road which is being made" the cement mixer taking part in it, and the men taking part living in the mound. Here we have horizontal movement which is carried to the left in the Tower bridge which implies the idea of a river; this bridge has a vertical movement as well as a horizontal one. Finally the buses on the right were containers (like the mound) and also moved horizontally – if and when "they are allowed out" along other partially imagined roads. Sand walls (said also to be hedges) separate the centre ideas from the bridge and the buses.

If we compare this World with Word 6, these two present a major characteristic of William's interior pictures and his presentation of them in Worlds. (The same characteristic also appears at times in his Mosaics). In both these Worlds objects from the real World appear which have no conceivable relation to the rest of the scene, but which in William's mind were part of it. These objects are means of transport (carts, ships and buses). William feels quite clear that they should be there, but when pressed to explain their connection, can only do so in a way which makes comprehension even more difficult: for example, the remark that the buses were "something to do with the animals".

In studying Charles' Worlds we have become used to Worlds which are divided into two parts quite different from each other. This is a World which consists also of two parts differing from one another, but the nature of the difference is quite different from that in Charles' Worlds. The difference here is not in the objects used, nor in clear and overt differences in their significance, as for example that between engines and farm animals, but in the type of presentation of the two elements. The "garden" shows a possible scene; the front strip with its bridge, buses, and the mound is a many-dimensional proto-system statement.

A letter from Mrs. Carter which arrived after this session reported the following story as recounted by William to his grandmother:

"There was a witch who was caught by a king and queen and had a rope put round her neck and was hanged. But she was rescued and the king and queen were sent away and the witch became queen and lived happily ever after." (William is reported to have told the story with an impish grin on his face).

Owing to various circumstances a four-week gap occurred here.

World 8 Figure 48 (7th session)

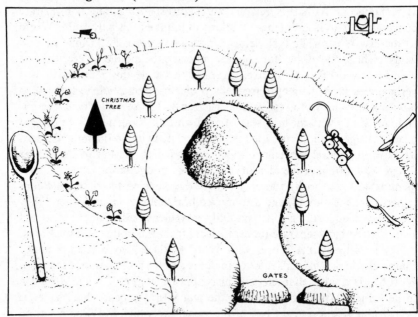

William fell eagerly upon the World tray and began mixing sand and water very vigorously. He moulded a round mound in the centre of the tray, clearing the sand away around it and leaving the rest rough; he then began to make two small ridges of sand from the side of the cleared space by the nearer edge and continually altered them; they were said to be "gates". He then made a kind of loop of trees surrounding the cleared space and began to flatten the sand in another loop outside this, saying he wanted to make a garden; flowers were put in all along the left-hand side and then the Christmas tree. In the corner by the further edge the cement-mixer was placed, with a wheel-barrow toward further left corner and a road-drill toward the right. The spoons which has been used in the making of the World were left on the tray.

Conversation. William was very vague about the World; all he could say was that the mound was "a castle", that "workmen were working there, but no one was living in it".

Discussion. Here the-mound-which-is-a-dwelling-place and "the work-

180

man's house" came together. This mound is a castle, i.e., a place made for people to live in, but it is empty. On the other hand there is a garden round it, and the Christmas tree of World 3 (placed first in the field and then on the mound) is now in the garden. The cement-mixer and another road-making tool (which appeared frequently later) were introduced casually without any organic relation to the whole design. It was a sign that this World was not really completed that he left his tools on the tray.

William's school reported occasional dry nights: that he appeared to be happy, and that there was some improvement in his school work, particularly in arithmetic. There was a three-week gap between this World and the next during which William had an attack of influenza.

At the next session all William's Worlds were gone through with him carefully and their interrelation pointed out.

Two weeks later, at session 10, William, on arriving from school, reported that he was no longer overcome with fears in school and had had no tantrums. This session was the beginning of a new stage. William started mixing dry and wet sand together in which he demanded my assistance. I was ordered about and told exactly what to do, William becoming completely absorbed in tactile sensation. This had, however, to be given intellectual cover and was therefore called "experimenting". Toward the end of the session he made a World.

World 9 *not illustrated* (10th session)

First he cut a road across one short side of the tray at the nearer end; then covered the rest of the tray with pink sand, leaving it rough. Along the further side of this road William made a hill extending the whole length of the road with its top in the middle. The space between the road and the nearer edge was divided into three parts, and a house was put into each division. William now made some small quantities of coloured sand and sprinkled these over the surface of each division, green sand to the left, brown in the middle and yellow to the right. He then took out a dozen very small houses and packed them closely together in a row along the nearer side of the tray. Finally he took out a large barn and "cemented" this into the face of the hill on the other side of the road.

Discussion. From the point of view of theory this is an interesting session. The cement-mixer and the "road", the expression given by this World to his inner sensorial exprience, my acceptance of it and my discussion with him of the whole series of Worlds, had released his desire to "experiment". The image of the cement-mixer made this possible on two levels: – the primitive (faeces derived) one of the actual mixing, and the increase in reality perception in his use of the houses on the road.

Play with mixing wet sand and coloured (pink) sand occupied the next session.

At this point William developed measles and did not return for the rest of the term.

During the Easter holidays he went away with his parents. At the end of the holidays his mother reported that "William is greatly improved and was dry for 19 consecutive nights, he no longer sucks his thumb at night before going to sleep"; he was, however, "excitable, noisy and rude". He "showed great affection for his father and had only two rages".

The next session took place 2 months later, at the beginning of the summer term.

World 10   Figure 49 (12th session)

William smoothed all the sand in the tray very carefully. He then placed a house toward the further side of the tray, in the centre; he found a bridge (designed for use within a station) and placed this over the house. He now took out a church, a long house, and a Swiss house and placed them in a triangle in the centre of the tray; over this he placed a big bridge. He put a woman and a little boy just outside the left staircase of the small bridge. He then took out 6 pieces of motor transport which he grouped in pairs, putting one pair on each side of the tray by the left and right nearer edge, facing inwards; the third pair was placed behind the right arm of the big bridge against the right-hand edge. He now began to move these vehicles one by one, making a pattern of tracks in the sand which circled round each of the 3 houses and around the back of the centre house and the small bridge, and then bringing each vehicle back again to its original position. He completed his World by placing 3 men on the sand close to the nearer edge, one woman in the first loop of tracks, 2 men walking from

182

left to right across the centre of the big bridge, and one man in period costume on the centre of the small bridge looking down over the scene.

Discussion. This is a most interesting World and brings out strongly the impulse toward patterning which is so definite a characteristic of William's Worlds. If World 4 is compared with this World, the close correspondence between the waterways in the former and the tracks in the latter will become apparent. On the other hand the choice and grouping of objects was different from any other Worlds heretofore and marked a significant change in William. These objects and this grouping, while still "fantastic", was far more coherent than any World made hitherto. All these objects *could* be found together, and compared with the use made of them by the other two children; it displays the third use children make of bridges. Here William used a large and a smaller one, both belonging to railways, and placed them squarely on the sand, not actually bridging anything. The people on the bridges and the tracks underneath link these with the Tower bridge of World 7 and make clear that to William it is not the "bridging-ness" of bridges which strikes him about them but the contrast between people on the bridge looking down and movement that happens under and through the bridge. William's houses in this World formed the four points of a diamond with the church as one "house": the vehicles were in pairs, a bus and a lorry (suggestive of male and female); as far as the people are concerned the focus seems to be upon the mother and boy who stand under the bridge: the other figures are undifferentiated and appear to have no connection with the design.

In something the same way that in Charles' series, Incoherent Worlds alternated with Coherent ones, the explosions of E in the former making possible the focusing achieved in the latter, so in William's series periods occurred of eager and absorbed sensuous play, alternating with attempts at objective constructions which seemed to enable him to achieve a momentary focus in a World.

The two sessions between World 10 and World 11 were of this nature. In these William worked hard with sand, water, sieves and slats of wood carrying out schemes of his own in the tray which were very difficult to follow. In the first session he used pink sand and said he was making a "fairy road". In the second he tried to "make a house" in the tray with sand, wooden slats and water, using the slats to cut wet sand with and to help in the making of walls, but failing altogether to achieve anything coherent.

In the beginning of session 15 he demonstrated quite clearly his inability to image shapes or to understand the relation of actual objects to each other by being altogether unable to manipulate the lorry and wheels of a constructional toy intended for children much younger than he. While these sessions were going on I began to talk to William about the body, about early physical sensations, about things that went in and things that came out of the body and to give very elementary explanations of how the body worked.

Discussion. This intense absorption in sensuous experiment fits in well with what had been reported of William and what he reported of his own interest in faeces and his own fears of what might happen in the W.C. The association of these "crude" ideas, experiences and fears, with his aesthetic pleasure in sand (which he had made pink with powder colour), and his idea of the fairy road, was one of the central characteristics of William's work.

World 11 *not illustrated* (15th session)

It happened that among my boxes was one containing numbers of small bricks of various shapes painted in gold and silver and bright colours, intended for making fairy palaces.

William took these and set them out in two oblongs following the shape of the tray, one within the other; in the centre space, facing the further edge, he placed a model of the Coronation coach and one of the queen on horse-back, filling in the remaining space with a star of coloured sticks laid flat upon the sand.*

Discussion. The making of this World arose out of the presence of the gold and silver "bricks". These do not form a normal part of World equipment but are often very useful. Here they carried on William's idea of "glittering", his desire to make a "fairy" something, the upright sticks of World 4, and his feeling for his mother. Having experimented as much as he had with amorphous play he was able to focus upon something nearing an ordered construction. This is still "fantastic" but is much nearer coherence than he has as yet achieved, and in its way is completely "ordered".

On the session following this I introduced the idea of painting and William took to it with enthusiasm. He thoroughly enjoyed mixing colours and covering large areas of the Mess Room walls with them. He was not able really to let himself go but nevertheless got a lot of fun out of it. Contrary to the situation with most enuretic boys he took no interest in using water in the water rooms.

As Mrs. Carter had reported earlier that William had told his grandmother a story he had made up about a witch, a king and a queen, therefore – as he stood beside the sand tray at his next session uncertain as to what to do – I said, "What about making a fairytale"? William seized on the idea and made a World.

---

*This was at the time of the coronation of Queen Elizabeth II.

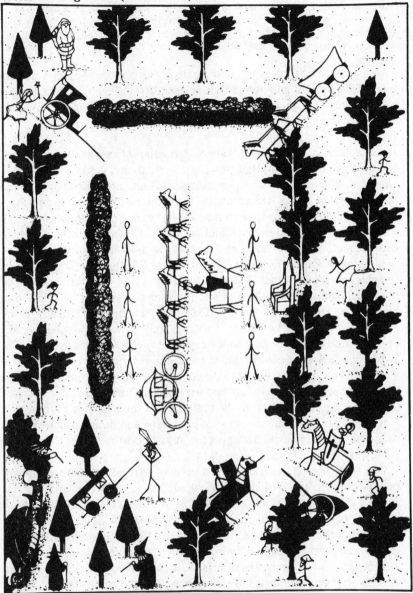

He took out all the large shady trees and hedges and placed them in two oblongs, one within the other, following the shape of the tray (as he had done with the bricks in World 11). He then wanted coaches and accepted the small stock I could provide, placing them one in each corner, facing inwards. The black and the white knights on horseback were put facing each other in one corner, with all kinds of gnomes, fairies and dancing girls dotted among the trees. He selected one female figure, which he called a witch, and then took an actual big witch and

185

another small one and put these in the opposite corner, well out of sight from the centre; he found a dragon and put it between the witches, "attacking them". The coronation coach was then set in the centre, facing away from the knights and witches; the queen on horseback was beside the coach, and flanking these all the people he could find dressed in scarlet and gold.

He now said he wanted to build a palace with a piece of apparatus with wires fitting upright into holes in a base; he insisted upon having the longest wires, saying that this was to be "a splendid palace"; but he was quite unable to accomplish anything with it at all.

Discussion.   These two Worlds are of particular interest as they show how one kind of imagination, that which gives rise to and is fed by fairy-tales, interacts with proto-system structures. In his previous Worlds and Mosaics William had laid emphasis upon things "glittering", and there had been glimpses from time to time of the type of symbolic imagination which finds expression in myth and fairy-tale. His profound involvement with his mother was obvious, and the fact that this was the summer of the coronation of Queen Elizabeth II made it possible for these trends in him to achieve a focus in the "apparently ordinary" use of current models of the Queen and the coronation-coach, to express one side of his relation to his mother, Here indeed she was the queen; on the other hand, in the corner of the same World are 3 witches and a dragon, expressing the opposite side corresponding to his expression in his witch fairy-tale. The rods of the "splendid palace" and the gold and silver colour of the bricks of World 11 were directly related to the coloured sticks of Worlds 4 and 5 and the "glitteringness" which had appeared several times; all this expressed the excitement William felt in the presence and thought of his mother.

It is worth noting that the sense of patterning and design which William showed in his Worlds did not appear in any of his Mosaics. At this time he made very few.

One more session completed the term and initiated an entirely different type of play. In this William used coloured sand, both wet and dry. He began by elaborately sieving dry sand in and out of various containers; then, finding a number of rubber tubes, he spent the second half of the session pouring water to and fro through a series of tubes fitted together. He showed great excitement and satisfaction with this.

Discussion.   As a general rule boys with enuresis spend a good deal of time in play with water in the water room, but the confusion of ideas in William's mind and his fears of his inner concepts had so far made impossible for him any direct play with water. This session marked an important development in that he found a way of permitting himself to "experiment" with water within the framework of a World tray.

This session completed a stage in William's treatment.

The summer holidays now intervened, at the end of which his mother reported as follows:

"I thought you would like to hear how William was these holidays. He was absolutely marvellous. There is a great change in him and I was delighted with him. He was much more self-confident and went on his own for two bus rides. He appeared to have no fears over this at all, which is quite different to the Easter holidays. He also went out alone to the shops, etc., without any misgivings. He did not have one single tantrum. He never once attacked either his father or me in the way he had done previously and his relationship with his younger sister was excellent. At the beginning of the holidays he was dry off and on for about three weeks, but for the remainder of the time he was wet every night. He was much calmer than I've ever known him and he managed to go alone to the lavatory after the first few days without any qualms. He was very affectionate to his father and to me. He was always so willing to help with little jobs about which he used to grumble and often refuse to do. The only thing that upset me is that at the last moment he was very reluctant to go back to school. He was chosen to be a gnome in the school play last term which thrilled him immensely and they told me that ever since being in the play he had developed into a chatterbox. They say that he seems to have settled down this term, but is rather quiet".

World 13 *not illustrated* (19th session)

The whole of this session, the first in the Autumn term, was spent in first emptying the tray of all sand, then patting small handfuls of mouldable sand on the tray and smoothing these very flat; very dry sand was then sprinkled with equal care over it so as to make an absolutely flat surface. A long time was now spent hooking together trains of a suitable size and running them slowly over the sand so as to make tracks reminiscent of World 10. The whole focus was on the tracks. Having achieved considerable satisfaction with this, William moved the trains on to the linoleum-covered floor where he spent the rest of the session chalking routes for them and running trains along them.

Discussion. This session illustrates very well the relation between temporary interests in a child and the permanent development of self-realisation. Having been away from treatment for 3 months, William picked up the threads of his work from World 10, by-passing Worlds 11 and 12. As already pointed out, World 10 picks up threads from World 4. Worlds 11 and 12 (see Discussion on these), although reflecting a temporary element, picked up elements from earlier Worlds. Taken together these series – the "glittering" series expressing affect and the movement series expressive of E – interweave with one another in a way that helps us to understand some elements of the structure of the psyche in children.

The part of the experience of children to which least attention has been directed is that of sensuous experience. In children such as Charles this played little part; such children seem to achieve a sufficient integration of the different aspects of their experience and their thoughts about it to

187

prevent confusions and conflicts playing a major part in their disorders. In other children, such as William, these two aspects, their actual experiences and their thoughts and fantasies about them, play a central role both in their development or retardation of development and in the production of their symptoms. In such children the process of development of interest in and understanding of the outside World becomes held up through investment of E in these early confusions and conflicts, so that insufficient E is available for overcoming learning difficulties.

It is the particular value of the World Technique that it enables direct presentation by the child to himself of the clusters of his proto-system. Such a child starts on his World without knowing what his hands are going to make, and it is this absorption which the process awakens in him that discharges the E which has been locked up in these clusters.

This session initiated a new stage in treatment.

The next session was occupied with a crucial revision and interpretation. My note reads, "Definitely more at ease and less tense". The contents of his mother's letter was taken up with him and he was congratulated on his progress; at the same time it was explained that it was natural in his situation that difficulties about excretion should continue. William replied that it was not the actual fears about excretion that troubled him, but that he wanted to have a grownup with him when excreting. The difference between the infant's and the adult's attitude to excretion was then discussed and related to his general dependence on his mother.

After this William found a large red tip-up lorry and spent the rest of the session filling this with wet sand, running the lorry round and tipping the wet sand out on the floor. Ice-cream carts were next taken from the World cabinet and put in the lorry. Then the cement-mixer was taken out and an elaborate ritual developed of pouring water into sand in one or another container, stirring it up, moving it round, and emptying the contents on to the floor. When he discovered that dry sand would spill through the screw holes in the base of the lorry he played at filling dry sand into the lorries and studying the tracks made by the sand on the floor as the lorries were moved about. During this play lorries were arranged in lines like trains.

While this was going on I kept up a discussion about faeces in general, pointing out the differences between the excretory products of different animals and the use of manure. It was characteristic of William that although he lived in the country in a house with a garden, he had not consciously noted or understood any of these facts. This has a bearing on his poor school work. As already explained he had been so absorbed in his interior difficulties that he had been unable to be receptive to teaching from the outside.

Discussion. One of the reasons for which this child has been selected is that during his treatment various pieces of play occurred which we have observed as essential and recurring elements in the play of children under treatment. This ritual play of mixing sand and water, filling lorries or barrows with wet sand, moving these round and emptying the contents on the floor is a constantly recurring feature of the play of children both with and without fears about defaecation and can occur at any age.

William's dependence upon the adults of his family was shown in his desire, when this piece of play was completed, to show it to his grandmother who had brought him to the Institute.

During the next five sessions William initiated and worked out various kinds of play with trains, seen as trains (going-along-ness); trains and lorries filled with sand (containers); pouring, mixing, and the use of rubber tubes and funnels through which dry sand or water was poured. The contrast between Charles' and William's use of the idea of trains is of considerable importance. To Charles the aspect of trains, as he observed them, that which caught his attention, was their power. They were to him huge and massive objects which moved along irresistibly with great force – and therefore an appropriate symbol for E. The fact that their purpose was to contain people or goods appeared only later. To William this aspect of trains did not appear at all, the essential of a train to him was its length, its sinuosity as seen from a distance, and its likeness to the behaviour of long rubber tubes. Both boys used their ordinary play at home to express what was going on inside them: Charles played with small cars which he moved forcibly about on the floor with suitable noises: William spent his spare time with an electric train set to which he adopted an attitude like that to the rubber tubes in his World play. Noises played no part with him and he did not identify with the trains he used in therapy.

About this time he developed a new element in play. He would bury the rubber tube or tubes for part of their length under the sand, and experiment with what he could put in at one end and make travel to the other. This made possible the use of a piece of technique concerned with the sand which we find valuable. One of the basic difficulties of children of this kind is with location of space; they cannot conceive of their bodies as having an "inside" or of the structure of that "inside". I therefore moulded a body lying on its back or its face in the sand and with the help of thin rubber tubes demonstrated the intestinal structure of the body, linking it up with his play. In this it had become clear that he was doing his very best to project his bewilderment, his phantasies and his fears about urination and defaecation on to his play and to sort them out there.

The effect of this type of play and our discussions of it was shown in a piece of objective train play with clockwork trains on the floor, in which his manual skill and power of realisation of reality factors showed definite improvement. One session was also spent in the playroom shop, wrapping up and selling food, with fair competence and understanding. My note says "each week just a degree less strained and anxious". On the 24th session it became possible to discuss the question of girls and girls' bodies and William demonstrated vividly his confusions and spatial identifications of one part of the body with another by stating that what came out of the vulva in girls was milk. He then ran off to chalk elaborate but very sketchy systems of railway lines on the floor with coloured chalks and to try and get small goods trains to run over them.

World 14 Figure 51 (26th session)

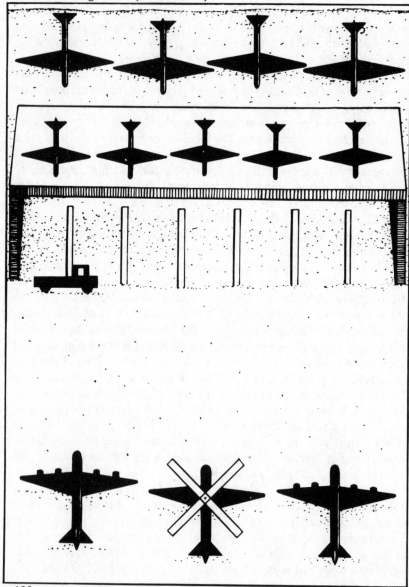

William arrived very eager, saying he was going to make an airport. As usual the sand was very carefully smoothed. He then fetched areoplanes and put a row along each short side of the tray facing inwards. He now began one of his curious muddled constructions in the centre which he said was to be "a garage for aeroplane-lorries". He made it of stakes on which he balanced wooden planks to make a roof, and then a further row of stakes outside; sand had to be spread carefully on the top of the roof. He then hammered it all down, not realising in the least, or being able to accept the fact that the roof must collapse if hammered. The roof was several times rescued and reconstructed and the collapses disturbed him a lot. He wanted pink sand inside the garage. Finally he placed one lorry by the side of the "entrance to the garage" and 5 small aeroplanes on the "roof". These, he explained, were fighter and bomber planes which rose from the ground, rested on the roof and then took off again.

He wanted to show this also to his grannie.

Discussion. In this world William moved on to express another element in the proto-system which has been described in the Introduction; its "global" nature. Up to this point we have been concerned with containers and contained, in their direct and inverse relation with each other, with movement along, and with ideas of depth. But up to this point there has only been fragmentary and short-term expression of movement up and down. Interest in this took place during one session in the period between this World and the last, when William discovered a crane and used it with enthusiasm to move his wet sand in containers up and down. World 14 is almost entirely concerned with movement up and down; and the confusion of ideas expressed in the central structure with its emphasis upon forcible down strokes (hammering), the smooth sand surface (as used for the base of trains and lorry tracks), and the idea that this is a garage, all indicate his struggle to express that this new element of up/down is somehow also part of all the other elements he has previously been working out.

This bizarre conception of aeroplanes which rise from the ground to rest on the roof of the garage and then take off again and which contain forcible objects that are ejected downwards from them, depicts a series of events which came to coherent expression very much later in the working out of large and elaborate structures with a crane in their centre, which lifted, mixed and emptied water and sand in imaginary building operations. This series illustrates that process of multi-dimensional "sensory/perceptual thinking", which seems to be necessary in some children before verbal understanding is possible.

World 15 *not illustrated* (27th session)

It was impossible to draw this World owing to the fantastic nature of what was attempted. William started as before with an elaborate sifting of sand and then mixing the sifted sand with water; the product was now "cement". William looked about to find a "base" for a "house", placed this on the tray and collected a store of wooden slats; from these he selected slats of equal length

191

with great care and tried to construct with them a house on the base, smearing the wet sand over the slats "to stick them together". When, with my help, some sort of a structure had been achieved, he was quite unable to accept the fact that a slanting roof could not be constructed with material of this kind (William's family house has a pointed roof). In the end he was able to persuade himself to accept a flat roof.

Discussion.   This World and the process of making it provides a clue to the nature of the perception of the outside world in children of this kind. Although William's manual dexterity had been steadily improving throughout treatment, it still remained at about a 4/5 year old level. He was unable to see the discrepancy between the materials he was using and the picture in his mind of what he wanted to achieve. The "cement" here picked up the theme of the cement mixer in Worlds 7 and 8 and showed how important this has been to him. The passage of time between that date and this showed also how much had had to be worked out in different lines of play before the significance of this object became evident to William.

On another plane the nature and the sequence of the two Worlds (14 and 15) repeats the sequence so often found in psycho-analytic work where emphasis upon the "masculine" (aeroplanes) with an aggressive and destructive element is followed by a "feminine" element (construction of house), with an attempt to restore what is phantasised as a possible destruction by the masculine element.

This session completed the Autumn term, and the Christmas holidays intervened. During these holidays the family reassembled at their own home and it was planned that William once more attend a day school. The holidays were spent with the parents away from home; the report on them runs, "He seemed happy, much more independent and there were no tempers; enuresis continued and defaecation fears were increased; apart from this, however, he is less timid and not so jumpy".

At the beginning of the next term William chose to play "Shop"; the fact that being inside the shop he could frustrate the adult caused him great excitement; his arithmetic was wild. The school reported: "some days he covers a reasonable amount of ground in arithmetic, at other times his mind appears to be a complete blank".

William's obsessional and ritualistic play with sand, water and colour continued. Exploration of his ideas concerning the inside of the body was taken up again. He denied any knowledge of the bladder, but had now become interested in discussing the structure of the body. A certain ability to conceive of structures as such and of their existing in an objective way apart from his feelings about them, made it possible to begin to separate out with him sensations, feelings, ideas and objective facts about the body. When, having got some of the objective facts straight, I asked him what picture came into his head when thinking about the bladder he said first "a fierce animal" and then "a great big man". He denied ever having done any urinary play himself. When we were talking of the making of babies he knew they grew inside their mothers and insisted that they were made of food. It was at this point that his mother ventured to talk about his masturbation to me, and William, when this was taken up with him, was very solemn about it.

William now changed his type of play. From having been "outside" his materials of expression, he, as it were, became "inside" them, making clear the importance of providing opportunities for other types of play in treatment of these children. For three sessions he chose the Mess Room and used the walls in the way he had previously used the floor of the ordinary playroom. On to the walls he projected a complicated series of lines, "going along" and up and down, which were at the same time railway systems. This play he alternated with periods in the shop. He seemed to be identifying himself with movements and procedures previously either imaged in objects in his Worlds, in the up/down movements of the crane and in manipulations of sand, water and tubes.

World 16   Figure 52 (35th session)

William cut out an oval road in the tray, exposing the blue base; it was important

to him that the outer bank should be high. He then placed an ambulance in the left nearer corner and a piece of fencing across this corner; the hospital to which the ambulance took people was said to be outside the tray on this side. Next he found a very big street-light and put it in the centre of the tray with a turnstile beside it. Then he cut a straight road across the sand to the left, parallel to the short side of the tray, and began to put traffic in. This was altered several times; the drawing represents the final position. A bus was placed by the ambulance, and a coal-cart and a large empty lorry in the straight piece of road. A "fire" was made with coloured sticks at the left far corner of the high bank, and a large petrol lorry was put exactly in the centre of the further stretch of road, and on the centre island to the right of the lamp a large ornamental metal gate. Road-mending-tools (road scoop, drill, break-down van) were grouped in the further right-hand corner, and a lot of time spent cutting the outer bank away to make "places where the traffic could pass". A coach was put in the near right-hand corner and beside it a dust-collecting cart, a new item to which William attached much importance; I was instructed to tear up a lot of paper and scatter it on the banks and in this cart. One other container, an empty trailer, was put in the right near corner. Traffic signs, telegraph poles and pieces of fencing were scattered without any meaning all over the scene, and one more street lamp added. In this whole scene there was one human figure: a "park-keeper" beside the turnstile.

Discussion. For all its confusion this is a very important World. Through projecting part of his proto-system into manipulative and part into symbolically acted-out play, William had arrived at a point when he had got his inner experiences sufficiently into order to attempt to put them into a collected objective expression.

This World introduced a number of new symbols and brought his objectification onto an entirely new line. The idea of damage-to-the-body, which had been latent hitherto, appeared in the ambulance and the concept of a hospital, while damage to machines was presented in the breakdown van. Fire appeared for the first time and the idea of a rubbish cart. William was emerging from complete absorption in sensorial experience to the formulation of ideas concerning it. The coal cart which appeared here for the first time is a particularly interesting feature since, in our experience, children at this stage so often use coal to link ideas of fuel, dirt, fire and excretion.

World 17 *not illustrated* (36th session)

At the beginning of the next session William said eagerly, as soon as he came in, "Can we do it again? There wasn't time last time to do it properly", the World of last time clearly appearing to him as a coherent "it" although so confused to anyone else's eye. Permission being given he reinstated the last World with all the details of World 16, but with the following differences.

This time William put two ambulances instead of one in the corner. He did not cut the straight road across the island. The road signs, etc. which seemed to me so haphazardly arranged were reinstated almost exactly as they were before. William's action all through were full of purpose and eagerness and it was clear that the whole had great significance for him.

Toward the end he said suddenly, "Now it is raining, will you get me some water", and when the water was brought he sprinkled it carefully all over the traffic, anxious that only a little should appear anywhere; but when by chance the road did get really wet, his eyes lit up and he seemed really to enjoy this.

Discussion. William's relation to this World and the nature of the World itself, resemble to some extent the attitude of primitive tribes to their tribal rituals, as observed by the anthropologists. To those who take part in the ceremony the whole is of deep significance and has interior coherence, but to an observer who lacks the clues, it may well appear an unconnected series of puzzling and often bizarre or trivial incidents.

These two last Worlds were carried out by William with eagerness, speed and intense concentration, and when completed they clearly gave him a feeling of intense satisfaction. Their "sense" seems to run as follows:

Layout. World 2 has a very similar layout except that the outer banks are missing; these banks, however, appear in World 4 where the outer oval waterway is almost exactly the shape of the road in Worlds 16 and 17.

Objects. Several of the items of traffic in these two Worlds appeared also in World 2, with the difference that while there was a fire engine in World 2 there is a "fire" in these Worlds. The apparent haphazard dotting of upright objects in these two Worlds strictly parallels the upright sticks in Worlds 4 and 5. The road-mending tools we have already met several times, but this time they are actually at work on a road. The dustcart is new; and this and the idea of rubbish scattered about the side aroused considerable excitement in William. As already pointed out the "fire" is also new and a great deal of attention was given to it. The odd pieces of fencing are reminiscent of those in World 7. The addition of "rain" at the end is an important point as this is the first time that water has been thought of as coming down from above rather than up from below; and except in the relation to the making of "cement", William had only played with water by passing it through rubber tubes. It was pointed out to William that although there was no danger in this World there were provisions against the possibility of danger.

At the next session William came in and said he wanted to make a bonfire. It was explained to him that this could be better done at home and his attention was deflected on to examining toys in the cupboard. An important "bridge" session followed. William found some toy bathrooms and with great excitement alternated between play with them and small quantities of water (showing much disappointment when the taps did not work and keen enjoyment when they did), and mixing "cement" on the World tray. He finally repeated his actions with the barn in World 9 and

195

"cemented" the bathroom into the sand in the tray. The whole play was impossible to report accurately or to follow, but clearly had important interior coherence to William.

World 18 *not illustrated* (38th session)

This World was William's first direct handling of water as such. He scooped all the sand away from one end of the tray, piling it up on the other side, poured in a little water and then more and more and floated boats on it; he became very excited and delighted with the real landslides that took place as the water undermined the sandhill. He then wanted to know how to get the water out of the tray and was shown how to siphon it out, but had great difficulty because he blew instead of sucking. Eventually he succeeded and then put it all back again, calling his mother in to see it. He finished by messing about with water and sand.

Discussion. This World marks a most significant step forward. Hitherto William's sensations, feelings, thought, phantasies about urination had gone into nocturnal enuresis, as those relating to faeces and defaecation had been expressed in daytime phobias. He had to some extent been able to express some of these in symbolic manipulative play, but had not so far arrived at a point where he could let himself experiment with water in mass. In this World water carried out for him "attacks" on wet sand, and this effect made a bridge for him from the "faecal" aspect of his previous play, to being able to make direct contact with water as a force.

It was then possible on the next session (39), the last of this term, to follow this up and to get him to spend it entirely in the water-room. Here William's play was very limited and devoid of imagination; his main activity was to fill the sink full with boats and to take great care that they should not bump into each other; his interest centered upon a long, pointed wooden boat.

Taken in connection with his enuresis, this last series of sessions is diagnostically revealing. Although continuously presented with the fact of fluid emerging from his own body, William had been quite unable to allow to himself any possibility of play either directly with urination in his home surroundings, or with water in treatment sessions. His imagination so far could function in connection with water only when he represented it to himself as a natural force, such as rain or the sea or as a strictly limited and controllable substance moving through tubes. His water-play in the Water-room gave a clue to the possible reason for this. Objectively on the level only of a 5-year old child, the form of this play suggested that the ideas explored by psycho-analysis in regard to the penis as a sexual rather than an excretory organ, and the phantasies connected with such ideas operated as an inhibition of all direct and/or aggressive play either with water as a force or with pointed objects in water.

During the Easter Holidays some mutual inspection play was reported between William and a neighbour's little girl, which was handled sensibly by the parents. William's mother reported that he had had a bicycle for 18 months but had never had the courage to ride it until this Easter when he suddenly began riding; he was dry that night. She reported too, that "if anything goes wrong he blames his mother". When he fell off his cycle for example he rushed up and said to her, "why didn't you prevent me falling off". When he hurt himself he was furious and crying at the same time.

At the beginning of the summer term my note runs, "William begins to look much more boyish and self-confident".

At the first session of the summer term (40th session) William made a Mosaic which gives valuable clues as to his perception of external objects and his capacity for arranging them. Up to this time William had made only five Mosaics, all of a very primitive type consisting in the main of a border of squares around the edge of the tray with blocks of pieces, mostly diamonds, in the middle. On this occasion, however, he settled down with concentration and started to make a line of red squares, each composed of 2 half-squares, along the left-hand edge (this used up 14 of the 16 available pieces). He followed this with 3 exactly similar columns of pieces in yellow, blue, white, the three together covering a third of the tray; having now used up all the half-squares available, except green and black (which colours he had avoided in other Mosaics) he set to work to try and see if he could use the scalenes. Here the same difficulty appeared as had been noted by Mrs. Lenore Schwartz while working as a member of Dr. M. Mead's 1955 expedition to the Admiralty Islands where she reported that the Manus were incapable of distinguishing between the isosceles and scalene triangles. William showed the same incapacity. He could not grasp the difference in length even after careful discussion; he used 20 of the available 24 red scalenes in an attempt to make a column of red, but in doing this did succeed in making two half hexagons as part of his column. He now thought he would try diamonds (with which it is impossible to make a vertical column), and made three oblique lines of all the available yellow diamonds. The top right-hand corner of the tray being still empty, he filled it with all available red diamonds. He would have liked to have used all the blue diamonds to cover the empty space at the bottom of the tray, but there was not room for them. He now surveyed the tray with pleasure, but noticing that there was a space at the bottom, below the four columns of squares, he filled this with 4 white diamonds and put the remaining 4 red scalenes in the gaps between this row and the yellow diamonds. He then began to cover the whole of this arrangement with a second layer of squares, fitting these exactly over his columns of half-squares columns. Then he had a new idea and alternated green and black in chessboard fashion for two columns, thus completing all six colours. Then he got stuck completely: he wanted to cover the whole of his first layer but, all the squares being now used up, could not think of anything to do. When I pointed out to him that there was a shape he had not tried at all, he was surprised but responded with pleasure, took out all the red equilateral triangles and arranged them in a column alongside the others. He then took all the blue equilateral triangles and attempted to do the same, but as he had started with a slight inaccuracy, only 11 would fit in, not 12. He continued with the yellow equilateral trainagles put together in pairs along the right-hand short edge.

While carrying out the second layer he commented on the shiny quality of the pieces, saying they "glittered". He was very pleased indeed to have been able to use nearly all the pieces in the box and remarked that the whole thing looked "very gay and very pretty".

Discussion. This Mosaic is an important indication of William's tendency to be dominated by a global form of thinking. In his constructions from now on he attempted to achieve 3-dimensional structures, even in the use of Mosaics. For a considerable period he made piles of Mosaic pieces which he endeavoured to compose into a design.

The next session began with a discussion of his work to date and an explanation from me. I pointed out the resemblance between 3-dimensional structures and bodies, explaining how houses were "mummyish" kinds of structures; I reminded him of his ideas that babies inside mummies were made of food, and linked this up with his own puzzled fears about what came out of the inside of his own body. I said further that although he knew now that this was *not* so, I thought he was trying to present to me and to himself in various media the earlier ideas that he had had about bodies in order to be able to look at them outside himself and to get them sorted out and discussed.

It was clear that this was on the right line because he became much freer, even becoming bullying to me.

World 19 *not illustrated* (41st session)

William cleared the tray and started making "cement", filling a truck on one side of the tray and emptying it on the other; he wanted to "make a house". When after a time he realised it was impossible to make this of sand, he reverted to the same idea as he had had in previous terms with Mosaics, and said he wanted to make a "wall" round the tray. I was told to help, and together we made a smooth wall around the four edges of the tray; when this was finished he emptied the truck in the centre of the tray and said he wanted to make a hill, but decided against this; he then heaped up about a 2-inch level of sand and smoothed it out into a square; he was vague about what this represented, but said it was something of the nature of a garden or a field.

Discussion. This was the first time William had demanded that his therapist take part in the making of a World and was a significant development. William's isolation from his environment was lessening and where his relation to his therapist had hitherto been almost entirely that of "containment" – that is his therapist's presence, interest and responsiveness had formed a "space" within which expression for William became possible – now it was a comradely cooperation in a task designed by William.

The interest of this World lies in the parallel between it and William's use of Mosaics and also in the example it provides of a typical piece of proto-system presentation. In William's use of Mosaics he first made frames around the edge of the trays with a something in the middle, and then later used all the pieces that the tray would hold to make a linear 2-layer design. In the World he made a "wall" around the edges of the tray and a square "field or garden" in the centre.

The fact that he set out to use "all the sand to make a house" (the essential of which is that it is a 3-dimensional hollow structure), and then made the walls of a hollow square with a solid block of "land" in the middle, is a typical proto-system presentation.

World 20   Figure 53 (42nd session)

William came in saying he wanted to make "a circus", but his conversation made it clear that he really meant a travelling fair and circus, not a circus in a town.

He smoothed the sand carefully and then dug out a circular ditch which had to be narrow, very smooth and very well defined. Within the arena he placed 9 circus items, but was really interested only in the triangle of acrobats, horse and ringmaster. He now began to look for objects which would do for the wagons; he accepted the covered wagon and team of horses, and put in a merry-go-round and a gypsy caravan; he then took the horses off and put them beside the wagon, and began to take out lorries and covered vans. He was particularly pleased with the milk-van which opened at the back, and excited about getting this filled with small beer barrels which he was prepared to accept as milk containers. He found two other carts, took the horse out of one, put it beside the cart, and added a swing and a foal. Near the caravan he put a small fire and an open seaside umbrella and two milk churns at the far right-hand corner. He now saw a couple of Bayko* rods and hailed them with delight; he started putting up rods around the edge of the outer circle. As soon as this was completed he began to struggle with the idea of balancing a rod across two uprights so as to construct an arch, and made his usual acute signals of distress when they would not stay on; the difficulty was overcome with the aid of plasticine and an entrance made on one side with an exit for animals opposite. At intervals while doing this William dashed to the drawer to get out ladders and piled these in groups in the carts. Taking more rods out, and using plasticine to fit them on, he made a ring round the arena. He then began to struggle with the ladders, trying to make them stand up against the upright rods. He was troubled because my fire engine was missing, not because he wanted to use it as a fire engine, but because he wanted the ladder which had an extension which could be used to make it longer or shorter; he also put in several other ladders at random. While making this circus he went on talking about a fair, making quite clear that the parts of the fair that were important to him were the shooting galleries and the coconut-shies. When this was finished William said it was very important that the garden tools which he had used in making it and then slung into the sand, should be drawn in at the opposite side.

He was very keen for his mother to see the World.

Discussion. A central point about this circus is that although William wanted to present the circus in action, the idea of spectators did not appear at all. In a way William was all the spectators. A second point was the eagerness with which the World was constructed, each item appearing as important as every other item. This World marked a step in development. Its underlying emotion is similar to that with which the model railway village (World 5) was constructed, but this World, for all its confusion, is very near to a realistic presentation of external fact with the facts in proper relation to each other. The area of Fair and circus were securely delimited from one another and there were very few irrational features. Milk for the first time appeared in a milk cart and milk churns and a primitive kind of "house" (caravan). From a psycho-analytical point of view the symbolism of this World brings it into the category of a tentative exploration of ideas of male and female, coitus, and the family, and links up well with and adds meaning to his circular Worlds.

The work tools which came in so often in his road Worlds as the embodiment of his struggle at realisation, appeared here in the scoop and

---

*A constructional toy.

miniature "World" tools used in making the World.

An important point about this World was the appearance of ladders. These were without function as ladders and William was so little interested in their purpose and used so many of them that they can only be regarded as symbolic.

The question of stimulus here is interesting. On his way to London William had seen a Fair on the road, and it is probable that this gave a shape to ideas which were struggling to find expression. Similarly, the fact that the Bayko rods were lying on the cabinet, suggested to him a way of putting thoughts into action. The similarity, however, between this World and his other circular Worlds, and its interior coherence, makes it probable that in any case he would have found other means for making the same pattern, or that, as in Mary's series, the circus would have appeared later, independent of outside stimulus.

World 21 *not illustrated* (43rd session)

William came in saying, "I am going to make the queen coming home".*

He started off to mix sand and water into a mouldable state, scooped up the sand along the centre of the tray saying, "this is the Thames", and made sharp-topped walls along both sides of the river; he then found the largest boat and put it in the centre of the river and in it a figure in historical robes which he called the Queen, placing a small boat behind it. He found the Tower Bridge, played with it for a little, and then put it ahead of the Queen who was entering from left to right. Along the side of the river nearest to him he set the Coronation coach followed by a band in single file. He spent the rest of the time choosing and arranging people in rows at both sides looking at the procession, with policemen to keep them in order. He was particularly keen to have country people who had "come up to town for the day to see the Queen".

Discussion. The fact of Queen Elizabeth's actual homecoming, which took place about this time, gave William an opportunity to focus and express the intensity of his feeling about his mother. She is for him "the Queen", the centre point and highlight of his world, the cause of excitement and the focus of emotion. Such a World, regarded from the point of view of the unfolding of expression of emotions central to himself, followed naturally upon the last World.

World 22   Figure 54 (44th session). See page 202.

William cleared the tray free of sand and went to the chest and got out building bricks, saying he was going to make the Forth Bridge. He took real trouble to fix these bricks together along each short side of the tray, and constructed 3 piers across the centre, laying slats on top of them to form a bridge on which he put a big train; he connected some small trains, placing them along either side. He

---

*Queen Elizabeth II had recently been abroad.

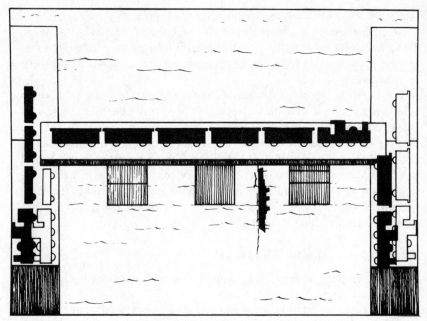

then got a lot of water and poured it into the tray, and put a boat going under the bridge.

Discussion.　　There was a marked improvement in this session in William's practical handling of objects. It is noteworthy that the chest with the big bricks had been available all the time, but William had taken no notice of it and instead had given me peremptory orders to fetch such building material as he needed. This time he opened the chest and looked for and handled the material himself, producing a workman-like structure. But it did not occur to him that, placed as he had put it, the trains could not get on to or off the bridge. This attempt to construct a massive bridge representing an outstanding one over which he had been in reality, fits in with William Carter's use of bridges. They are not real as Charles' has been, but were part of a symbolic idea: this construction was the combination of bridge and trains *on* bridge, water, boat *under* bridge and was more a realistic presentation of a global conception of movement.

At the next session William made a Mosaic which he said was "a maze" although not in the least like one, and then attempted to "build a house" with Bayko. Although his ability to manipulate objects was considerably improved, his use of it showed that the symbolic values of the rods and the tiles which fit between them, dominated what little power he had to plan. He achieved only the front of the house with two bay windows.

World 23　Figure 55 (46th session)

William went straight to World tray and began smoothing the sand, then pulled

202

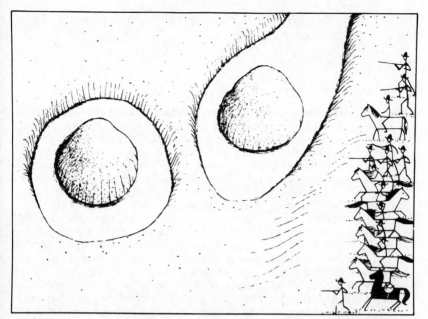

out the drawer of Indians and started selecting single Indians, inspecting each carefully and rejecting all on horseback. These were placed in a row along the furthest edge of the tray facing inwards. Khaki soldiers of all sorts were then chosen and placed along the end nearest him, and to begin with the numbers of the two sides were equal; later this was not kept to. Among the khaki soldiers were a number on horseback and several of the very big horses (one rearing back "startled").

Across the middle he now built a wall of sand and reinforced this by the addition of two rows of fencing on the side of the soldiers. When all was ready he said the fight was to begin. He took the soldiers, but from the outset the Indians had no chance whatever. He took firm hold of the rearing horse and charged with him all over the tray "killing" all the Indians and trampling them down. I did my best to put up a fight for the Indians but William was quite ruthless. When all the Indians were dead, he collected roughly half of them, saying, "they were all dead and must now be buried", and putting them in a pile he heaped sand over them so that it made a circular hill. Around this he cleared a circular moat and then repeated with the remaining Indians making an exactly similar mound and moat. His movements throughout were quick and definite. He showed his mother the finished tray but did not explain what had brought it about.

Discussion. As with Charles, at the moment when he wished to express aggression in his play, the conventional figure of the Red Indian provided William with a means of doing so. This is the first time that William had made a fight. It is a curious one in that no actual fighting took place. All the horsemen were on one side, and one large horse was the instrument of massacre of the whole of the other side. These (ideationally) "bad men" were now buried in breastlike mounds with moats round them; they are probably the "bad breasts" of his early feeding history. This is

203

the first time that what William had done in play had a direct connection with his personal history.

World 24 *not illustrated* (47th session)

This session was a very confused piece of play.

William was very eager to make another fight, and while I was explaining that people in olden times did bury their dead in mounds of this sort (referring to his last World), he was carefully selecting two kinds of soldiers and setting them out at opposite ends of the tray. One lot was his side, the other mine. I was, however, allowed no cannon. As soon as they were arranged William said it was time to begin; but he had no idea at all of playing in any fair or orderly fashion; instead he took one of his own men and drove across at mine with overwhelming force, and said they were "all dead". He then said he would bury these and started making a mound as at the session before, fetched water to fill the moat round the mound. During the making of the second mound he lost interest and it was only perfunctorily completed. At this point I was called away for a short period and on return I found that he had abandoned the mounds, had got the large hollow bricks out of the chest and was experimenting with various arrangements of them, combined with soldiers and cannon. In the end he set up two towers of the bricks on top of which military bands were put and were said to be playing very loudly. On the sand beside the towers were some military transport and between the towers a lot of standing soldiers. He was particularly keen to show this to his mother.

Discussion. The development of the World of the last session into this World shows an alteration between explicitly feminine and explicitly masculine symbolism which occurs very frequently in children's Worlds. In my handling of World 23 the question also of interpretative technique arises. The World of the two mounds and the buried soldiers was the first appearance of any direct material of this sort. It came suddenly, with a terrific burst, and there was no evidence at all from previous work as to how William would react to such an outburst. There was a gap of eleven days between World 23 and the next session.

I felt that the fighting/mounds World had to be anchored to reality at some point; but the richness of significance which had been packed into the last World and the absence of any prepared ground for direct interpretation made me wish to wait a while, knowing William's explosive nature, until there was more evidence as to his outer reactions to this inner material which was bursting up through him. I therefore decided to take the other line and link for him the side of his World which was the "burial of the dead" with old customs. This may or may not have steadied him; as far as the development of his second fighting World was concerned, it probably had no effect, as this developed in an "expected" way. William started off in this World as he had in the previous one, only with me as the antagonist. Here appeared a characteristic about which his mother had told me shortly before, i.e., that he could not bear not to win in a game. The free expression

204

of aggressiveness in this World signalled a big increase in confidence, and William was no longer afraid to let himself go. He repeated the actions of the previous World and these acted as a bridge to the phallic masculine aggressiveness which he now found a way to depict.

All was going well and from that moment on progress would probably have been rapid. But this was, in date, toward the end of June and an unfortunate illness of mine interrupted treatment, and the Summer holidays followed.

In August of that year a letter was received from the parents, saying they wished to discontinue his weekly session on the grounds that they had had a good school report and that William was about to move up to another form where absences from school for treatment would be adversely commented upon by the other boys. The letter continues, "we are so pleased with William's behaviour now and his ability to deal with life as it comes; he has in fact greatly improved and we are sure he will be able to stand on his own feet successfully".

Treatment was therefore discontinued.

Reporting Visits

Arrangements were made for William to come for a reporting visit during the Christmas holidays. This appointment however was not kept owing to the father's being posted away from home. Mrs. Carter reported two weeks before the end of term: "William is behaving very well, enjoying school and doing well, seems to have more confidence; bedwetting improving": the appointment was therefore postponed to the Easter holidays.

Before the date of that visit Mrs. Carter wrote, "He has been getting on well with the exception of a tempestuous time before Chrstmas, but has improved a lot during this term".

At the time of this reporting visit Mrs. Carter was interviewed by the Social Worker and reported: On the whole good and calm but round Christmas William began to bite his nails and say he was dreading going back to school.

Exploration of this by the parents ascertained genuine bullying at school, which was checked by the Headmaster and a rapid improvement followed. "He bicycles to and from school and is helpful to his mother". The enuresis was inconsistent, periods of dry nights coming at times of strain and wet patches when he was apparently happy. He is "mad on bonfires and makes two or three a day, putting them out with water". At the end of the interview Mrs. Carter casually mentioned that over Christmas William had had influenza, "looked awful" and had been constipated. *Concerning the Easter holiday visit* my notes run:

"Wlliam has grown a lot and filled out somewhat; manner still jerky but definitely more at ease than when last seen".

He began the session with a Mosaic* which was a combination of a "house" and a "fountain", untidily extended. He then made a World which broke new ground for William. This was a type of World which occurs constantly in the Worlds of children of all ages and which is, to some extent, a natural derivative from the "farms" that form an ordinary item of toy shops.

World 25 Figure 56 (1st follow-up visit)

William smoothed the sand most carefully and collected a large number of fences which he arranged without gates, across the short side of the tray, thus enclosing one-third of the tray. Into this field he put 3 trees, 8 cows and a calf and a farmhand with a fork near a sheaf of corn. The left-hand near corner was enclosed by a semi-circular fence, in which was placed a tree and 3 bulls. He then fenced in a third field, next to that with the cows and along the further edge of the tray; in this he put 3 trees and 6 horses. He then took a lot of trouble to find a farmhouse that he liked and placed this in the near right-hand corner with a patch of "grass" to the left and a small chicken-run beside that; the farmer stands outside the house by the grass. Above the house was a barn and above that a man sweeping; between the house and the barn were another farmhand and a woman with a hen; at the far right-hand corner a tree with a tractor beside it. In the centre of the tray he put a farm lorry with a trailer and a milkmaid passing it.

Discussion. William worked with great concentration. When finished the World was very neat, tidy and well constructed. This was a very normal

*Described in detail, page 243, no. 9.

sort of World and different in every way from anything William had done before. The one unusual feature was the three bulls in the one small field.

An appointment was made for a second reporting visit at the end of the summer holidays.

In July (just one year after treatment had ceased) Mrs. Carter wrote: "William has made great strides this term. He has learned to swim at school which was not easy for him as he has always feared the water. He is getting on well at school and having lots of fights, which he nearly always wins. The change is quite astonishing, he looks happy and is so full of himself. He no longer goes to school reluctantly and he returns calm. We have had a few dry nights but not many".

In September William came for his *second reporting visit*. My note runs, "still apt to be stiff and compulsive but very glad to be back". He started straight away on a World.

World 26   Figure 57 (2nd follow-up visit)

William asked if we had some pink sand, smoothed the sand in the tray carefully explaining that he was going to make a farm. He took out a very large number of farm animals, put them in a heap; he said he was going to use very many fences and wanted a gate that swung open. He arranged the fences to make a very large field in the centre of the tray, reaching to the further edge which formed the fourth side. He then took out 2 farmhouses and placed them at the left edge, one at the far, and one at the near corner, and carefully constructed a path made of pieces of mock pavement leading from one to another. He next got out two farm carts, moved them about and finally placed them at the far right-hand corner. He placed a pond at the near right-hand corner of the field. He now began to put the animals in; he called attention to the cow and the pigs, put a bird on the pond (which pleased him), and he said he wanted many horses ("I like horses"). He then put a man carrying milk pails on the path between the houses, and a shepherd in the field. When the enclosure was full of mixed animals, William began putting cows outside the fence, between it and the edge of the tray; these were arranged in a procession, moving round the corner to the right toward the open gate, where a farmhand stood as if to see them safely into the field. Behind the cows he placed 2 bulls saying that they were being driven into the field. Near the front house was a man carrying a lamb. A farm cart with a trailer (he wanted a tractor, but we could not find one) were on the left between the pavement and the field with a farmhand standing beside it; 2 other farmhands were placed among the animals in the field, and one outside to the right. Although it appeared that the animals had been put in haphazardly, one bull was about to toss a lamb.

Conversation. When the World was finished I asked William to consider what would happen if it came alive. Very reluctantly he concluded that a number of fights would arise. He slowly worked out for himself that the two bulls would fight on account of being jealous about the cows; and he agreed that the lamb, about to be tossed, was himself and that the bull stood probably for his father.

It was then suggested that he make a Mosaic.

*Mosaic.** William made four widely separated columns of squares, which he said were "pillars". In the centre between these pillars he made what he called "a fountain" with red scalenes, arising from a green base.

As the situation presented in this World and the mosaic embodied so many features characteristic of the Mother/son relationship which were now coming to clearer expression, a second session was arranged for in order to explore the situation further.

Construction. At this session William was shown a new apparatus for large scale construction; he was interested and set to work. His control had improved but he stuck at any point where a temporary solution had been reached and could not see the next step, or when he had made a mistake could not see what to do about correcting it. (Mrs. Carter reported that with similar material at home nothing would induce him to do anything but copy set designs and he demanded her presence all the time). William recounted the following *dream:*

He was on a very high bridge with two boys from his school; there were railway lines along the bridge but no trains in sight; along the lines were several small structures resembling huts facing the railway lines. The boys from school went into the first hut, but stopped short because the ground fell away in a sheer drop toward the back; he nearly fell down it but quickly recovered himself and came out. William went into the next hut and had the same experience. He then woke up.

We discussed his last two Worlds and in the discussion it became clear that

*Detailed description, page 243, no. 10.

everything that had previously been grasped about bodies and their workings, sex, and its functioning, had been pushed out of his mind.

Putting all the evidence together it was pointed out to the parents that if he was to recover from his enuresis, treatment must be resumed. They agreed, and as my timetable was completely full it was arranged that William be admitted to the I.C.P. for treatment by a staff therapist (non-medical) as soon as a vacancy could be found.

Second Period of Treatment

Two months later treatment was resumed. His therapist notes: "William has grown into a tall, slim boy, determined in what he wishes to do, clear about what he is looking for and critical as to whether the objects fit his purpose or not. Works quickly, not on impulse, but following a pre-conceived plan".

World 27 Figure 58 (50th session)

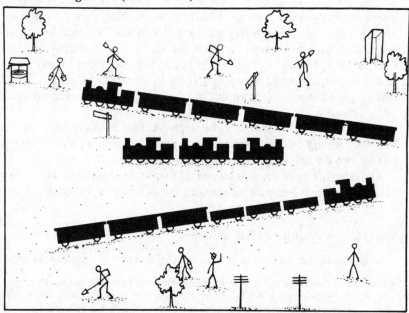

He asked for pink sand which the therapist set out to make while William constructed the World. He smoothed the sand and constructed two long banks, one parallel to the nearby and onto the further edge of the tray. He then drew railway lines in the centre of the tray in the flat sand on which he put 3 trains; one was a long-distance train going to Glasgow, another an ordinary goods-and-passenger-train without specified destination, and between them two engines towing a third engine. The trains were first made to go in the same direction, then the nearer one was turned round. The pink sand was now spread over the banks which were said to have caught fire owing to a long dry period; firemen

209

were placed along the banks to put the fire out. On the banks were 4 trees and 2 telegraph poles. A well was placed in the left further corner, its bucket filled with water, and beside it a man carrying two pails. A workman's hut was put in the further right-hand corner. Finally 2 signals were placed at appropriate points.

Discussion. This World began a new phase. William now made Worlds which were in the main realistic in that while it is very improbable that exactly what he set out *would* happen, there is no denying that it could.

Railways and a high bridge with a train on the bridge had appeared in World 22; in this World there was no idea of movement nor would it have been possible. The concepts of trains which move, and of a high bridge now appeared separately: the high bridge in a dream*, the moving trains in a World. In both, the idea of potential danger was present. What is very interesting about this World is that it presents exactly the situation William had been earlier playing out at home (making bonfires and putting them out with water) combined with his earlier train symbol. The small train is between the two big ones (Mrs. Carter had reported William getting into her bed in the morning), but the water puts out the fire: the enuresis quenches the fire of the emotional feelings within him toward his mother. Here an obvious question is: "why was this World, and particularly its connection with his enuresis and his getting into his mother's bed, not interpreted to William?" The answer is that this was a first World with a new therapist; there had been a long break in treatment before this World and no preparation laid down out of which such an interpretation could grow naturally.

About this time William's mother reported that he still wetted his bed but was "getting on fine at school; he would now go to a public lavatory, but still would not use the one he is afraid of at home".

At the beginning of the next session a *Mosaic*† was suggested. He made a "magic Christmas tree with decorations out of doors in the snow".

World 28 *not illustrated* (51st session)

William said he was going to present the making of a new main road.

A strip along the centre of the tray was hammered hard and flat and the therapist was asked to provide slats of different lengths. William drew 2 parallel lines in the sand, to mark out this strip and put a big red lorry in the centre with another lorry and a road-mending machine beside it. Signals with "road work ahead" and "no entry" were placed at either end of the strip of road, and a steamroller near the front edge of the tray. In a workman-like fashion he began to dig a narrow strip along each side of the road, hammered the remaining sand, and fitted the slats in as pavement. Various workmen were now put along the further and nearer sides of the road.

---

*Page 208, second follow-up visit.
†See detailed description, page 244, no. 11.

Discussion. This World is in its way an illuminating statement. In starting treatment again William is indeed "laying foundations for a new main road". In the World the work is well advanced; "No Entry" signs keep interfering traffic away; the usual road tools were present and the work was orderly. It is interesting that the outline of the road was so firmly made as this had not happened before. There was also a process of "digging down" to make the foundations firm, whereas up till now the "going-down" direction has been either a sign of danger (as in World 18 and in William's dream) or to a secret place as in earlier Worlds.

World 29   Figure 59 (52nd session)

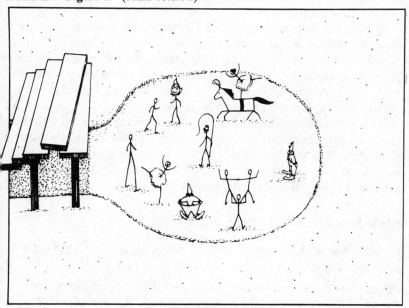

William rushed in saying he knew exactly what to make, and asked the therapist to collect "circus people" from the cabinet while he started with the sand.

He casually drew an oval in the sand, using a small spoon. He then asked for sawdust, but as there was none, he accepted pink sand instead and used this for indicating the line. He then started to build the archway to the circus on the left. He seemed to have a definite idea in his mind and took great trouble with the help of his therapist, to find the right sticks to carry over the roof and the right wooden slats which would cover the entrance completely. He worked on the construction of this archway for the whole session, using plasticine to stick the roof on to the edge of the tray; and as time was now up he asked the therapist to put the circus performers in; it didn't matter in what order, except that the ballet girl had to be put on to the back of the galloping horse.

Discussion. William's return to the theme of a circus after a "road-

211

making" World, is an interesting example of the spiral movement of "thought" which so frequently appears in this process of self-realisation. In Worlds 16 and 17 William made a circular road, and used the road-making tools, stating that they were "mending the road". In World 19 he used wet sand to build a wall, outlining the edge of the tray, with a field in the centre "to grow things in" (this took place at the beginning of a new term). He followed these with the elaborate circus of World 20. World 29 is circular too, but it is the centre of the circus only that is presented; William's own interest was focused upon the entrance, not upon the circus itself. In his previous circus World, an entrance and an exit "for the animals" has been indicated and it was at and around the entrance that the ladders were placed.

In World 29 there appeared another aspect of the 3-dimensional space-concepts implied in the arrangement of ladders and entrance in circus World 20. His use of slats and his struggle to manage these and to find out how they could be made to stay up and to form an enclosure, links back to his earlier struggles with the same slats when he endeavoured unsuccessfully to build a "house". In World 29 the entrance to the circus was roofed over, nothing went through it, and William saw it essentially as an enclosed space leading into an oval-shaped arena in which human movement took place. The implication of a womb symbol is clear and is further stressed by the fact that the only circus performer that William was concerned about was the girl on the galloping horse.

World 30 *not illustrated* (53rd session)

Again William knew exactly what he wanted to make and worked with great speed.

He piled mouldable sand up against the right-hand short side of the tray and made a hill sloping toward the centre which he said was a skiing hill; he then asked for a toboggan, but as there were none exactly of the type he required, he accepted the only one available. He then placed a male and a female figure (said to be a daddy and a mummy) on the sledge and explained they "had to go first"; he then changed his mind, removed the female figure, and seated it at the back of the hill saying, "she prefers to watch". He next put a girl on a sledge behind the father, and a boy walking up hill. He then sprinkled dry sand over the hill, saying it was "snow", and asked the therapist to take out some pine trees to be placed on both sides of the hill.

Discussion. This World illustrates another aspect of picture-making. William's family was not one which went to Switzerland for winter sports, so that although it was made in December it could not be a representation of actual events. It reproduced the spatial qualities of World 18 with the difference that instead of the emphasis being laid upon "that which is below" attacking the hill which stretched above it, the emphasis was now

212

upon the hill as the starting point for a descent. This hill was built in the same part of the tray as that in World 18; but whereas in World 18 the "sea" undermined the hill and carried it away, in World 30 the hill itself and its steep slopes formed the basis of satisfaction. Around this hill conical fir trees were placed (these were the trees which throughout his series of Worlds carried with them an aura of "Christmas tree").

The following two sessions were spent in making a World which was meant to be a representation of the London railway station he arrived at when coming for his session, "with Christmas decorations". (This was in December, and during his last visits before Christmas).

The first of these sessions was spent making the preparations: measuring out the tray, planning where to put things, and looking up all the objects required so as to be ready to make the World next time. The therapist noted that William was looking very pale at this time.

World 31 *not illustrated* (55th session)

William put 4 coloured sticks upright in the tray, each one a short distance from the corners, and 4 other sticks upright between these, but nearer the centre. To the tops of these sticks he tied green cotton connecting the corner ones diagonally, and the others across, the lines meeting in the centre of the tray; these were for the Christmas decorations to be attached to. Two boxes for ticket collectors were placed at the right-hand side, with a crowd of people passing them. A cardboard box was painted like the station and placed at the far right-hand corner. Steps were carefully made in the sand supported by small wooden slats, leading down to the Underground Station. At the far left-hand corner was a letter box. To the left two cars were leaving the station and in the middle at the nearer edge of the tray parcels were being unloaded from a lorry by 3 porters.

Discussion. This World completed the cycle of 5 Worlds made during this term. The first (27) was concerned with trains on the surface (not underground), and the banks were on fire. In World 31 trains were implied but not presented. The station is represented with a dual purpose: on one side it is the terminus of electric trains arriving from the nearer counties, on the other is one of a series of stations of an underground railway, leading into the centre of London (real). William knew about this underground Railway but did not travel by it. The World repeated the general idea of the circus World in that it was the entrance which William presented; but in calling it "the entrance to the Underground Railway" he gives it the additional dimension of depth. Through concentrating upon the ticket collectors, he combined this with the concept of "going in and out".

These Worlds were made on December 13 and 20 when there actually were Christmas decorations in the station, but it is interesting that in describing these William did not use the world "glittery" which he had so often used before. The concepts of containers and contained which had been presented in so many ways in previous Worlds also appeared here in the lorry with the porters unloading parcels, and the private cars turning out of the station.

The Christmas holidays intervened here. Mrs. Carter reported that William had had 4 dry nights running and that he was now going to the lavatory in trains.

Work in the spring term opened with the making of a Bayko house. William showed considerable progress in constructive power and ability to plan.

At his second visit William made a World in which he returned to the theme which has so far only appeared in his isolated follow-up visits.

The therapist noted that he looked better, and was eager and full of initiative as usual.

World 32 Figure 60 (57th session)

William started by smoothing the sand. He asked for farmhouses and found two identical cottages which he placed together at the further left corner, saying they were one farmhouse. Further along the edge he placed 2 stacks of corn and hay, fencing them in all round ("so that the cows shall not go and eat it"). He continued putting in fences and making fields with odd corners here and there. In the centre of the tray is a large field with 6 cows, a calf and two drinking troughs; it has open gates to the right and 5 horses are entering it; by the open gates are 2 farmers and 2 dogs. Attached to the nearer side of this field was an irregular rectangular enclosure in which William put 4 bulls in pairs opposite to each other. He said they were "having a fight, but not a serious one". At the right-hand further corner were 2 chicken houses with chickens inside them, and outside them one hen and a man. All these were fenced in. At the short edge of the tray to the left he made an irregular enclosure in which were 2 cows with piglets and a pig, and in the near left-hand corner another enclosure with 4 sheep and a shepherd. Outside the farmhouse are the farmer and his dog, with another farmer outside the pigs' field.

When this World was finished William sprinkled it all over with dry sand, which he said was "snow, covering it all".

Conversation. William had spent his holidays on a farm and he had enjoyed it very much, and he hoped to be going there again. He explained that in the World there were gates into all the fields which could be opened everywhere. He watched the World being drawn by the therapist to make sure it was recorded correctly.

William then made a *Mosaic** which he said was "a fountain with walls".

Discussion. This World, as frequently happens in the course of therapy, shows the same influence of contemporary events as the station World. The scene it presented was possible, and showed William's increasing power of grasping and presenting external facts. The central feature of this World is the field with the four bulls and later the coming of snow. This is the clearest statement of antagonism between males that William has so far permitted himself. The Mosaic in its way was also a clear presentation of his enuresis.

Part of the next session was occupied in conversation, the therapist pointing out how "islands" of energy and force had been appearing in his Worlds, but separated from each other and needing to be put together, with himself steering the whole. The fact of the four bulls being penned in a very small field in which they were fighting was connected with the bright red fountain of the Mosaic enclosed between strong walls.

Meantime William has been using a new construction toy to build a big bridge on the floor; he put an arch over it, ran trains along and on to a ferry boat with other trains in a station beside it. His manual dexterity showed considerable improvement.

World 33 Figure 61 (59th session). See page 216.

William went straight to the tray and smoothed the sand. He then collected from the cabinet all available road signs and some lamp posts, put them on a table near the tray, and then looked for lorries and cars. He put the big street lamp in the centre of the tray with a smaller lamp post to the left and a telegraph pole further down to the right. He then arranged a row of traffic going across the further (short) edge of the tray, headed by a fire engine, with an overturned bus in the middle. Another line of traffic was arranged coming from the nearer left-hand corner, crossing the tray diagonally and passing to the right of the big street lamp. He next rearranged some of the cars at the nearer end of the tray, turning them in different directions; overturned a green lorry as if the tip-up lorry behind it had run into it (all this was *arranged*, not played out). An ambulance was placed

---

*Detailed description, page 244, no. 12.

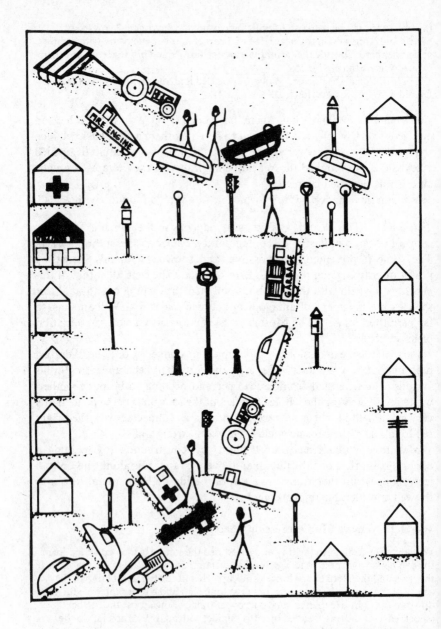

nearby "to take people to hospital". The traffic- and road-signs already selected were now put in at various places, and 5 policemen distributed at the critical points. Finally William placed a row of houses along the right- and left-hand (long) sides; the house to the left, at the further end, was "a hospital" and the one next to it "the village inn". On looking through the drawers, William came across some farm machinery, and found a harrow which he liked very much, and placed it with a tractor at further left corner.

Conversation. The therapist discussed the World with William, and drew particular attention to the fact that the overturned bus and lorry at the further and nearer ends were presented as events which had already happened. Also that the traffic was arranged in such a way that if it were to start moving, more accidents would happen. The contrast between the overturned bus at the further end (about which William had said nothing) and the overturned lorry at the nearer end where an ambulance was provided, was discussed. The whole scene was compared to blocks in the movement of E. The interesting fact that the scene presented accidents that had already happened, made it possible to explain to William that this blocking was due to factors which "had already happened", and further that, in spite of the policemen and the best that they might be able to do, the arrangement of the traffic, would inevitably cause future trouble unless something was done to reorganise it.

Following this conversation William used a rubber building toy to make a long solid wall expanded in the middle to form a solid rectangular block, which he called "the stationmaster's house". He did not realise until it was pointed out to him that although he called this rectangular block of solid rubber a "house", it was impossible to get inside it and it had neither doors nor windows.

Discussion. As was pointed out at the beginning of this series of Worlds, especially with reference to World 6, the really surprising characteristic about William was the divorce between the true character of the objects put in his Worlds and his use of them. William's ideas concerning his own body and its relation to the outside world was so fantastic, and at the same time so hidden from William himself, that his Worlds stand in a class by themselves. In the three years between the making of World 6 and World 33 William had made great progress. Not only was he now three years older (nearly 11) and had therefore a more reliable and extensive knowledge of the outside world, but he was also able at last to picture interior conflict and stress in terms of everyday possibilities instead of highly obscure symbols. In this World accidents are something that had *already* taken place but the cause of which was not known to him; it was in rescue and not in the accident that human beings appeared. Further the accidents appeared to arise from the vehicles themselves rather than from any idea of human beings driving them.

The rubber house. In World 9 a "barn" was "cemented" into a hillside. The question of whether this wooden object was thought of by William as hollow or solid cannot be determined, because the possibility that he might think of it as solid had not then been thought of, and in the nature of the case the toy used was hollow, being intended to represent a barn. The fact that William made his present "stationmaster's house" a part of a long solid wall, parallels the construction of the World of the cemented-in "barn" with the road upon which it stood.

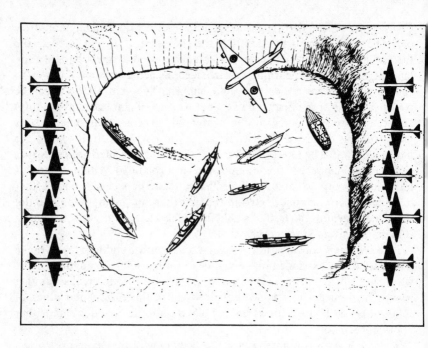

World 34   Figure 62 (60th session).

William scooped the sand away from the centre of the tray, leaving fairly high banks along all the four edges. He then took out 6 warships and placed them in the cleared space, which was the sea; in the centre of this he put a submarine, a liner lying on its side, with a coastguard's boat at the right further corner near the liner. He next selected aeroplanes of a similar size and type, and put 5 planes on each bank, to the left and right of the sea, facing each other. He then wanted a big aeroplane "flying right over the sea" and took great trouble to fix it on to a stick with plasticine (the therapist promised to draw it flying). He explained that the liner had been escorted by warships and a submarine, and had been attacked by other warships and sunk; the coastguard had come out and rescued a few people from the liner. Finally he poured water into the "sea".

Discussion.   This World has been selected as the terminal point for this extract from William Carter's case because it presents so much of the material symbolically represented in World 4, but now embodied in real life objects. It therefore enables us to make a survey of the whole series of Worlds up to date in relation to the themes we are considering in this book.

In this World all three dimensions were present and movement took place in each. The use of still water was new, the surface of the water took the place of his usual surface of land. Nothing moved on the land although 10 planes rested on it; but 6 gunboats and a coastguard's boat moved over the surface of the water, and below the surface a submarine. An aeroplane flew overhead. Partly on and partly under the surface lay the result of disaster, an overturned liner which had been attacked by a warship. Some of the people in this liner were being rescued by the coastguard's vessel.

In World 4 these themes were presented through the medium of fish, crocodiles, seals and men; the whole scene being entirely fantastic. In World 34 these same themes reappear through presentation of men-who-live-under-water (submarines), machines that move aggressively above ground (aeroplanes), and ships that move on the water (islands of "land" in the water); these are attacked by war machines operated by men.

Although this is a convenient moment to complete our series, nine months later William made a World which so neatly completes part of his series that it is appended here.

During these nine months William had made steady progress in the development of his personality. His relation to his sister had become satisfactory; his mother reported that rages were a thing of the past. His relation to his mother had also improved considerably, his dependence on her had become much lessened and he was more able to find his own occupations. His relation to his father, however, remained unsatisfactory. At school he had become a normal school boy and was able to make friends with his fellows, although school work remained poor. Certain fears remained; he was inhibited in the use of certain lavatories and his enuresis continued in a patchy manner.

At the beginning of the Autumn term, when he was $11\frac{1}{2}$ years old, he made this World which is the last of our illustrations.

World 46   Figure 63 (76th session). See page 220.

William first smoothed and flattened the sand carefully. He then drew with his fingers a pattern which he called at one moment "roads" and at another "streams", and smoothed their edges. The stretches of sand between these he called "islands", exactly as in World 4, but with the difference that the surrounding circle which in fact makes them into islands, was in this World not drawn, the edges of the tray to some extent fulfilling this function. William now quickly picked out some trees from the drawers, working with intense concentration and delight. He was, he said, making "a garden of trees of all kinds", "it was an experimental garden with little streams between the trees; it was very well guarded because the trees were very valuable; some of them had never been grown in England before; there were instruments to tell if the trees had water enough and if their roots went deep enough; they were guarded day and night". By this time he had set out a lot of trees on his islands. He now asked for water; but when it was pointed out to him that if he added water the shape of the islands would melt away, he accepted the blue bottom of the tray as a substitute.

While he was talking about this it became very noticeable that to him the "road" and the "stream" were identical. For example, the further, direct way from the centre to the right-hand edge he called a stream, pointing out that the water fed the islands on both sides of it. The oblique way, on the other hand, which also leads from the centre to the right-hand edge, he called a road, whereas the oblique way to the left corner was a "stream". The direct way in the middle of the left-

hand side was "a kind of road", while the one to the further left-hand corner was again a "stream". When the setting out of the trees was finished William began to take out all sorts of different men with rifles; these were to guard the trees day and night; they were dispersed among the trees over all the islands in pairs; one pair on each side of the centre way; they were, he said, standing "at the mouth of the stream". William was asked what the guards were doing; he said they were there "to guard the trees from people who might want to damage or steal them". Discussion made it clear that he had no idea at all of a spatial localisation of this "danger"; there was no barrier of any kind round the islands, and the guards faced all ways and were in all positions, so that the danger was "just there" without any specific location. Finally William arranged the military band marching in single file along the centre road. As he was finishing William said, "wouldn't it be nice if it was all lit up".

Discussion. World 46 repeats a great deal of the structure of World 4 seen from another point of view; it therefore illuminates a good deal which has already been discussed.

Three ideas predominate: Firstly, that of preciousness – something that needs to be very carefully and continuously guarded, or to which "people" might cause damage; this preciousness is, however, not expressed as gold underground (as in World 6) but in living trees that grow. These trees take the place of the coloured "dry" sticks of World 4 and several subsequent Worlds. Secondly, the idea of gaiety; this idea of festival, decorations and lights which has appeared many times in the Worlds and Mosaics, is expressed here in the marching bandsmen and the wish that it was all "lit up". Thirdly, the identification or confusion of road and river; William feels the presence in his World of *movement*, of water soaking into the ground, of streams flowing along the ways, of men "standing in the mouth of the streams", and that all this helps the trees to grow. Here we have all the feeling of excitement and preciousness of urine and of phallus that lies behind his enuresis and which will continue to take this form until he has found a way of expressing these feelings and ideas in real life.

General Review of William Carter's Worlds

In almost every respect William's response to the possibilities of the World apparatus was radically different to Charles' (Case 2). If we now review William's Worlds under the same headings as we have used for Charles, this difference can be studied.

Time

William's attitude to time, as expressed in his Worlds, was peculiar. In as far as they were concerned with time at all they represented "the present". In none of them was there a story or anything corresponding to a story: in three Worlds only (18, 23, 24) the final state of the World was different from the first layout: in two (33, 34) something definite was presented as having happened before the making of the World: seven Worlds (21, 25, 26, 28, 30, 31, 32) follow the usual pattern of realistic Worlds in presenting a moment (after the pattern of a "still" in a Cinematograph film) in a relatively normal realistic scene. World 5, the model village, was an attempt which failed to do this with a remembered actual scene, and World 9, where the barn was cemented into a hillside by a road, falls more into this group than into any other. Worlds 15 and 19 were manipulative and constructional and did not present any kind of a scene.

In the remaining eighteen Worlds (1, 2, 3, 4, 6, 7, 8, 10, 11, 12, 13, 14, 16, 17, 20, 22, 27, 29) time stands still and it is a strange kind of time which holds William's consciousness in thrall, as the "strange knight" in Keats' "Belle dame sans merci" was held by the "faery-child". There are relationships between the objects used in the scene and to some extent things happen – as when the idea appeared in World 4 of the huntsmen arriving from their boat to shoot the seals – but these events are recounted, not acted out, and take place only in the mysterious framework of the World.

This aspect of time is characteristic of productions made by children whose psyche and relation to life is dominated by a fantastic and unrealised proto-system. Everything "is" "at once" and the only time that exists is that demanded by the reality process of constructing the World. Time stands still as in the Rip van Winkle story or Mary Rose. Without treatment of some sort directed to the expression and sorting out of this interior world, these children do, in fact, remain static, the world around them goes on, but in them development does not take place.

Dimensions and Movement

In their relation to dimensions and to movement William's Worlds are in striking contrast to Charles'. In his constructions and his use of materials

Charles was throughout firmly rooted in reality. Not so William. His Worlds, regarded from this point of view, are astonishing creations. Nothing in Charles' series resembles in the least, for example, Worlds 1 and 4 of William's. The sand in the tray, the dimensions of the tray, the objects of the cabinet are used more as indications, as crystallised points in a multidimensional cloud of real and imagined perceptions, than as presentations of fact.

In World 14 for example, what is presented has no content, there is no reason (in contrast with the strict "sense" of Charles' use of planes) for the planes to leap up on to the "roof" structure, nor could they do it. The structure of the scene as a whole has both up and down movement, in/out expressed by the lorry, and violent "down" implied in the statement that the big planes were bombers. The scene was called an "air port" and William was perfectly familiar with airports, but there is only the slenderest thread of connection between what he knows and what he presents here. This World was more an essay in an attempt to represent several dimensions of space and several types of movement simultaneously and to connect these somehow with colour and texture (pink sand). Similarly, in the multidimensional World 34 (air, surface, underwater), the scene is "impossible" though each object is, in a sense, anchored to reality. Again what is presented is the idea of various planes and movement on them, and of a fictional inter-action of movement on these planes.

The dimensions of "outer" and "inner" are equally misty in their presentation. Many children make mounds and tunnel through them from side to side; very few imagine people as living within such a mound. No children in ordinary play imagine "a lot of people who slept and ate within the mound and when they come out a Christmas tree moves from a nearby field to the top of the mound." In this World (3) some reality movement actually took place as the lorry ran round the tray; this lorry was a kind of "within", containing hay and ran on a horizontal plane but quite unconnected with the mound or the Christmas tree. In World 6 many pools supplied drinking water separately for each animal to drink, that is to say to go into the animals; the boats at the side, conversely, provided somewhere for the animals to go into if the water rose around them, i.e., "in case of flood". In World 4 the fishes' houses in the rocks presented the dimensions of "inner" and "outer".

The direction of the streams in two Worlds (4, 7) is in both directions at once: the "pools" in the "streams" in World 4 were seen as separate from the streams, though the water in both was continuous. When making World 4 William cut out the channels of the streams with his finger, regarding the tray with a dreamy air; the emerging pattern was, as it were, movement precipitated into static form; the "pools" had for him the feeling more of pearls on a chain and it was only when words came into it, as he went to the cabinet, that he saw the patches of sand as sand and not as part of the pattern of water he had been drawing. This is characteristic of William's inner perceptions, if such a term can be used. Feelings, sensations and perceptions were blended in a manner that seemed obvious and natural to him.

In World 10 William took hold of a number of wheeled vehicles and using them in the way he had used his own finger in World 4, made tracks on flat sand in curves suggestive of the pattern of World 4. The upright sticks placed all over World 4 brought into this flat World the feeling of height, which was part of the total concept and which, with the "depth" of the fishes' houses, completed the "global" setting which is characteristic of this type of World. In World 10 some progress had been made with the movement of growth out of this "global" inner world since vehicles and tracks are "real" in a way that "pools" and streams flowing both ways are not. The bridges here bring in the dimension of height, and the people looking *down* from these reproduce his own position of "looking down" on the tray. I would venture the idea that the mother and child standing between the bridges is a statement of himself-and-his-mother, with whose involvement with each other this World may possibly be concerned.

In Worlds 16 and 17 William struggled to reach a further working out of movement in a circular manner, combined with up/down and in/out. The sticks of World 4 became the traffic signals of Worlds 16 and 17. The cut across the central island of World 16 repeated the central "cut" of waterways in World 4; in this cut are an empty lorry and a full coal cart; William knows that coal comes from "within" a mine.

Several other aspects of "through" and "within" were expressed on the larger half of the central island of World 16. The big gate was specially chosen for the centre; beside it a turnstile with a man emphasised "a-man-and-going-through-ness"; the road drill placed at the back brought in the concept of "boring *down*", and the big light put in the centre of both Worlds carried the usual symbolic meaning of "I-am-trying-to-throw-light-on-all-this." When we study the vehicles on the circular roads this within/without aspect is further subdivided and expressed; rubbish goes into the dustcart; the purpose of buses is for people to sit in them; petrol, within the petrol lorry, is designed to go into motor vehicles and so on. As already pointed out, on the outer banks are fire, rubbish and the ambulance into which hurt people go. Rain finally added water-from-above (World 17) where in World 4 there was water-below, and in World 6 the danger of floods appeared.

It would seem that in the sequence of Worlds 18 and 19 that followed, William was wrestling with and trying to express concepts of movement and fixity. In World 18 (his one coherent and reality World of this period) the actual action of "sea" on cliffs of sand gave him a chance of working with a force which was "down" but which in its nature moved forcibly "against" and "up", and so cut up solid masses which then came "down".

The facts of circuses (Worlds 20 and 29) provided a further link between inner and outer perceptions and experiences, and made possible a fresh step forward in the emergence from this inner "cloud" to the realisation and perception of external reality. Movement and juggling with up/down and their dangers are the essence of the work of circus performers; the hoops of clowns make a going-through addition possible. These now occupy the centre of the picture and the natural circle of the circus arena gives a reality model for the circular road. That, however, it is the movements of the circus performers which is their expressive power to William, was shown by the complete absence of spectators. The up/down sticks of World 4 became, as already pointed out, the rods and ladders of World 20, the latter placed against some of the rods, one against a cart, and one, as if to emphasise their symbolic rather than reality value, placed alone in the sand at the back. But no movement up/down these ladders was suggested.

By this time William had made considerable progress in gaining mastery of his inner expereinces and relating them to external reality. The actual existence in the reality World of the river Thames, of the Queen and her coronation and of the fact of William's real experience of going over the Forth Bridge, made the next step to reality perception. The "movement" of Worlds 21 and 22 was expressed almost wholly on the reality plane.

For the first time, three weeks later, in his first fighting World (23) William became able to allow himself to conceive of force moving in a horizontal direction meeting a counter force moving against it. But this was only a transitory achievement, since as soon as the implied "battle" was set out, with a giant-sized horse William trampled and killed all the symbolic human beings on either side. The original concept of the mound in World 3 was then repeated, but this time as a burial mound instead of a "house" for the living, the enemy Indians being "buried" in two separate breast-like mounds.

For the understanding of the process by means of which consciousness finds its way out of proto-system confusion, fighting World 24 is of particular value. At the outset the layout of the previous World was repeated and it was possible to make William aware of what he had been doing in this World. This "awareness" took immediate effect. William lost interest in repeating the previous World and moved away from this and on to a struggle to achieve instead a use of reality material in a reality manner. The sense of elation which so often in these children accompanies a movement of consciousness from a confused inner to a more coherent outer expression, came to life here, as in Mary's series, in the incorporation in this World of all the military bandsmen William could find. These he placed on the top of his tallest towers and said they were "playing very loudly".

These two tall towers have no "sense"; they convey nothing of external reality either to the maker or to the observer. They embodied nevertheless a considerable increase in the comprehension of and manipulation of external reality in the sense of size, weight and the force of gravity.

In World 27 William attempted another form of symbolisation: what he appears to be trying to work out is non-aggressive force moving in a horizontal direction, with its three possible train embodiments (passenger trains, goods trains and engines pulling engines), and to combine these with ideas of danger, fierceness, and "fiery feelings".* The trains move between banks on fire. This World was the beginning of his second period of treatment and is party "real" in conception. William had emerged by now so far out of his absorption in the proto-system that he was able to conceive of a "new way". World 28 is a reality presentation of the making of a new road.

William was now sufficiently "at home" with the conception of horizontal movement to be able to work at the combination of this with "going-in" as the central aspect of a concept (World 29). The reality of circuses supplied him with a possible ground-plan for this (as it had provided for him a ready-made instance of movement up and down, excitement and danger within a circle) and made possible for him intense concentration upon a "going in" to an enclosed space.

Once again, in World 30, the factual existence in the outer world of hills and toboggans and snow made it possible for him to concentrate on the presentation of swift movement downwards, this time in a joyful context rather than a disastrous way as in World 18. In the Station World 31, external reality again provided William with the possibility of combining swift horizontal movement, up/down movement and the feeling of Christmas decorations so prominent in his Mosaics.

The element of danger which had been implicit in a large proportion of William's Worlds emerged in the traffic World 33. The accidents here "have happened", that is to say, before the construction of the scene (in contrast to the deaths caused by William's actions in the battle Worlds or by an impersonal force in the World of sea and cliffs); the World presented the consequences only.

Having now gained enough courage and clarity to present an actual disaster, in World 34 William moved on a stage and from accidental damage arising through competition for space on an (implied) road, this World presented a disaster to a-container-carrying-people (cf. the overturned bus) deliberately carried out through hostile intention. This disaster took place in and on water and so linked this World back again to World 18; only in World 34 rescue was present also (the coastguard ship). Rescue as a clear concept in relation to reality damage had been present previously only in World 33.

To sum up this development therefore, we notice that in the earlier

---

*This phrase is often used in therapy to express to boys their sexual drives.

226

stages of his treatment, where his normal skill and perception of reality was low, movement in William's World was circular, either completely so as in the circular road Worlds, or partially as in those of loops and partial circles. This did not arise, as in Charles' Worlds, from some aspect of the facts in the World, but was of the essential nature of the World itself. It was only after the circus World 20 (the last of the Worlds with circular movement) that powerful horizontal movement was depicted. Movement in a vertical up/down direction when it occurred in early Worlds, as the fantastic Worlds 6 and 7, was connected with imagined movement of human beings – it is only in the later Worlds that the movement up and down of powerful machines occurred at all.

Table 3 Table of Movement

Circular	Vertical	Horizontal	"Static"
2	6	21	1
3	7	22	5
4	14	23	9
7	18	27	11
8	30	28	12
10	31	29	15
13	34	33	19
16		34	24
17			25
20			26
			32

Coherent and Incoherent Worlds

The balance between these two types of Worlds in William's series is the reverse of that in Charles'. The term "coherent" can only be fairly applied to William's realistic Worlds. Leaving out the model village World which, although an attempt at the presentation of a real scene was so peculiar that it belongs more to the incoherent series, William made twelve coherent Worlds. The table on page 228 shows the distribution of the 34 Worlds between the various types.

Incoherent Worlds

Since Incoherent Worlds are the dominant factor in William's series, these will be considered first. The importance of these Worlds is their demonstration of the impossibility for any child (or for that matter of any adult in the same position) to translate into words what is going on within his mind. This series of "incoherent" Worlds is of great value since it demonstrates to any critical observer the extreme confusion within the mind of a boy whose response to life is such as William's was, and the fact that the probable source of that behaviour lies in these "global" tangles and complex patterns of identifications.

Table 4

	Incoherent	Composite	Coherent
Fantastic			
1–2–3–4–6 ⎫	1–2–3–4–6	(7)	
7–8–9–10–11 ⎪	7–8–9–10–		
12–13–14–16 ⎬	11–12–13–14		
17 ⎭	16–17		
Constructional			
15–19	(15)–(19)		
Factual Scenes			
Model village 5	5		
Sea and cliffs 18			18
Fantastic			
20–21–22–	22		20–21
23–24	23–24		
Factual Scenes			
Farms 25–26			
Road 28			25–26–28
Fantastic			
27–29			27–29
Factual Scenes			
Toboggan 30			
Station 31			
Farm 32			30–31–32
Fantastic			
33–34	34		33
Total	**20+2**	**(1)**	**12**

The second illuminating element a study of William supplies is the speed with which radical improvement took place in his response to life once the opportunity for direct expression of his interior concepts, affects, and urges had become available and had been made use of by him.

Taken as they stand and without any background knowledge of or experience with the proto-system, it is very difficult to make these Worlds intelligible. Many of the features that appear in them are familiar to those who use this technique, and understanding of them is aided by the appearance of the same constructions and arrangement of objects in the Worlds of many children. One child's series of Worlds can be compared with other children's series and the comments of one child on his Worlds used to aid in the understanding of others. In this way a "total" understanding grows up in the mind of the therapist using this technique which is again constantly checked against new Worlds as they appear made by new children.

William's first ten Worlds form a group. Of these the River-and-islands (7) has elements of coherence and is therefore also grouped as Composite.

These ten Worlds fall again into two sets: those concerned with animals, eating and sleeping, traffic, tracks, and a road (2, 3, 5, 8, 9, 10) and those concerned with water (4, 6, 7); World 1 is unique in form and in the idea of robbers; the hidden "gold" is met with later. It is only in this World that the idea occurs of a single person ("the face") both possessing and being robbed of the gold. World 2 is a kind of first sketch for later Worlds and contains the two sorts of objects able-to-move-about, animals and vehicles. World 3 is also a kind of trying out of features which are elaborated in later Worlds. The last action of this session was the putting of the Christmas tree on top of the mound. At the next session William made a Mosaic (said to represent "two fountains which make the Christmas tree all wet and glittery") which linked World 3 to World 4 and initiated a series of water Worlds. World 4 (seals) started as water in a formal design. The feeling this World gave one was that as near as the materials made it possible for him to accomplish, William strove to make an ovoid water scene with depth and height to it, within which other "withins" occurred.

World 6 was, in design, in marked contrast to World 5 and carried the squareness of the Mosaic made just before. Here water, as well as being nourishing, became threatening – animals might need saving from it, as gold again needed protection from potential robbers. The only object which had occurred in previous Worlds was the crocodile (2 and 4). It is just possible that William may have thought of carts as "things you *sit* in" and therefore connected with excretion, but this is pure speculation. The connection with his own "flooded" beds is obvious; and the inclusion of a hidden and guarded preciousness (gold) suggestive.

Grace and symmetry returned in the next water World (7) together with the many upright structures of World 4. The water here is separated from the proto-system ideas of "withinness" and "up and down" but still carries a union of opposites in that the flow goes both ways. World 8 was an experimental World. William kept on altering it, striving, it would seem, to get the ideas of the previous Worlds somehow combined together. The fact that he started by moulding a mound (said later to be a living place now deserted) and cleared a circular space around it seems to link backwards with the mounds of Worlds 3 and 7, and forwards to the two mounds surrounded by moats of World 23.

The inclusion of the Christmas tree among the trees of a "garden" connect directly with the form of World 3.

It is unfortunate that owing to some accidental fact which I forgot, or to carelessness on my part, William made no Mosaics during this entire half year, and it is not possible therefore to tell whether or not "glitteryness" continued in his mind.

In World 9 William struggled to combine his tactile experiments with his concepts of "a house" and "a garden" and combined these with the "road" which had been part of the "movement around" of World 2.

In World 10, made two months later, William was no longer completely overwhelmed with the ideas, experiences and urges within him; he could draw his designs with objects whose nature is to move instead of using his own finger to do this. His vehicles were still as irrational as the buses in World 7 but their arrangement makes part of the fundamental design of the tracks. The "bridge" element is no longer a symbolic Tower Bridge tucked away in a corner, but a fine structure which dominates the picture. This bridge is a "something-you-can-look-down from", and what is contemplated is houses and a church and a mother and little boy. A little real contact between William and the outside world was coming into being.

It is natural and right that this World should prove a stepping stone to an expression of his passionate feeling for his mother. The fact of the coronation of Queen Elizabeth and the presence in toy shops of models of her state coach facilitiated this (World 11). Without these external facts it might have been some time before William succeeded in bringing this feeling to expression. These facts, together with the existence of my box of gold- and silver-painted bricks made it possible for him to conceive of and execute a new design – a rectangular pattern in some relation to his last Mosaic. Here "the queen" drives in splendour.

Exactly what would have happened had I not suggested to him "a fairy tale" on the next session there is no means of knowing, but his spontaneous story earlier on of the witch and the king and queen seemed to demand exploration. Three witches and the gypsy caravan (which was to appear again in the first circus World) were placed together in the left-hand front corner (World 12) with a standing knight with upraised sword in front of them. Behind them the queen drove, and this time trees replaced the "fairy" bricks. This World brought one block of work to an end.

With the Autumn term William entered on a new phase: with his finger he had made a pattern of water, with vehicles a pattern of wheel tracks; now he moved to trains, and in World 13 made patterns in the sand with trains. This initiated a stage of experiment with rapid movement in several planes with powerful air symbols (World 14), balanced by an attempt to build a house in the sand (15).

It was only after two months of experiments with different types of play that William worked out a new kind of World. He had finished for the time being with rectangular forms and returned to the circular road of World 2 in the important road Worlds 16 and 17. In these the circle does not touch the outside of the tray but has both an outer and an inner portion. The same exaggeration of upright symbols occurs, but light is suggested in the large street-lamp in the centre of the scene. On the outer rim both fire and rubbish appear, and on the road an ambulance and a breakdown van. Although these Worlds cannot be said to be coherent, yet a number of ideas and fears appeared in them in direct form which had hitherto only been expressed in very disguised symbols. They were in fact portals to a series of three coherent Worlds (18, 20, 21) with one constructional World among them (World 19).

Two months later efforts at construction were combined with a quite unreal use of trains and William achieved in World 22 the most successful construction so far.

Having achieved something satisfactory to him with trains, he came to the point where he could carry out direct expression against a "shadow" opponent in World 23 and finish that World with a disguised reference to hostility to his mother's breasts. This was followed by a triumphant expression of masculinity in the towers and bands of World 24. At this point his first period of treatment ended. The only three coherent Worlds made during this period are discussed later under Coherent Worlds).

William made one more Incoherent World (34) at the end of this chronological series and we have added to this a final drawing of a World made nine months later which completes the series of Worlds 11 and 12.

In World 34 he returned to the theme of water and presented powerful engines moving in three horizontal planes, and up and down in a vertical direction: aeroplanes in the air, ships on the surface of the water and submarines below. On the surface and within the water both attack and rescue took place. Aeroplanes were stationary on either side of the central "sea" and one aeroplane flew overhead. All these contain people. The concepts presented in confused medley and obscure symbolism in the earlier Worlds were now stated in clear and direct terms.

Coherent Worlds

William's coherent Worlds carry both different problems and a different significance from those of Charles Robinson. Charles expressed himself directly in objective symbols, used throughout in a realistic way. It was only in World 18, made on the 38th session, that William achieved a World which was both coherent and which presented a realistic scene. This World is of particular interest both in the process of treatment and also in its exposition of the theory underlying the World technique. From the "seals" World (4) onward William had made a number of Worlds dominated by the idea of water. In all of these "water" had been symbolised by the blue base of the tray. In World 18, for the first time, he made use of actual water and the fact that this water "attacked" the cliff and made it eventually crumble into water delighted him. The boats on this water formed a "rehearsal" of "attack and destruction" occurring in water which he put into explicit expression in World 34.

On the 42nd session he broke new ground with an imaginative World of a Circus. This was coherent in itself but fantastic (using this word in the dictionary sense) in its components. In design William adapted the general plan of Worlds 2, 16 and 17 to the idea of a circus and showed very real progress in his grouping and arrangement of the objects, but his treatment of the poles and ladders was purely symbolic.

The working out of this circus gave him keen satisfaction and set some spring of reality perception free in him, so that one week later he was able to return to his series of Worlds expressing delight in his mother, with a World of the Queen coming home down the river, with a band and her coronation coach in a procession alongside on the banks of the river. For the first time William sought out and enjoyed the arrangement of masses of people on the further side of the procession, kept in check by police. This was the last of that series of three Worlds: frank admiration of and devotion to his mother came to expression much later in the building of "palaces for the Queen". The 16 months break in treatment occurred here.

Both Worlds done on his Reporting Visits were coherent and realistic, the first (25) a pleasant and satisfactory scene of a farmhouse and fields, showing considerable development in observation, and with the "symbolic element" of the bulls in a field in a corner. World 26 was in many ways an echo of World 2 and had as indiscriminate a collection of animals within its central space, except that these were all those which could be found on a farm. In this World William personified himself for the first time as a lamb about to be tossed by a bull.

When treatment was resumed William had made considerable progress; he was able to use trains both directly and symbolically. World 27 is again a World coherent in its arrangement but fantastic in its conception. It is a scene of excitement and danger – a little train between two big ones, banks on fire and men putting them out; a very good statement of the sexual situation he felt he was in and the calming effect of enuresis.

Both William's power of organising external scenes and at the same time the integration going on within him was steadily increasing. In World 28 he collected together many of the road-making symbols he had scattered through previous Worlds, and focused them in a clear-cut World of the building of "a new main road".

As before, success in a realistic presentation gave William confidence to break new ground in a symbolic one – so, following the roadmaking World he returned to the circus theme (World 29) and endeavoured to do something in a three-dimensional way which would express for him something of his feeling about the female. The Queen symbol was no longer easily available (public festivities about Elizabeth II having by this time ceased) and William had to do what he could to work out a symbol for himself, in this case a strongly emphasised entrance to a womb-like circus. Again in this World, which is both coherent and fantastic, the drive of his feelings obliterated what little ability he had to perceive the shape of slats and to use them practically.

Two weeks later William became very lively and repeated the construction of the World of sea and cliffs (18), this time making the hill a tobogganing ground (30). Mummy and daddy were put on a sledge to go first and mummy was then put to watch while a girl sat on the sledge and a boy toiled up hill. This was the nearest to the presentation of a family group that appeared in any of this set of William's Worlds.

Problems of direction and movement, of in and out and up and down, still dominated William, and the elaborate World 31 of an Underground Station was a "realistic" embodiment of them. He took immense trouble over the making of this World and for the first time really persevered and wrestled with material objects until he achieved the effect he desired.

This achievement and his Christmas holidays gave him confidence, and at the beginning of January he returned to the subject of a farm to present male rivalry in four fighting bulls: horses are streaming past them and sows and young fill a field at the side; the content of William's fears were coming nearer the surface.

Finally (for this extract) in World 33 William nerved himself to produce a real life disaster. It was again coherent in itself but from a realistic point of view impossible. All the accidents had already happened when the scene was made, the ambulance had arrived and the village included a hospital. William was no longer swamped by emotions and submerged in proto-system confusions, but began to be able to present his problems directly.

William's Use of Symbols

In studying the symbols used by Charles we divided these into two groups: the use made of the mouldable qualities of the sand and the employment of objects from the World cabinet. In William's series so important a part is played by the sand itself and what William did with it, that this is considered in a separate section on Interior and Exterior space.

We therefore pass immediately to consider the objects from the cabinet William used in his Worlds.

Animals. A fundamental difference is to be seen immediately in the way animals are treated by Charles and William. This difference in the two boys' use of the commonest World objects illustrates well the fact that the same object, often even used in something the same way by different children, can have entirely different significances for the child. Charles' use, both of wild and farm animals was always realistic, though this realism was adapted to serve his own purposes. William's use of animals is an exact opposite. It is difficult indeed to gather what the exact significance was to William of the animals he put in the Worlds made during the first period of treatment. It is impossible to separate the significance of wild and farm animals in these so they are considered together.

In the first World (2) in which animals appear, wild and tame animals were mixed indiscriminately. In World 4 it is fairly clear that the crocodiles

233

were felt as dangerous and the seals as the "prey" of the hunters – but this is on a relatively superficial layer of meaning only. This point will be returned to later under the heading "people".

Animals appear next in World 6. This is a World with two basic themes – food (i.e., things to eat and to drink) and water. The latter is presented in actuality in the World in the form of small pools for the animals to drink from, but water in quantity forms the underlying thought of the World (William is a boy who wakes in the morning to find his bed in a flood). The choice of the animals seems to have some relation to water. A crocodile (already seen as inhabiting water) was put in the centre of the picture. On one diagonal line were a duck and a camel (which have opposite relations to water), and on another diagonal were two hippopotamuses which revel in mud and water. If it had been possible at that time to discuss these Worlds with William, probably the significance held for him by bears and rhinoceros would have come to light. As it is we are without a clue to these. What is remarkable is that this World contained nine of the most formidable jungle animals, but William says these "are friendly". It is impossible for a boy, even if only 8 years old, brought up in William's surroundings, not to know intellectually that these are dangerous animals. So with them he presents a fusion of two opposites – fierce and friendly.

One other animal remains, the single horse, the one "ridden by the caretaker"; this horse features only as part of the caretaker's protection of the animals.

Wild animals do not appear again in this series of 34 Worlds.

William used horses eleven times, and apart from Worlds 2 and 6 where they are incidental, the mode in which they were used is instructive. In three (11, 12, 21) they drew the Queen's Coronation coach or were ridden by the Queen; in two (20, 29) they formed part of the performers in a circus; in three (25, 26, 32) they were part of the equipment of the three farm scenes, and in one (23) a giant horse rode down and killed all his opponents. As has been pointed out in the earlier description, it was as if William worked up through the earlier peaceful uses of horses figures to this final and cataclysmic one just before treatment was broken off.

William resembled Charles in that he used farm animals for the expression of feelings and ideas directly connected with maleness, femaleness, mating and babies, and the one direct statement of hostility from an adult male to himself was embodied in a bull and a lamb. In contrast to Charles, apart from this one incident William never worked out directly the relations of human beings to farm animals and of animals to each other.

Road Traffic. Apart from the farm scenes, road vehicles appeared in twelve Worlds (2, 3, 6, 7, 10, 14, 16, 17, 20, 28, 31, 33), but the place given them and the use made of them varied considerably. William became attached to certain vehicles, looked for them carefully and used them repeatedly: many of the key ones appeared already in World 2; in World 7 he partially personified buses, which he said, "were not allowed out on account of the animals", although there were no animals in the World. None of the "traffic" was neutral nor expressive only of force, as Charles' traffic was; each piece chosen was individual and charged with significance for William.

Single vehicles or two at a time appeared in three Worlds, the-lorry-carrying-hay in World 3, the lorry-in-the-garage of World 14 (both fantastic Worlds), and two cars as part of the Underground station of World 31. The completely fantastic World 6 contained carts, and the fantastic front strip of World 7 buses as part of the many-dimensional concepts presented by these Worlds. In World 6 William provided no clue to the way in which he regarded the carts, but his remarks about the boats combined realistic and fantastic ideas concerning them. In World 7 on the contrary, what he said about the buses was entirely fantastic, both because there were no animals in the World and even supposing there had been, it is difficult to see what the connections would have been between animals and buses. In World 10 the patterned tracks were made by pairs of vehicles, the only ones in William's series where movement of vehicles formed the kernel of the scene.

The central feature of Worlds 16 and 17 was the circular road which carried a number of highly specialised vehicles: the dust cart, breakdown van, tip-up van, and ambulance seemed to be of special importance and appeared in the road accident (33) and in several Worlds subsequent to this series. They represent measures taken to deal with disorder (rubbish cart) and disaster (breakdown van and ambulance), to assist in constructive work by moving earth about (road-scoop) and buses which move people. In the first circus World (20) a motley collection of vehicles was arranged on a semi-circular space, but their relevance was dictated by the assumption that this was a country fair.

No further motor vehicles appeared in the first series of Worlds. The farm Worlds, being realistic, contained the sort of vehicles that belong to farms.

It is in World 28, the making of a new main road, that the idea of traffic and of a road became completely realistic. It is such a simple scene that William was able to keep all the elements of it completely in focus. World 33, following that of the Underground Railway, brought all the traffic elements of the previous Worlds together and into some kind of focus – almost as if it were the circle of Worlds 16 and 17 on a higher turn of a spiral. Here they enabled him at last, using his familar vehicles, to express a real life disaster, a crash which had happened and which had to be repaired.

Horse-drawn vehicles were used in three ways: as a coach for the Queen; as a caravan or covered wagon; and as a milk cart for circus people. In World 6 five carts were introduced without horses and with no connection with the rest of the scene.

Upright Objects. Although William made a lavish and in some ways extreme use of upright objects, in none of his Worlds did he use these realistically. In World 4 the symbolic nature of the element of upright poles is most marked; their significance can only be understood when studied in conjunction with his Mosaics. It becomes clear then that these, together with those in the model village (5), were part of the cluster he called at times "a fountain", and at times "a glittery tree". Miscellaneous upright traffic signals, telegraph poles, etc., were used in the cluttered Worlds 16 and 17 and appeared more sparsely but with similar significance in Worlds 27 and 33.

Road signs when included in Charles' Worlds were always functional in conception; in William's they formed part of the series of "many-upright-posts".

In the circus World (20) the place of the "ring" was really a collection of upright posts joined together, with their symbolic significance emphasised by the placing of useless ladders against certain of the posts.

Trains. Apart from those in the model village, trains only appeared three times in William's series of Worlds. In none of them did they form part of a realistic scene such as, for example, Charles' train-in-snow. They marked however crucial stages in development. Trains appeared first in World 13 where their significance to William was not the trains in themselves but the use of them to make tracks in the sand repeating the tracks made by road traffic in the Bridge World 10. The next appearance was in William's successful construction of the Forth Bridge where the position of the three trains blocked movement in each other. The third World with trains is the highly significant World 27. Here their use is purely symbolic, and expresses a complex state of emotional excitement; he seems here to state that water from oneself quenches the excitement of emotion aroused by his relation to his parents.

Aeroplanes. As we have seen in the study of Charles' case, 'planes, to Charles, were in the main symbols of force, parallel to motor vehicles, and on occasions masculine symbols; in every case they were used realistically and in the coherent Worlds formed a reasonable part of the picture. William only twice used 'planes and each time in a completely fantastic manner. In World 14 they leaped on and off the roof of a "garage" and in World 34 they were drawn up on either side of the central sea with one big plane flying overhead.

Boats and Ships. In Charles' Worlds the boats which appeared were functional parts of a realistic scene. William used boats both realistically and symbolically. In "the Queen coming home" and in the World of the sea and cliffs, the ship and the boats were entirely realistic. The boat which goes through the pillars of the Forth Bridge was also a normal component of a realistic element in that scene. The boats in World 6 however are fantastic elements in the scene – they were intended to float on water – the normal destiny of boats, but also to rescue animals. (Is there perhaps here a hint of Noah's ark?) The ships in World 34, while behaving in a way that any ships might in an ordinary sea, are in fact symbols in a symbolic scene. They expressed for William ideas of damage and rescue which he had put into the traffic scene (33) only this time in relation to his central problem – water.

Bridges. Bridges do not function realistically in any of William's Worlds. A bridge appeared in the "seals" World but as an afterthought and not as any essential part of the World. Similarly, in World 7, a bridge connected two islands, but was a quite unimportant feature. On the other hand in the front section of that World the Tower Bridge, though completely without functional significance, had, as already discussed in the passage on that World, considerable symbolic significance.

In World 10 two bridges dominate the scene, and as already discussed, carry an up/down significance which fits in with that of the Tower Bridge, and suggests that it is this vertical dimension about bridges which characterised William's thought about them, rather than the horizontal functional significance they carried for Charles.

Enclosures and Fences, which occurred frequently in Charles' Worlds and always with a realistic purpose, appeared in eight of William's Worlds. In two of the farm scenes, 25 and 32, they were used realistically. In World 2, however, and World 26 the fences enclosed a quite unrealistic collection of animals. In World 3 the small enclosed field contains first the Christmas tree and was then left empty, while in World 7 the fences appeared to be intended to enclose the "garden" or "park"; they really fail to do so, and are in a way irrelevant, as are the odd pieces of fencing in the circular road Worlds 16 and 17.

Trees. William used trees in three ways. The "Christmas tree" which first appeared in World 3; ordinary trees in a naturalistic setting as those in the farm scene, and those in the "fairytale World", which links with World 46 which has been added to this series of illustrations.

If Mosaics 2, 9, 10, 11, 12 be considered together and the comment following Mosaic 9, it becomes clear that "a tree" is part of a cluster containing "Christmas tree", "fountain", "glittery", "house". The sexual significance of these identifications is obvious and so is its direct connection with William's nocturnal enuresis; the excitement, expressed in other ways as in the bands accompanying the Queen coming home or standing on top of the towers, is expressed in this also. The fountain which is within the "house" in Mosaic 9 resembles the Christmas tree taken from an enclosure to be put on top of the "house/mound" in World 3. Trees appeared in the "park or garden" half of World 7 without much apparent meaning, but formed a major element in the expressive and dynamic fairytale World 12, where all the forces of good and evil hide among the trees surrounding the

Queen in her coach. It is this World of which World 46 is the fulfilment. On another connecting line these trees carry out the suggestion of the upright sticks in World 4 and so link to the whole question of upright objects.

Trees therefore carry a significance for William that is entirely absent in Charles' use of World objects, and express for William a very complex many-sided cluster of experience and emotion something resembling the use of trees in myth and ritual.

Professor Erwin R. Goodenough of Yale, in his exhaustive study of Jewish Symbols in the Greco-Roman Period,* treats the significance of "The Tree" in Mesopotamian, Egyptian, Greek, Etrurian, Roman, Jewish, Christian and Apocalyptic tradition and art. In all these, he writes, the tree is thought of as a symbol of triumph and of more abundant life, as bringing victory and healing, and as being itself a symbol of divinity, and particularly of feminine divinity. In Mesopotamia and the Near East the tree is both the female principle and represents the mother (Adonis was born from a tree in Syrian tradition). The combination of water with trees appears powerfully in both Jewish and Apocalyptic tradition as in Ezekiel's great vision, chapter 47.

(1) "And he brought me back unto the door of the house; and behold, waters issued out from under the threshold of the house eastward, for the forefront of the house was toward the east, and the waters came down from under from the right side of the house, on the south side of the altar. (2) Then he brought me out by the way of the gate northward, and led me round by the way without unto the outer gate by the way of the gate that looketh toward the east, and behold, there ran out waters on the right side. (5) . . . and it was a river that I could not pass through: for the waters were risen, waters to swim in, a river that could not be passed through. (6) And he said unto me, Son of man, hast thou seen this? Then he brought me, and caused me to return to the bank of the river. (7) Now when I returned, behold, upon the bank of the river were very many trees on the one side and on the other. (8) Then said he unto me, These waters issue forth toward the eastern region, and shall go down into the Arabah (desert): and they shall go toward the sea; into the sea shall the waters go which were made to issue forth and the waters shall be healed".

In this vision the trees are planted by the side of four streams, but in Apocalyptic and Rabbinic tradition four rivers flow from the roots of the tree to the earthly Eden. In the Zohar all the waters of creation are gathered into the tree and in turn flow out from it to nourish the earth. In another passage the tree is said to grow out of a "house" which is itself at the centre of creation and in this tree male and female are united.

This compares with William's World 4 where "the streams flowed both ways" and with Mosaic No. 9, where the fountain is within a house, which is also a tree.

---

*Bollingen series XXXVII 1958. Vol. 7, pp. 87–134.

The men with rifles who guard the trees in William's World (46) express his anxiety lest this essential source of life within him, which is also E and the Freudian and Jungian libido, may be threatened with loss or damage. Only when he is sure of the safety of the tree, of life within him, will his confidence in himself be secure. He is, as we all are, impoverished by the fact that no great corporate ritual exists in our modern life through which his striving to make contact with the source of life within him can be strengthened and enriched, bringing him into communion with his fellows in this striving, so he must find his way alone.

Buildings. Apart from the model village actual buildings logically used appeared in the three farm Worlds, in the realistic primitive road World (9) and on two other occasions: in World (10) and lining both sides of the traffic crash scene World 33.

People. William's handling of the idea of people was curious. A number of his Worlds contained the idea of "people" though no figures were used; for example the "robbers" in World 1: the people living in the sand house in World 3: the men making the road and living in the sand house of World 7. Actual people appeared in quite specific ways in the earlier Worlds: the "hunters" in World 4: the "caretaker" of the gold and the animals in World 6: the woman-and-child and the indefinitely characterised people in World 10. In World 11, however, and in all the other Worlds where "the Queen" appeared, she was most definitely presented, surrounded with pomp, and great care was lavished on the scene. The circus people in World 20 were the first that were "active" in themselves, and led on to the two "fighting" Worlds of 23 and 24 where fighting men appeared. These two ended a series, and when William resumed treatment his handling of people was quite different. The three farms had ordinary farm people as part of them; the World of trains with banks on fire had labouring men pouring water on the fire, and in World 28 making the road. "Activity" returned in the girl on the galloping horse in the second circus World (29) and in the World of toboggans running down a hill (30). As already pointed out these are the only people in the series having relationships with each other. In World 31 ordinary "token" people returned, and the only instance of definite "character" figures in this second series were policemen in World 33. In the final World 34 specialised people such as "coastguards" were again implied but not embodied.

Special Symbols

Water. Real water was used by William in three Worlds: "the seaside and boats" (18), the "Forth Bridge" (22) and the last one, the "sea battle and rescue". The blue base of the tray was used to symbolise water in three Worlds; the "seal" World (4), the "river" of World 7, and the realistic World of "the Queen coming home" (21). Water was implied around the mounds of World 23. In addition a well provided water in the railway scene with the banks on fire, while in the farm scene (26) the huge enclosure contained a small pond. Water formed the central motif, as we have already described, of World 6. The underlying "feelings" of these water Worlds is the opposite of that in Charles'. Charles' rivers flow, they are barriers and they equate with E. Water for William is circular, it rises into flood and becomes dangerous (6 and 18); it contains danger (4), it can be used to combat danger (27), it can nourish (6): it does not "flow" (except in World 7 where in answer to a leading question William stated it flowed both ways at once).

Fire. Neither in Charles' Worlds, nor in his play did fire appear. With William the making of bonfires played an important part at the end of his fourth term of treatment. Fire appeared directly in three Worlds; Worlds 16 and 17 where it was thought of *as* a bonfire, and World 27 where it was "a danger to the trains": Fire engines appeared in two Worlds (2 and 33). In all of these Worlds and in real life, bonfires stood to William for keen excitement, pleasurable and dangerous. The last Mosaic of the series represents "a magic fire".

Myth and Fairytale. Fairytales played no part in Charles' scheme of thought, but myth and fairytale make their presence very much felt in the background of William's play. He was much preoccupied with magic, which finds expression in his Mosaics; he made a story of a witch and a king and queen; he used the fairytale bricks to make a fitting "surround" for "the queen" (11): he picked up my suggestion of a fairytale and put the queen (in World 12) in a completely fairytale setting, and in Worlds 1 and 6 he has "hidden gold". The relation between gold and faeces is universal and gold is also "the treasure within".

Design

One of the most interesting aspects of World-making in children from the theoretical point of view, is the occurrence in them of definite designs.

The collections made by Rhoda Kellog* and published in her book "What Children Scribble and Why", suggests both an ontological development of design and form and the possibility of a natural and inherent impulse toward patterning in children.

In Worlds this feature appears strongly in some children, occasionally in others and not at all in some. It seems to have a relation to two factors: the degree in which the child is enclosed in his own inner world, and the appearance in children of factors of a universal nature, such as the Mandala design. In the series of William's Worlds studied here, four main patterns occur which to some extent interact with one another. These are:

---

*Golden Gate Nursery Schools, San Francisco.

Series 1. Ovals

World 2 is a primitive form of a central "island" with traffic around it which is developed in Worlds 16 and 17 and in later Worlds following this series. The general shape of a central oval unit in the centre of the tray with its contents differing from that of the surrounding area occurs in Worlds 4 and 34.

Series 2. Ovals with pattern inside

World 4 has not only the oval shape belonging to Pattern Series 1, but also, within this oval, an elaborate patterning of islands and water – this recurs in the interlacing tracks of vehicles in World 10.

Series 3. Circular

World 3, although classified as without pattern, contains in the centre of the tray a circular mound with half of a circular surround to it which relates it to the group of Worlds with circular patterning. The mound, as a mound, belongs to another category, that of structures arising above the level sand, but taken as a circle it is the first of a series (7, 8, 23) of Worlds where circles appear within circular surrounds. The Circus in World 20 is a plain circle only, repeated in World 29.

Series 4. Rectangular

In Worlds 11 and 12 two oblongs placed one within the other following the outline of the tray resemble each other, while the star in World 11 is repeated as the central feature in World 31. The final outcome of World 19 was a rectangular oblong within a wall along the sides of the tray.

In making these patterns William treated the sand in a characteristic manner. Apart from the three farm scenes, World 2 and a small field in World 3, William did not use rectangular fencing but used the shape and area of the tray as his rectangular outline. William, like Charles, treated the area of the World tray and its objects quite differently from the way he treated the Mosaic tray and its pieces. Worlds 11 and 12, and particularly World 11, in which the coloured bricks were used in a geometrical manner, express a type of patterning very commonly used by children and which one might have reasonbly expected to appear in William's responses to the Mosaic Test material. On the contrary it was only comparatively far on in treatment that William used the Mosaic pieces in a patterning manner. For the most part the pieces stirred in him the desire to use them in a semi-representational fashion.

To sum up. Patterning appeared in fourteen Worlds while eighteen Worlds have no pattern, and two Worlds (15 and 19) were constructions with "cement". It should be noticed that except for the two "feminine" Worlds 23 and 29, unpatterned Worlds occur roughly in series following the patterned ones, World 34 returning to the oval shape of World 2.

Mosaics

During the period under review William made 13 Mosaic designs. These were of considerable help in understanding what was going on in his mind. They were:

No. 1. (made in the consultation interview) see page 169.

No. 2. (made on 2nd session, followed by World 4).

A confused irregular arrangement of big and small triangles in 3 half-rows vertically across the board on the left, described by William as "two fountains which are magic and make the Christmas tree all wet and glittery".

No. 3. (made on 3rd session, after the model village).

A frame of diamonds within which all the squares were arranged in irregular rows vertically, some pieces on top of each other in a clumsily rectangular lattice work. When he had finished it William said it was "glittery".

No. 4. (made on 22nd session).

The available eight squares of red, blue, yellow and white placed along the four edges with a mass of red, blue and yellow diamonds projecting from left to right inside the frame; an irregular mass of red triangles placed at the top.

No. 5. (made on 27th session before attempting to build a house in the sand tray).

Twenty-eight diamonds and eight red squares placed in a disorderly fashion around three sides of the tray. None of these fitted together although William seemed to want to make them do so.

No. 6. (made on 40th session). *A double layered pattern*, which is described in detail in the case.

No. 7. (made on session 44. *Forth Bridge World*).

Consisted of piles of four and five pieces of identical shape mainly in the same colours as before, placed along the bottom and left edge of the tray, but with little lateral coherence with each other.

No. 8. (made on session 45).

This was the first Mosaic in which William exercised control over the pieces instead of the shape of his pattern being dictated to him by the number of available pieces of a given shape or by the shape of the tray. He placed 10 squares in pairs of white, green, red, yellow, blue, along the bottom edge of the tray, piling 3 additional squares on each (thus using up those available in each shape and colour). When five colours had been used, however, and the length of the edge of the tray filled, he was unable to check his actions there, as one colour, black, remained unused. He therefore put a pair of piles of black squares above the two whites against the left-hand edge. William now took out the whole pile of green half-squares and put them, long side toward the row of squares, by themselves, to the right of the two black piles of squares. Two piles of black half-squares (using all available) and one of white placed by themselves in a row above the squares completed this line. Next above this William repeated the arrangement with large equilateral triangles, beginning again with a pair of red side by side with two piles of blue fitting into them. These were followed by a yellow pile, two white, one yellow, two green and two black – in each case using all the available similar pieces superimposed.

Having arrived at this point in his pattern William said "*This is a maze*". He now added a row of piles of half-squares above the equilateral triangles, this time with the colours put irregularly, and not in pairs. This completed the series of Mosaics of the first period of treatment.

It is interesting and informative as to his "intentions" with his Mosaic that he followed it by an attempt to construct a house with Bayko, a construction set where wires fit into holes in a base and pieces of plastic rather resembling the Mosaic pieces, are slid down between each pair.

No. 9. (made on first reporting visit).

This was a very interesting Mosaic. William took out all four squares of white, red, yellow and blue (the same colours he had used before) from one side of the box and arranged them down the left edge of the tray to form a larger square with each colour. He repeated the arrangement along the right edge with the squares from the other side of the box and in reverse colour-order. This left the middle of the tray bare. He now took out 12 green diamonds and made an irregular vertical loop with an open end at the bottom; this he said was "a house". In contrast to the untidiness of the arrangement of these diamonds he made an orderly pyramid shape of three red, three yellow, one blue, one white triangles arising from the bottom and pointing upwards within the loop and topped with a red diamond – this he said was "a fountain". The columnar spaces each side of this he filled with blue, yellow and red scalenes laid flat one under the other. These he said "were a decoration".

This Mosaic is particularly informative. In its completed form it represents a tall thin "house", in the centre of which a fountain plays. It happens, however, that the vertical loop said by William to be "the house" was made of green diamonds, a colour William has previously used once only. The loop of green, therefore, combines "tree" and "house" and the design puts the fountain firmly within the house – and tree.

No. 10. (made on his second follow-up visit).

For the first time William here used the *space* of the tray deliberately, constructing four "pillars" each of four squares placed first against the right and left edges of the tray in identical sequences of blue and red, then using the whole of the yellow and white squares to make similar "pillars" free in the space and each a quarter way across the tray.

Within the central space he placed three green squares one against the bottom edge and one each side slightly higher up, and arranged a rod of red scalenes rising vertically and tapering to a point at the top; this he said was "a fountain".

No. 11. (made on the 51st session: World 28).

Here the ability to manage space has developed. For the first time he started in the centre, placing a vertical row of six red squares from the top edge downwards and filling in a block of four blue squares between the last red square and the bottom edge of the tray; five yellow scalenes were placed at intervals standing out horizontally one each side of the central column with their points touching the points of junction between the red squares. Five red diamonds were now placed on either side sloping horizontally outside these with their points touching the outer points of the scalenes. Between the row of red diamonds and the outer right and left edge, and equally disposed in space, William placed on either side four white equilateral triangles broad side down. The whole he said was "a magic Christmas tree out of doors with the snow falling".

No. 12. (made on the 57th session: World 32). William showed considerable advance in management of his ideas and his materials.

He started this time in the centre and constructed what he said was "a fountain" with the sixteen available red diamonds extending from a projecting diamond at top in four curved and vertical lines to the bottom edge; horizontally across the point at the top he placed three, and at the bottom one, yellow diamonds. Against the short edges of the tray he used all the red squares on the left and the blue on the right, putting a similar column of yellow on the left and green on the right, about half-inch inside the outer one. These he said were "the walls of the fountain".

No. 13. (made one week after World 34).

This is the last Mosaic of the series we are studying. It shows movement from the edges into the centre. William made a three square wide column up from the bottom of the tray of blue, yellow, red, white, white, red, yellow, blue bands. Stretching horizontally from the middle to each side he inserted a band of squares in the same colours. He now flanked the centre column with a fringe of red diamonds sloping up above the centre and down below it, each red diamond with a yellow at its tip. This design William said was "a magic fire".

Summary. In these 13 Mosaics three responses (3, 4, 5) are partial or complete frames. No. 5 is very rudimentary and empty, No. 4 is complete and partially filled, and No. 3 is a lattice work. One only, No. 6, completely filled the tray and did it twice, one layer on top of the other; two (Nos. 7 and 8) were small blocks of pieces piled on top of each other, one of these called "a maze". The remaining seven were representational, four (2, 9, 10, 12) of "a fountain", two (1 and part of 9) "a house", one (11) a Christmas tree, and one (13) a magic fire. The same type of patterning was followed throughout.

The Concept of Space

A central characteristic of William's Worlds is their peculiar relation to space. This appeared at the outset when, in his first Mosaic, the four black squares, placed in the outlined house in positions usual for windows, were called by him "corridors". To William therefore these four Mosaic pieces were not solid objects but the blackness of narrow channels running through and at right angles to the paper.

This concept of depth below/or behind the surface presented to the eye, came out clearly also in his first World. All that appeared were shallow surface markings on the sand, but William's fragmentary remarks about them made it obvious that to him the "robbers" and the "gold" were "real" and existed below the surface of the sand.

Now, both exterior and interior space have three dimensions – and if a plane surface exists, like the Mosaic tray or the surface of sand in the World tray the two other dimensions can exist above and below that surface. There can also be movement or the idea of movement connecting any part of these inner or outer surfaces. Furthermore, clusters arise out of accumulations of identified fractions of experience and ideas. In these clusters, concepts and experiences of space are essential parts of the cluster.

Worlds 3 and 4 supply examples of the expression of clusters in structures below the surface of the sand in the tray.

World 3 is a network of ideas about "within" and "without" and movement between them: little is constructed, much is conceived of, and this in parallels of larger and smaller, after the manner of a Russian doll; the mound contains people, they go in and out, they eat within; the lorry contains hay which comes out to form another mound and then goes "into" horses: the Christmas tree is first in a field and moved to the top of the mound and so on. In World 4 an essential spatial element is conceived of as below the surface of the tray. The water contains mound-like rocks, the rocks contain "houses", the fish live in the houses: at the same time the "upper" dimension is provided by the sticks. The guns of the hunters (which appear only in this World) are also long objects out of which fire comes; the sand mound here is an inverted container.

In World 6, as we have already pointed out, several kinds of "space" are implied and several "withins" and "withouts" both in relation to water and to "cubical space" where the "underground" to which the caretaker goes down and up is implied as beneath the sand.

In World 7 the mound reappears, this time although it is specifically stated that people live in the mound, it is not tunnelled to admit of entrance and exit, the "tunnelling" in this mound is vertical and not horizontal and this vertical hole was seen by William as a projection (chimney) not a hole. William's treatment of the cement mixer and buses suggests that it is these as "containers" that impressed him. The "standing up" element supplied by the sticks in World 4 appear here as many telegraph poles and street-lights. The third mound was the centre of World 8 – this time conceived of as hollow but without occupants.

World 14 is a kind of essay in different kinds of "space-above-the-sand-in-the-tray" and movement within it, the aeroplanes being conceived of as moving about in that space and the lorry as moving within and without the schematic "garage". This construction is to some extent repeated in the Forth Bridge World (22) where the single ship between the pillars of the bridge corresponds to the single lorry between the pillars of the "garage".

Mounds reappear in World 23 but this time to contain the dead rather than the living, and in World 24 this idea of a-structure-above-the-sand containing the fruits of victory changes to large structures above the sand on the summit of which a band plays boomingly in the mood of victory.

William is a boy who lives in sophisticated surroundings and the well in World 27 has therefore more point than it would in a rural boy: in this setting a well seems to be "water beneath the earth" and to resemble other ideas of treasure and help below the surface of the tray and so to belong to the same series of ideas as appears in the last World of our series, World 34. This is a World in which all three dimensions of "outer" space appear – the aeroplanes (peripheral in this scene instead of central as in World 14) in the air, the ships on the surface and the submarine and the wreck below the surface of the water. At the same time the idea of "men within" was included, the sunken liner was thought of as containing people and the coastguard ship as containing coastguards.

As it was in the first Mosaic that this relation to space was first expressed, so it is in the Mosaics that the unexpected relation between what he actually put on the tray and what he saw in his mind first showed. This is the relation of a very young child to what he has drawn and suggests that if he could have found words to describe the layout of his Worlds and the objects he put in them, they might well have contained ideas quite un-suspected by me. Later when William started to attempt to build a house in the sand tray, the Mosaic he made (5) reflected his inability to manage factual materials in that the comparative order achieved in Mosaic 4 was lost in 5. In Mosaics 7 and 8 William attempted to use this material to build in height, for which it is patently unsuitable.

On William's first reporting visit he combined in a Mosaic the ideas of fountains which had been dimly in the background of much of his work with that of a house – the fountain not "outside" as in the model village World, but "inside" the house. At the same time the Mosaic pieces used to form the house are green diamonds and outside the walls are "decorations" suggesting that the "house" is also the "Christmas tree", a suggestion which is given support by Mosaic 4 which represents "a magic Christmas tree" and where the same pieces were used to form the branches.

In a single study it is difficult to show the help that this type of expression has given us in our understanding of the inner world of childhood and the psychogenesis both of school failure and of behaviour disturbances, but it is hoped that enough has been said to give some indication of the nature of the proto-system and of the value of the World Technique in giving it expression and assisting in its understanding.

Review of William's Treatment

Every experienced Child Psychiatrist has met boys resembling William when first seen and many accounts have been published of similar cases, studied and treated from other points of view. During the period covered by the extract under review, sufficient progress had been made to show that this was an adequate sample of the process of treatment. This period of William's treatment then makes possible a study of the relation between the proto-system and other aspects of the psyche.

From the beginning it is obvious that William was deeply involved with his mother; his dependence on her, his identification with her is almost classic in its completeness. Regarded from the point of view of instinctual theory there is little that is unknown about this situation. The purpose of this study is to suggest the possibility of regarding these familiar facts from a different point of view.

Even a short acquaintance with William made it evident that he was driven by an interior anguish; that his behaviour both in its active aspects of rages or the negative one of phobias or his school failure proceeded from forces within him which were not "willed" by him. It was clear that these were concerned, in part at any rate, with his emotional drives. His Worlds made it evident, however, that other events were also taking place within him. The question is where does the emphasis lie? What is the nature of that anguish which is not affective, from which this child – and similar children – suffers and which finds expression in their Worlds?

It is the purpose of this study to suggest that the nature of this anguish is concerned with the structure of the proto-system and with the problem of truth. The kernel of every neurosis is isolation, the being consumed with and shaken by experiences which no one seems to share. An infant on the breast is in an intense, almost symbiotic, relation with his mother, and this sense of unity is the matrix through which his inner development takes place. As a child develops, not only does he suffer the exaltations and satisfactions, denials and frustrations which have been so intensively studied by other methods, but also his whole existence is shot through with vivid constantly changing experience of all his five senses. To every small child the basis of life is the assumption that everything that goes on within him is known by and shared by those around him, his mother centrally and in a lesser degree other adults. Their behaviour to him seems to him directly and intimately related to the knowledge they have of him. However frustrating or painful his mother's handling of him may be, or however terrifying to him his feelings about her, the fact of her unity with him remains to him the core of everyday life.

When therefore discrepancy arises between "truth" as it happens to the child, that "truth" which is so "real" that it cannot be denied, as in William's phobias of the lavatory, and the "truth" told him by his mother about that same situation, there arises in the child the most acute of all human conflicts; that between his own "truth" and the truth of the outside world. The child knows that what he feels and fears he does indeed feel and fear; the pictures that rise within him and the connections and interconnections between things his senses have told him, have an absolute reality for him. He does his best to make them into a whole, to relate them to each other and his central self to them; he works hard at it, but there is a gulf between what he feels the world to be, and what is told him about it by the powerful adults outside him; the two are in essential conflict. What then is he to do? His position is that of the adult individual in whom the same conflict occurs at the onset of a psychosis. As this is an unendurable position, expression of it must be found, together with relief from the tension so aroused, and bit by bit the various elements of the "disturbance" develop. There are therefore present in such a child two types of anguish: that arising from emotional conflict and that arising from conflict of truths. What we need to ask is how do these affect each other?

The study of human biography shows that it is possible to achieve an inner integrity and to achieve a workable relation to reality, even in the absence of love given or received. It is not however possible to achieve a working relation to life and a sound integration of the self, however excellent the interpersonal relationships, in the presence of beliefs concerning the nature of external reality which are in conflict with each other and also with the facts.

But, it will be argued, do not these false beliefs arise directly from confusions, fixations and failures in interpersonal relations? It is to seek the answer to this query that the World Technique has been adapted. Here, there is no question of a specialised form of interpersonal relationship with the therapist with whom what develops is a normal atmosphere of trusted fellowship. As has been studied in Mary's World series, a wide range of interpersonal relationships can be and frequently is, directly as well as symbolically, expressed in Worlds. It depends upon the point of view of the therapist where the emphasis in discussion with the child and interpretation is put.

The explanation given to the child at the outset by the therapist, that there are pictures in his head which are important but which will not go into words, breaks at once the worst of the child's isolation: the child feels "here is a human being who knows what it is like inside me". Confrontation with the World apparatus and experimentation with it, brings to him the feeling that here is something which can be made to "say" something of the inner torments that boil within him. The act of expression is in itself a relief.

The central impression one had in working with William, particularly in the early sessions, was his complete absorption in the Worlds he was making.

Viewed from this angle William's first World is illuminating – "Robbers" and "gold" and "a face", put in an order which is expressive of his urgent need for "sense". This is what his inner "self" feels; "there is gold" – value, within him, richness somewhere: "there are robbers" – some force is battling to get the gold: "a face" – it is something to do with people (the face is the epitome to a child of "a person"). This presentation, with itse sense of depth (the robbers and the gold were felt somehow to be within the sand), gives the clue to the sort of child this is. This is a child driven, not like Charles by excess of unintegrated E who is able to express his experience in direct symbolism, but a child caught, like the humans in fairytale (or myth), in an inner world which is totally different from the outer one which surrounds him, and which is completely incomprehensible. That is to say a child in whom the proto-system, instead of being a part only of his experience, has come to flood the whole of his inner consciousness and distort both his real sensorial and emotional experience and also his contact with the whole outer world.

It is this distortion of the normal relation to outside objects that forms part of the evidence that this is the inner situation of such a child. The degree of difficulty children in this state can experience in grasping the simplest facts about weight and mass has to be seen to be believed. For example, William would constantly attempt to set quite heavy objects on the thin edges of planks fixed on their sides in sand, and exclaim in a depressed fashion "oh dear" when they immediately fell down. It was clear that he saw in his mind as a completed solid the structure he wanted to make, but was quite unable to analyse this out into its component planes and realise the facts of gravity. The same haziness of comprehension covered his attempt to combine and manipulate objects of different sizes where the force of gravity was not involved, or to understand the construction of his own body. Everything was fluid for him: liable to turn inside out, or for the elements to rearrange themselves within exterior space.

This situation penetrated to his school work. As his headmaster wrote "at times he seems to understand quite well and makes normal progress, at other times his mind is a complete blank and he knows nothing".

On the basis of the theories we are attempting to expound this is perfectly reasonable. At the moments when E was energising the Secondary System, that of ordinary cognitive thought, his ability to understand, and so to manipulate abstract symbols, such as number etc., was that of the ordinary child of his intelligence and age. In the moments when E was mainly investing the proto-system (where there is no "time" and whose construction is multi-dimensional) this "system" became projected on to the outside world and the normal procedures of language and number (which essentially function in a time/space continuum), became incomprehensible.

250

Perhaps the difference between these two types of experience can best be illustrated by the statement of an able adult man patient under treatment for asthma, who said, when asked about his own experience of the proto-system: "it is as if the continuum in which you are, is broken open, and you have a direct experience of all the senses combined in one; very intense. It is like an explosion; there is no distance in it. It is to me the source of ideas; everything is equally vivid as, for example, a colour is loud".

It is my belief that much of the common "blocking" of normal children in relation to their school work if of this nature, and can only be relieved through expression and resolution of an abnormally charged and also fantastic proto-system. Once the E which is over-charging the proto-system can be released from it and set free to energise the normal components of intellectual work, the processes of learning can, and in our experience most usually do, begin to function normally.

This is what happened with William. When William was first tested on Terman-Merrill Form L, his mental age was 10–6 as against a chronological age of 8–9, giving him an I.Q. of 123. At this age there is no sub-item dealing with arithmetic or rote memory. When he was tested again on Form M at a chronological age of 12.11 where sub-items of this kind are included, his I.Q. had fallen to 106. When however at an age of 13.10 he was tested on Koh's Blocks his mental age was 15.8. The psychologist's report runs "The perseverance shown by him when doing the Koh's Blocks was quite extraordinary, so was his determination to succeed – which he did". Concerning the boy himself she reported "you have made a person of this boy, his capacity for concentration and his will-power were astonishing". What has happened is that the confusions of a fantastic proto-system having been cleared away and the fears, nightmares, and irrational impulses arising from these, resolved, the E which was entangled in them had become free to energise the normal processes of thinking.

In the child's relation to his emotional experience and conflicts something of the same sort seems to happen; tensions between different aspects of inner emotions and outer semblance, which in the presence of distorted images of the self and the world outside, tend to increase to an unendurable point, become so reduced in intensity and menace, once the proto-system confusions are cleared up, that the child becomes able to face and cope with them. Increasing sureness in comprehension of himself and his factual surroundings brings a sense of confidence which makes the tackling of other problems possible.

My aim in describing the treatment of William Carter is to convey an impression of the process by which this detachment of E from a proto-system of abnormal content is brought about, and the resolution of that content. Once having established, through William's performance at the Consultation session, the fact that he was a child whose disturbance in all probability arose from the clusters in his proto-system, it was clear that the

World Technique would be an exactly appropriate method of treatment and the road led straight ahead. This, one's reasoning ran, is a child who needs all that human ingenuity can offer him of multi-dimensional technique and sensorial possibilities to make possible the externalisation, study, dissection, realisation and correction of his distorted inner world. He is in urgent need of four things: to have the nature of his distress recognised and accepted as real by an outside person; to have a means of presenting this inner content to this outside person; for this person to understand it and to find a means of communicating this understanding to him; and to have possibilities of giving vent to the energies, excitements and interests so long dammed up within him. All these we were able to provide. The one thing we were not able to provide was a modification of his parents' characters and outlook so that they should understand what was going on within him and be able to change their handling of him.

For William's sake this was regrettable and both time and suffering could have been saved both for him and for his parents had this been possible. From the point of view of theory however this was advantageous as it makes possible the demonstration of the possibilities of this approach and the value of the World Technique to cope with situations in which suitable access to the parents is not possible.

What happened therefore in William's treatment is an example of the process through which children who have failed to find their way out of absorption in the proto-system, through working hard at successive presentations, gradually come to make contact with, realise, and sort out their own interior preoccupations. Explanation to the therapist of the associative background, the interior significance and the feeling tone of what is presented, coupled with explanation from the therapist of the reality meaning of these presentations, brings the child gradually into contact with reality and finally to mastery and direction of his own power in relation to reality, inner and outer.

When treatment was completed William had in all had 76 sessions of treatment extending, with constant breaks, over many months (the last sessions being of the nature of supportive sessions during a period when he had left his Preparatory School to attend a coaching establishment in preparation for his Public School).

As regards his personality, as his phobias declined so his interest in and ability to respond to his environment improved; the school began to notice that William was becoming a leader; his parents began to allow him to travel to town alone; an interest in rhythm appeared, and William would have liked to learn Scottish dancing; he developed ease of manner with adults and a good relation with boys; his relations with his sister became normal and in the end a friendship began to develop with his father.

On the subjective making of a World

The purpose of this chapter is to study the subjective aspects of the making of a World, and to give some idea of what actually takes place within the individual who sets out to make a World. Observation of both children and adults during the process suggests that there are differences between the inner experience of children and adults during the construction of a World. In children there is more excitement and less reflection. In adults, for the most part, the reflective element is stronger; yet in both, the same complete absorption in the process is observable. But since children cannot give a coherent account of what they are experiencing, it is to adults we must look for a verbal description of their experience.

But before we embark upon a study of this aspect, we need to pause a moment and reflect upon the nature of language and the nature of the communication that can be conveyed by this means.

During the past quarter of a century, emphasis in philosophy has come increasingly to be laid upon the study of words and on their relationship to the facts or experience they purport to communicate. Only those words or statements for which there exists some means of verification of their generally accepted significance are accepted as valid evidence of the existence of that which the word sets out to signify. In this examination, also, it is the usual or common use of the word which is taken for study. We will return to this aspect later. Apart from the question of the meaning of single words, it is, however, in their syntactical use that, for the main part, words either describe or communicate an experience.

This being so, it is held in many quarters that, for language to function as communication, what actually takes place is a process of coding from the experience with the words used by the speaker or writer and of subsequent decoding by the hearer or reader, through which process approximate communication is established. All languages are grammatically constructed, and both time and space are involved in this structuring. At one time and occupying one space in printed matter, only one thought, description or experience can be communicated. If, therefore, an event or an idea of any complexity is chosen as the subject of the communication, in order that it may appear in grammatical form, the event or the idea must first be present as a whole in the mind of the communicator. It must then be divided into sections in that mind, the sections arranged in a significant order and, finally, the material in each section set out in the type of grammatical form demanded by the structure of the language in which it is expressed. Time is essentially involved in this process at two points: during the period of sectioning and arranging, and in the procedure of articulating the ultimate sentences into which the original material is coded. If the language be written or printed, space is involved as well.

A communication of this kind from A to B, therefore, if satisfactorily accomplished, gives the appearance of a unity. This unity is, however, entirely illusory because, whatever the nature of the subject matter of the communication, or wherever and in what circumstances this "coding" takes place, a number of other events will also be happening, traffic passing, changes of light or sound, interior sensations within the body of the communicator, associated ideas and so on, all of which have to be excluded by an effort of will, if the communication is to have a unity. If the communication, moreover, is to have a scientific validity, some general body of meaning for each word to be used must be previously agreed upon between A (the communicator) and B (he who receives the communication).

For most general purposes, adequate agreement is usually present, so that a sentence such as "he put the book on the table" would be understood by all hearers in exactly the way intended by the speaker and would correspond with an exactly definable action capable of being directly and exactly recorded by photography.

It is here we come upon the recent advances in observation and recording of human behaviour by the use of photography in anthropology, of which the wholly admirable photographs by Dr. Margaret Mead, reproduced in "Growth and Culture"* can be taken as an example. These photographs portray attitudes of hands and arms taken by Balinese adults in relation to children and the point about the photographs is that they portray something which differs, in a fundamental manner, from the attitudes which would be taken by Europeans in similar situations. Moreover, because of the nature of the situations photographed and their effective implications, out of these differences in objective posture certain direct deductions can be drawn concerning the interior feelings of Balinese and European parents, when in these situations; their likenesses and differences.

These intuitive inferences are possible because the situations involved are wholly familiar to us and have been familiar for many centuries and in an unlimited number of variations. We have, as it were, in our own experiences of ourselves and our own people, a standard against which unfamiliar variations can be compared. Such photographs, with such standards for comparison, are therefore more than objective records of human figures, they are records which, through the fact of our previous experience of similar situations of other human figures "talk" to us on two levels and convey several layers of significance. Such double layers of communication are always possible when time enters into the record – when, that is, the immediate record is either of an individual of whom earlier similar records exist, and where therefore the one individual can be compared with himself at another date or in another situation, or where one example of a general species, other examples of which are already known, can be compared with those examples.

---

*Margaret Mead and Frances Cooke Macgregor, C. P. Putnam's Sons, New York, 1951.

254

These general propositions underlie the view that has recently been several times expressed that the proper recording of World-making would involve the cooperation of cine camera, tape recorder and shorthand observer either present or behind a one-way screen.

The validity of this type of record of the process of World-making as a means of communication needs however to be carefully examined. To do this let us revert to our sentence "he put the book upon the table". This is a clear statement of limited meaning, and although a dozen individuals in carrying out an identical action might have been motivated in a dozen different ways or intend to achieve very different ends, yet the action in itself is unequivocal and unless the exact position of the book on the table had a secondary importance, known or unknown to actor or observer, the words used to describe the phenomenon observed do so economically and accurately.

The camera and the observer in the second case who record that a World-maker standing in front of an open drawer containing a number of representations of houses of different shapes and sizes "took up a medium sized house and put it on the flat sand in the World tray" are making a record of an action of an entirely different nature. To the individual who has taken up the house it *may* represent "a house", but it may also and with equal possibility represent nothing of the sort. It may be the nearest object he can find to stand to him for the idea of "safety" of "being under observation" of "the restriction of urban life" of "family" or simply of a conveniently sized and shaped rectangular object he can use as a plinth later to put a horseman on to form a statue.

This situation arises because, although some unusual objects can be found in the drawers of a World Cabinet yet in comparison with the variety of experience any adult or child using the cabinet might wish to express, or with the number of words, in even an average vocabulary, it is only chance whether an object will be found in the cabinet which exactly expresses the "meaning" desired by the maker and in all other cases an approximation has to be made to serve. Without knowledge either of previous constructions, made by the same individual, or of the customary use by individuals of his age and type of objects of that kind or at best from the description by the individual of processes going on in his own mind during the performance of that action, no comprehension of the action can be gained. It is here that with children, and particularly with children of a certain type, the tape recorder can give genuine assistance, but with adults it helps us but little.

Without a record, therefore, of the whole process as seen from inside by the maker and a graphic reproduction of the construction made, we have little material to study. Since small children are unable to introspect or to report their experience, for enlightenment we must turn to adults.

In this chapter therefore we present three excerpts from work by adults, one long and two short, as illustration of the process of World-making as seen from the standpoint of the adult who makes it.

World made by K: Figure 64

This is a drawing of a World made by an adult, K during the course of training in child psychotherapy at the I.C.P. An account of the making of the World, the circumstances in which it came to be made and of the World itself is given in her own words.

K's Account:

"During the period covered by a personal analysis (vegeto-therapeutic character analysis in type), while training in Child Psychotherapy at the I.C.P., I experimented with the techniques which I was learning to use with the children* in order to see whether personal material arising in my analysis would appear in these or not. My object was twofold: a desire to experience subjectively what the making of a World felt like to the maker, and to test the validity of these techniques. On my own initiative therefore and apart from the process of training, from time to time when the urge to do so arose, I made a series of Worlds. These interested me but had no affective impact. Toward the end of the second year of analysis however I made a World which (illustrated in fig. 64) aroused powerful and un-expected affect at the time of making and set interior processes going which only reached their ultimate clarification and resolution about four

---

*Mosaics and Worlds.

years later. I made records of the previous Worlds but did not consider them further.

This World occurred in the following way: at the end of a day's work a fellow student and I went down to the playrooms at the I.C.P. to make Worlds, working silently side by side at separate World trays, as we had often done before.

The World

I started manipulating the sand with my hands, trying to find out what I wanted to make. There first arose some small hills spread over the tray, but these did not satisfy me. I destroyed them, scraped the heaps of sand into one big heap and then built quickly and without hesitation a long, strong wall of sand diagonally across the tray from the left nearer corner to the right further corner, stopped and looked at it, and then removed the parts of the sand that connected the wall with the corners of the tray. The wall was now free of the edge of the tray. From the drawers of the World Cabinet I selected six exactly similar pine trees, placed three at each corner at the end of the wall and some bushy vegetation on top of the wall. On the further part of the tray I placed big, dark forest trees in strict lines, like a wood, looking to me heavy and stern; I remember I searched carefully among the trees in the drawer in order to find the darkest ones. Using a small lid I made a circular hollow in the sand in the nearer part of the tray and filled it with flowers like a small sunken garden. Finally I selected from the drawers some wild animals, all fierce mammals, such as tigers, leopards, lions, bears, and stuck their heads firmly into either side of the wall of sand. The kind or type of animal was important, not the number; (the number here represents those of that type that were available in the drawer.)

Reaction

Till now I had worked quickly, allowing the World to develop of itself; I did not stop to think or to plan at all. But when I had finished, a strange emotion caught me; I sat down on a small chair at the table nearby, put my head on my arms while a violent sobbing shook my whole body. I was very perplexed, but gave way to the flow of emotion as long as it lasted. Afterwards I felt exhausted and bewildered as I had no plausible explanation of my reaction.

During the next two months, in the course of analysis, and starting with a re-living of the joyful feeling I had had when a child while playing that I was a horse, the factual element of a traumatic experience from early childhood, hitherto unknown to me, returned to memory as follows.

Childhood experience (age 2¾)

I am with my mother at a party; it is at a biggish farm; the people there were close friends of my parents, the wife my godmother, it is summer, late afternoon; people are about in the garden. I am the only child present and am playing by myself; I am dressed in my best clothes, am happy and gay. I play to myself that I am a young unbridled horse galloping along from the house toward the farm buildings some way away from the house; the setting sun is on my left-hand side. In the farm buildings there is a big barn door, with a piece of chain attached to it; I grip the chain; the wild horse has been chained and opposes violently; it kicks and pulls. Dislodged by this movement the heavy barn door (which had become detached from its hinges and was only propped up) falls on me.

257

.. I am stretched out on the ground, face down, with this heavy object on top of me, unable to move; I see a bit of light coming in from the top edge . . . – I hear running footsteps and several men lift up the barn door . . .

The next thing I know is that I find myself sitting on my mother's lap, leaning against her shoulder, stiff and motionless; I do not cry; my mother wears a black dress; she is sitting near the fire in the kitchen; grownups are standing round us, all looking very grave and stern and big – like a solid black wall; I am just sitting there; the grown-ups talk . . .

Check-up of the event

Three years after the incident had come to light in analysis, I had an opportunity to check it up with my father. I brought up the subject with him and asked if he remembered its occurring and if so what he remembered of it. He was rather startled at my asking this and the said that what I described was true, and had really happened. I was 2¾ years old. He had not been at the party but had stayed at home, he remembered, as if it had happened yesterday, that he had been out in the backyard when he saw my mother standing on the steps leading down from the house. "I can still recall the spot where she was standing", he said; "I was surprised to see her back so early". She said to me, "You had better go in and see K, she has been put to bed; I nearly did not bring her back with me alive". My father said that I had been found with a small arm stretched out under the heavy barn door; nobody knew for how long I had been lying there.

My father admitted that the event had never been talked about in the family; he didn't know why. I was the elder of two, and my sister, four years younger, had never heard about the happening.

The Link

About three months after the making of the World, during an analytic session, this childhood incident, which considered as a fact had already been recalled to memory a month ago, but without any accompanying affect, came up once more and was worked over. I brought myself back to the moment when I was sitting on my mother's lap, stiff and motionless; then suddenly I turned on the couch on to my left side, huddled together in a bundle, and a violent sobbing broke out. When the outburst of emotion had passed I got up, saying, "The World! That was what it was about; I cried just like that after having finished it".

After that, all the repressed emotions connected with the actual experience were little by little released in analysis and worked through so that neither the incident itself nor the World any longer carried affect. Some weeks after this I put the World up again in order to study it as objectively as I was able to do.

Immediate asscociations

The stern dark wood at the further part of the tray I saw to be the crowd of dark serious-looking grownups, looming high about me as I sat on my mother's lap; the rigid placing of the trees gave a picture of the rigidity I felt in those people: "what are they doing? why are they all looking at me?" The three stiff pine trees at each end of the wall I saw to be a picture of my father, my mother and me. We were alike, we belonged together, yet were isolated by our lack of ability to give way to strongly felt emotions. The frightful event that the fall of the barn door must have been for each of us was never released in a mutual sharing of the anxiety and of the joy that all was well and I was not killed. Each "forgot", and it was never talked about as far as anyone remembers.

The strong solid wall cutting across the tray I realised was a picture of the emotional blocking that this caused in me. I captured and arrested within me the drive of emotional energy, here presented by fierce wild animals with their heads firmly stuck into the wall. (I am aware that many other aspects and intepretations can be linked with just this choice of symbolic representation; these are omitted as they are irrelevant to the purpose of this account).

I grew up and became a shy, introverted girl, living my own inner life, represented here by the small sunken garden filled with flowers in the nearer part of the tray.

When I had worked out these associations I found that I had completed a description for myself of all the items in the tray. Having found the meaning of the objects I had chosen, their interrelationship, and that of the general layout of the World structure, I was aware, as a therapist, that this wall had to be broken down and the animals set free. But I could not see how this could be done. The only solutions which occurred to me were either to pull the animals out or push them through, or to break down the wall by external force; none of these could I do, so I left it as it was.

The answer to this problem appeared in a dream about 18 months later:

Dream I
The World I had made was spread out in front of me like a landscape; it had a certain quality of being alive; I saw a strong flood of water coming as from an underground current bursting through the surface in the nearer part of the ground near the middle of the wall, making its way through the wall toward the further part of the tray; more and more water welled up, turning into a real river; I watched the wall crumbling bit by bit as in a slow moving film, till there was an opening through the wall connecting the two parts of the tray . . . and still more water welled up . . .

I woke up the following morning with a feeling of inner reassurance, the dream having made me aware that the liberating forces would come from *within* myself; the wall in my World could not, and was not, to be broken down by external force. In this dream I was unaware of the animals.

During a subsequent stay of eight months in my home country a second relevant dream occurred which made use of the symbols of the World, this time of the animals.

Dream II (about two years after the making of the World)
I was in a house and some big wild animal cubs were playing about it; I made

259

friends with the cubs as one does with cats, let them into the house at night for shelter; I was especially fond of a young camel. An older one (a leopard?) appeared; it had an evil look in its right eye; I was afraid it would attack the others, so a shadowy person (myself) lets them out at the other side of the house (the front) while I let this one in at the back, hoping it would not discover the others. At night it wanted to get out too, and I dared not prevent it, so I opened the back door and it disappeared in the dark while I stood in the door waiting in anxiety to hear a cry that would tell me the leopard has attacked one of my friends, the wild cubs; but it did not occur.

The symbols of the World were still the media used in this dream to present to myself the changes that had taken place in me during analysis. The wall had been broken down, the wild animals had become free and friendly, except for one which is hostile to the others, a fact that filled me with anxiety.

The meaning of this "hostile" animal with an "evil eye" came to light in a dream later and was found to refer to an actual event which took place shortly after the making of the World. This event presented a sudden, completely unexpected and severe threat to the continuance of a project to which I was then committed. I responded to this shock as I had to the barn door incident with a "sham dead" reaction, sitting motionless for hours as frozen. In this dream the animals did not appear.

The animals appeared some time later in the final dream relating to this World:—

*Dream III**

I am walking toward the village in my own country on the road along the stream and have just passed the old bridge; am going to visit the people to whom I have let my cottage; with me is one of my grown "wild" animals on a lead like a large dog; he is walking at my right-hand side; I am very fond of him and a bit worried as I know the people I am going to see have a big dog and the two of them might fight; I decide to leave my "wild animal" in my neighbour's field while I pay my call, hoping they will not get at each other.

Maker's Comments

This has been an attempt to show how the Lowenfeld World Technique fits in with other kinds of analysis, producing as in my case a possibility of externalising a not yet realised, heavily charged experience in early childhood in symbolic form. The World described does not picture the actual event in any way; the only resemblance one may find is that the animals caught in the wall unable to get free may represent the feeling I had myself

---

*Dream III was inserted after the writing of this chapter and is therefore not commented on in detail in the General Discussion that follows. But its conclusive evidence is obvious as it solved the final question:— making friends with the grown wild animal in the World.

while trapped under the barn door.

The vegeto-therapeutic analysis I was undergoing at the time released the muscular tensions caused by repressed emotions connected with an event far back in early childhood. And it was the opening up of this flood of emotion that gave the clue to the meaning of the World and made it possible for me to give the symbolic representation its real content and context, to "read the language" of the World.

Next the dream activity took over. What was not possible for the cognitive mind to imagine or accept at the time when I rebuilt the World, namely the way of breaking down the wall (a process taking place during my analysis), was brought into consciousness through a dream and the procedure shown as on a cinema screen in a slow moving picture. This was followed by other dreams taking up the theme of the wild animals being accepted into my house, first as cubs, then as grown up walking with me towards home, friendly and accepted.

The choice of symbols is never a chance happening, even if it may seem so at the moment. They carry the personal, individual meaning as well as the universally accepted meaning in every case. As for my choice in 1952 of wild animals I should like to quote from E. W. Smith's "African Symbolism" (p. 191):

"Wild animals roaming the surface of the land symbolise at once the mystical 'livingness' of the earth and the mystical force of the ancestors, their efficacy in the lives of their descendants . . ."

The wild animals in the World were for me not only a picture of arrested "E", but carried too the deeper meaning of presenting a challenge to my willingness and ability to accept "the mystical livingness of the earth" and the inheritance from my ancestors way back and back in the culture to which I belong. This I conclude from the fact that dream II occurred when I had established a "home of my own" in my home country in a small village on a site inhabited in pre-historic times. Also the final dream III about a wild animal related to that particular place.

The symbols used in the World have not recurred in any subsequent dreams. It might, however, be of interest to add that, parallel with the dreams related here, a series of dreams occurred with a horse as the main symbol, the first of these dating about half a year *before* the making of the World. In reality, and without ever being able to account for the discrepancy, I had always had a panic fear of horses at the same time as an intense desire to learn to ride. This fear of horses, till now unaccounted for, disappeared gradually as the affects resulting from the traumatic barn-door experience were worked through and released. Through the help of an understanding riding master it now became possible to take up riding and to enjoy the experience keenly.

General Discussion

The World described above and the three dreams that follow, together with the maker's comments, have been selected for presentation because of the way in which the intimate relation between reality and affect, the process of World-making and its symbols and the process of dreaming are shown in it, and their eventual working out related to present day circumstances and feelings.

This World, the factual incident from which it all arose, and the mode in which its effects upon the personality of the child to whom it occurred are revealed in World and dreams, throw considerable light upon the nature of the process of World-making and the mode in which violent events register themselves in the minds of small children. To consider for a moment what exactly is involved and what comes to light in these four symbolic presentations, we have three facts to consider.

A. An accident which happened to a child of $2\frac{3}{4}$ years.

B. The making of a World in middle life which did, in fact embody the subjective aspects of this experience though these were not known to the maker at the time.

C. Two dreams employing the same symbols as appeared in the World, and a third dream four years after the making of the World which exhausted its meaning and brought the affectual aspect of the situation up to date.

A. The factual incident

This was an external assault upon a child of $2\frac{3}{4}$ which was not caused by anyone and in itself had neither meaning nor factual consequences; it was unique in the child's experience either as happening to herself or to other people. Since there was nothing to which it could be compared there was no mode by which it could be cognised and so none by which it could be assimilated to the fabric of experience. The incident itself therefore became encapsulated and shut off, inaccessible to the ordinary processes of assimilation.

In order that such an experience, thus encapsulated, become integrated again with the personality it must first be "remembered". The question then arises: how and in what form could an incident of this kind be "remembered" by a small child? The answer appears to be that, (1) as an actual incident, it could only be remembered if it had been described to the child by the adults who took part in it, or if she could have heard discussion of it at some time and in some form that she could have understood. This, however, did not take place. (2) It would have been possible for this experience in different circumstances, to have reappeared in the form of a nightmare or a somatic symptom; that is to say, while at $2\frac{3}{4}$

years the development of the child is too immature for exact cognition and recollection of an experience of this kind to be possible, yet the general content of bewilderment, horror, and shock, etc., could have made themselves apparent in the shapelessness of a child's nightmare. The fact that they did not do so is therefore significant.

The incident, as an incident, therefore was neither realised and understood at the time, nor was it interpreted or explained to the child then or later. We have to ask ourselves therefore, from the child's point of view what then was the essence of this experience? It would appear from what we now know that this was *an abrupt arrest during a play situation of the whole course of being:* that is, a wholly spontaneous and natural outburst of joy and gaiety expressed in absorption in the physical playing out of identification of the self with a rebellious unbridled horse was cut short suddenly by an outside force of overwhelming power, wholly blotting out consciousness. This arrest was further reinforced by waking to see the ring of stern and frozen faces.

Finally there was the complete absence of any expression of emotion on the part of the grownups concerned or of any explanation to the child of what had happened.

This was a real experience and as it could not be cognised by the child there came about an inevitable dissociation between consciousness and a crucial real experience really experienced.

In this way the reality-sense of the child became pitted against its emotional spontaneity, so that an intrapersonal conflict of the most profound type developed, the spontaneity and play impulse of the child meeting head on, as it were, the adult pattern of immobility. Moreover this experience, buried as it is in the unconscious of the child forms also a basic pattern for expectation of future experience.

We have therefore a set of subjective experiences referring to an event shared by adults, which for a child would have been totally incomprehensible, since no reaction was shown by these adults. This lack of reaction established for the child a pattern of behaviour in which the normal, and therefore expected and right, concomitant of experience was absence of movement and of emotional expression.*

To continue, the effect of such a total experience upon the development of any child will depend upon the relation between the experience and the general atmosphere of the family. Its impact could have been neutralised had warmth and freedom of emotional expression existed in other parts of the child's experience. But if, as in this case, this attitude was a permanent pattern in the family, then the impact could not fail to be very powerful, reinforced as it was by absence of any proper treatment for shock or warm comforting on the part of the mother.

---

*Cf. the biological "sham-dead" reaction.

It seems inevitable that in such a situation there must arise a fixed attitude regarding feelings of all kinds that these are dangerous and taboo and must under no circumstances be allowed to appear.

As, however, the intrinsic nature of a child is the spontaneity, the violence and volatility of its feelings, such an interior and unconscious attitude must bring about a condition resembling the endogenic depression of adults. The heartbroken sobbing therefore which appeared on relaxation of the physical tensions induced by this long-term arrest was both the appearance for the first time in actual expression of misery felt so long ago but never expressed, and also the weeping of the adult for the child self. What therefore is crucial about this situation is not the incident in itself, but the effect the total circumstances and surroundings of this incident had upon the intrapersonal development of the child.

B. The World

Taken as it stands, or as it would be recorded by the camera, this World is meaningless and the actions which might have been photographed or recorded of K during its making would yield no clue to its meaning. The outburst of sobbing which followed its completion would be totally irrational.

On the other hand the very fact of this affective storm makes it clear that the arrangement of the sand and the objects on it either stated something or described something with real significance to the maker. The essential – and to some extent the puzzling aspect of World-making (especially when it is a World of the type described above) – is that conscious planning plays no part. The process of making this World arose spontaneously, each step leading to the next, but without deliberate design on the part of the maker.

Four elements are to be distinguished.

(1) The symmetrical arrangement of both the moulded sand and the objects used taken in relation to each other and to the space of the tray.

(2) Plastic use of the sand.

(3) The use of objects such as trees, flowers and bushes which occur in any ordinary landscape and their grouping in a normal way.

(4) The selection and use of animals familiar from films and books, but which to the maker essentially represented living creatures who roamed in unrestricted space, and which are commonly used as symbols of violent feeling.

These four elements appear in the World with great precision, and when the meaning of the World is known it is clear that each is suited exactly to what it is used to present. What then does the World express?

The answer is curious and unexpected. It appears to be the conclusions of a mind, looking backward and within upon itself concerning the effect upon itself of a violent and totally uncomprehended experience which occurred to itself at the age of 2¾ but *of which the maker of the World was totally unaware*. To arrive at representation of this effect a number of different "modes" are used:

(1) Patterning

The use of patterned arrangements of colour and line in formalised statements of magical or emotional significance occurs in many cultures. The impulse to shape expressions of emotion into formalised patterns seems to be deep and widespread in many human societies. Here the arrangement of the component parts of the scene determines at least half of their significance. For example: the high ridge of sand runs obliquely across the tray. It has therefore the direction of a line drawn crossing out something, since the deliberate detachment by the maker of the ends of the wall from the corners of the tray precludes the idea of the line indicating merely a diagonal. Here then we have a barrier which does not entirely block one side of the scene from the other, but which has the effect of stating that something which might be imagined to take place in the centre of the tray is crossed out. The passage of time is part of this statement, expressed as is so often the case by arrangement of objects in space, the tray in this case appearing as what one might call emotional space.

(2) Plastic use of sand

Without the presence in the tray of mouldable sand, this World could not have been made, since no other way exists on a flat surface which would express what is conveyed here by this moulded ridge. In moist sand, used in this way, there are latent potentialities of sculpture, especially of sculpture seen from a modern viewpoint. Several instances of this use occur in the illustrations to this book.

(3) The symbolic use of conventional objects

The care and exactitude shown in the selection of objects to form this World is a commonplace of World-making, and it is that very exactitude both in selection and in placing which conveys the meanings of the World. For this reason it is worthwhile considering these in some detail.

The use of trees to express aspects of human relations goes back very far, and the contrasting shapes of the two types of trees selected here carries out well the difference in affect and atmosphere represented by these two elements in the personal background of the child. It is the tallness and darkness of the big trees which renders them suitable for the presentation of "grown-ups".

The duplicated group of three trees at each end of the obstacle, and between the end of the obstacle and the edge of the tray, on the other hand, uses the conventional pattern of 3 to present the relation of parents and child as this relationship was really experienced. That is to say, this was a stable family with a reliable interior structure, responsible and dependable, but without intimacy, the barriers to expression of affect or affection between the members of the family never breaking down.

The bushes on the ridge were inserted as camouflage to disguise its presence.

The isolated circumscribed little garden on the nearer side of the tray, diagonally opposite to the forbidding trees, with a barrier between them which would shut out all communication, expresses directly the experience of this child, as a child toward older people in her family, from contact with whom later her own withdrawal shut her out.

(4) The symbolic use of animals

The choice of wild animals and the negation of their freedom through fixation of their heads in the ridge, present another aspect of the same statement. Here conventional symbols of instinctual energy have been chosen to present the emotional forces of the maker, and these are presented as blinded by and caught in the barrier, across the tray. That which is symbolised in this World is states of being – the arrest of force and violent movement (the oblique ridge and the wild animals caught in it) the impact of awe and terror of towering immobile adults (the dark trees), the general emotional situation of the child/mother/father (the pine trees), and finally the little garden, which represents a sense of separate identity in the child herself, not blending with or in real relation with other people but nevertheless with the potentiality of growth and flowering and an implication of interest in the self and willingness to give time and trouble to the tending of the self.

To the maker of this World a disaster had happened which had powerfully affected emotional development but the fact of its occurrence was unknown to her. Through the loosening and reassuring effect of analysis, the adult who had grown from this child came into a position where a facing of the fact of this disaster and its results became a possibility. The World expressed this in symbolic pattern, demonstrating that, notwithstanding the distortion of affect-development that the incident brought about, we are here dealing with a personality in whom such an incident, although producing a profound effect, has not given rise to a hysterical or schizophrenic distortion.

The creation of this World therefore crystallised and shaped cognitive and non-cognitive thought about the various aspects of the maker's situation, enabling the energy of meditation to be focused upon it and used to arrive gradually at understanding and resolution.

C. The Dreams

This World has been selected to illustrate the nature of the World process because of the clarity with which it expresses the relation between certain aspects of World-making and certain aspects of dreams.

Dream 1. This is an important dream for the understanding of Worlds because it embodies something about the World which is vividly present to children but often very difficult for the onlooker to grasp. To the child who makes a significant World the often incongruous collection of objects placed in and about moulded sand in a tray is alive as dolls and furry toy animals are alive. The vivid vitality of the World carries through to the dream. The dreaming mind wrestles with a problem which is central to the personality – How is the barrier of the sand ridge to be broken down? How were the heads of the animals to be released?

Thinking in terms of the presentation, two possibilities were presented by the maker to herself – i.e., either the action of a powerful influence coming from outside (such as might for example be exercised by a powerful personality impinging upon the maker, a change of work and of external atmosphere, or the sudden occurrence of new and very demanding challenges from the outside world), or an attempt forcibly to pull the heads of the animals out of the obstacle (by, e.g., such courses as going out to seek emotional experience hitherto avoided). Both were regarded by the maker as unsuitable and also probably ineffective. A certain amount of depression was present at this time owing to the apparent fixity of certain personal characteristics. In this dream the part of the personality which is aware of what is happening takes up the symbolism of the World of the previous year and adds to it a living feature which cannot be presented in a World but which is the peculiar characteristic of dreams. By this device a means was found to present the removal of the barrier in terms which are consonant both with the idiom of the World and with universal practical experience. A natural spring arises breaking down the barrier so effectively that the river comes to flow in the opposite diagonal across the World tray. To the dreamer the fact of this river and of its source in a spring comes as an assurance of safety; not only has the barrier been broken down but it cannot build itself again because at the point where it was, a counter-force now runs.

The force of this dream, in the context we are considering, is its use of the same technique of presentation as had been employed in the World, and the completion of the pattern in the World by an opposite diagonal.

The unawareness of the dreamer, at this point, of the animals in the World is a very interesting fact, since in the World, their heads were fixed in the barrier. It now became possible for the symbolism of the two elements to become separated, and thus for the way to be made clear, in due time, for the second dream.

It is this possibility of simultaneity of aspects or trends in the presenta-

267

tion made by a World which is one of its richest qualities. After such a presentation it is a commonplace that subsequent Worlds (or in this case dreams) take up first one and then another element in the composite World for further elaboration and development.

Dream 2. It was felt by the dreamer as of guiding significance that this dream occurred after she had established a home in the countryside of her own country. This time the only element of the World which appears is a metamorphosis of the arrested wild animals. In the World they were caught, blind and immovable; but had they been free, they were of a type potentially dangerous. The animals in Dream 2 are different: they are faithful and friendly; they are young and playful; they are free to move and are approachable. Toward them the dreamer feels protective. They are to be admitted into the feeling part of the personality (house at night), to be given "house room", and to be trusted.

One element, however, of the old situation remains. This is a leopard which is regarded as dangerous to the practical side of the feeling life (the right eye); and the danger is toward the other feeling aspects. The dreamer takes trouble to separate these from one another. But what is remarkable – and which shows how thoroughly the problems expressed in the World have been surmounted – is that this separation of element from element takes place not by the erection of a barrier between them, but by an attempt to delimit their spheres, the delimitation being expressed in symbolic terms of front and back.

Relation to reality

The kernel of the original incident was the child's identification of herself with an unbridled horse. Such identifications in childhood are often powerful psychic events and continue in something the way that totem animals function for primitive peoples to "carry" the "picture" of the self for the self. It is therefore in line with all we know of symbols of this nature that it should have appeared in the real life personality of the dreamer as a mutually contradictory attitude to real life horses. These embodied for her both an intense fear and an equally intense urge toward learning to ride. As she carried this out it became clear that the effort was toward a real life mastery of the symbols.

This World and these dreams illustrate the subjective experience of the making of a World during a course not only of analysis but also of training in the psychotherapy of children. This is in a sense a special use.

World and dream are therefore aspects of a language of communication between the creative part of the self and the self's actual experience. Supposing, however, a World were to be made by an adult not "in analysis". Here follows an account of the making of a World by an adult interested in the idea of a World but unconnected with psychology or

268

psychotherapy. He was an Englishman whose work was concerned with the designing and supervising of film sets. Becoming interested in the author's work he decided one day to try out the possibilities of representation offered by so fixed and technically limited a set of apparatus as the World tray and cabinet and he reports as follows:

'I approached making a 'World' with a certain scepticism. To avoid making a conscious design, I deliberately worked at random, risking that the result might be quite meaningless. I shaped the sand into a rough landscape of land and sea, which was *absolutely* suggested by its formation in the tray. Then I went through the drawers of toys one by one without looking to see what was in the next ones, and selected objects, on impulse, putting them straight on to the sand, and consciously resolving not to change their positions. On looking through the toys, I found that I was either indifferent to them or else I reacted. I was aware that the reaction was emotional and that I invested the objects with feelings and meanings, but did not wait to enquire what they were. As I placed them on the tray, I felt it was necessary to rearrange the landscape, to scoop out channels or erect mounds to stand things on. As the 'World' progressed, I became aware that sections of it had an intention and I began to hunt for symbols to make that intention clear. I knew which figure was myself. I knew that one area represented something in the past, and I knew that a 'secret pool' was beautiful and desirable. In the end I was urgently looking for jewels, shells and flowers with which to embellish it.
It was like a dream in which one knows one is dreaming and which one wishes to go on with. But I had no idea of the relations of the parts to one another. Eventually I knew it was finished. The process took a grip on me, as when one struggles to remember a forgotten tune; or as if I had previously been trying to describe colours in words and had now, for the first time, been handed brushes and paints.
I drew a record and studied it over several days and was irritated by inconsistencies and meaningless patches. I attempted to translate it into ideas about myself or the world. I did not know if it referred to my present situation or to the world in general. Then I began to see it as having two layers: first a basic structure or landscape consisting of hills, rivers, bridges, islands and figures which expressed my egocentric view of life (and which revealed my contradictory state of mind: for instance the past seemed to lie between the present and the future); and secondly a superimposed arrangement of figures and objects which represented the present situation, enacted as it were upon the basic landscape as on a stage.
If the 'World' had coherence, this was the only way in which it could be described. I conclude that the 'World' is a natural means of expression for the level of awareness upon which metaphors are made, such as 'the world is divided into two camps', 'the world (or life) is an uphill struggle', or 'life' is a pleasant garden'. In the same way, one's personal situation is depicted upon this subjective stage.
The 'World' is not a work of art, since it bypasses aesthetic manipulation of a medium for its own sake, such as words or paint. It is, like a dream, the direct expression in symbols and images of experience, which is the raw material of art. Therefore its intention is not primarily to communicate, and it is egocentric and ambiguous. The handling of a physical means of expression allows images to be released from the depths of the mind or memory. What is being represented is a

269

situation, and as the symbols by which the situation is depicted are ready made, the 'dreamer' does not require the artisitic ability to manipulate words or to draw or model".

This example illustrates a way in which World-making can appear to an adult who is without any previous knowledge of psychology.

We conclude with an extract illustrating the relation of the making of a World to an analysis of a different type. N was an adult also in training for child psychotherapy, and simultaneously in the process of a psycho-analytical personal analysis. Much of N's childhood had been spent in mountainous country, and in the course of analysis she described to her analyst how she had treated the mountains as if they were a friend, singing on them when happy, kicking them when angry or frustrated, etc. This feeling of devotion to and personification of mountains was interpreted to N by her analyst as expression of an intense wish to explore her mother's body. The interpretation was rejected by N who felt both that this inter-pretation was not correct but also that mountains had some deep sig-nificance for her.

In thinking about this subject, N decided to experiment on a World tray with a presentation in World terms of her favourite mountains, and set to work on a World, letting it develop spontaneously under her hands. When the World was complete and she could contemplate it, she was startled to note that what she had actually made were two mounds, undeniably breast-like in shape, from between which a stream ran downwards. Studying this World she saw that it was obvious that the mountains did indeed stand for "mother" and it suddenly dawned on her that the mountains had taken the place of the mother she had rejected.

In this example as is the World of the wild animals two facets of World-making appear: the power of the World technique to amplify and in-tensify the material brought to light by analysis and to relate it to personal experience, and the need for great exactitude in finding out *exactly* what the symbols used by the maker in a World mean to the maker.

The subjective experience therefore of an individual making a World is of meeting a slice of reality; almost as if unexpectedly meeting oneself in a mirror. It has the effect in well-balanced subjects of enlarging the boun-daries of one's comprehension of oneself, and in patients of giving them a tool of expression which can present to their therapists and themselves aspects and subtleties of feeling and thought which both speech and gesture fail to present. As one adult has expressed it in a letter to the author: "It is only now that I have experienced the truly astounding mental and emotional clarifying of your techniques of non-verbal languages that I have begun to overcome my own prejudices."

Appendix

The Theory of E

It would appear that the parts of the Introduction dealing with the theory of E have either been lost or were not written by Dr. Lowenfeld.

The clinical material produced by the children she treated led Dr. Lowenfeld to formulate an hypothesis about the nature of the energies that activate human personality. As the source of these energies she postulated the existence in the psyche-soma of a single, neutral force, which could manifest itself in a number of ways. She chose not to give a descriptive name to this force, but to refer to it instead simply as "E", thereby avoiding the dangers of specifying its nature (which she thought could only be speculated about) or of creating confusions by associations with other theories of energy.

We are fortunate that, in 1960, Dr. Lowenfeld dictated a statement for a student-psychotherapist to use in her final dissertation. We are indebted to Mrs. Lilian Grant for the following quotation from that dissertation, which amplifies what has been said above:

"The theory of E postulates a primary neutral force as basic to growth and function, comparable analogically to electricity. The mode in which this force is manifested is determined, not by its intrinsic nature but by the nature of the structures through which it flows. This force is termed E. There are three distinguishable ways in which E is manifested:

i. E.p: Physical, accounts for growth, the activity of the smooth muscle in blood vessels and viscera, the activity of endocrine secretion, the tone and behaviour of the skeletal musclature.

ii. E.i: Intellection, thinking.

iii. E.f: Feeling, that form of energy which finds expression in the emotions and the affective life generally.

"When any one of these functions is unusually highly charged, for example at the end of a close race, at the height of sexual experience, at the crucial moment in the solution of a difficult problem, the other modes of functioning will be inhibited. Although normally E flows along all the three channels simultaneously, there may at any time occur a comparative blocking of the other channels, leaving one channel open exclusively.

"It appears probable that all these channels branch off from a common stem, and the blocking of one channel will tend to increase the discharge of E in other channels. Certain consequences follow: partial or complete blocks across any arm of a stream may cause floods which cut fresh channels in awkward places, or produce a stagnant swamp. Deepening a shallow channel may drain excessive water from the other arms of the river; since the flow of water is continuous in all arms of the river there is constant possibility of communication between them.

"If no appropriate channels exist for discharge or E, it may be experienced by the individual in a number of ways, as anxiety, physical symptoms, inability to think rationally, or as outbursts of anti-social activity which may or may not have an aggressive content. Schools of dynamic psychology state that such blocking can and does arise from unconscious conflict; our material suggests that this postulate is by no means essential. What emerges from our studies is the perhaps surprising fact that severe blocking can arise from quite other factors.

"If these symptoms and states, hitherto regarded as exclusively deriving from one form or another of unconscious conflict, can also arise from a situation unassociated with conflict, then it is clear that this is a fact of major importance. Our purpose is not to suggest that one explanation should replace another but to call attention to the existence of a second type of causal mechanism which exists side by side with the accepted one.

"Many schools of thought tend to regard destructive and violent phantasies, feelings and actions as manifestations of an aggressive instinct. It is worthwhile to examine also the possibility of a different interpretation.

"High charges of force, whatever its nature, tend to bring about explosion, the moment of explosion and its force depending upon the relation between the energy involved and the strength of the container. The effect is destructive and could therefore, in relation to what is destroyed, be regarded as aggressive. In fact in such a case, the resulting destruction is due solely to the absence of other paths of dispersion for the energy, once it has reached a certain pitch.

"Dammed-up E can and does frequently reach a point where some detensioning process must take place. These may take many forms, from an epileptic fit to hyperkinesis, or acute anxiety. Our experience with children suggests that it is not essential to postulate an aggressive instinct but that they also, in a certain proportion of cases, can be both understood and resolved through application of the theory of E."

The theory of E is further amplified at many points throughout the present volume, by Dr. Lowenfeld's comments on its relevance to particular aspects of the clinical material under discussion.

The Proto-System

When formulating her ideas about the nature and structure of pre-verbal thought, Dr. Lowenfeld first used the term "Primary System" as a name for these structures and processes. She abandoned the use of that term because of verbal confusion between it and the psychoanalytic concept of "Primary Process", substituting instead the term "Proto-system".

The Lowenfeld Mosaic Test

The Lowenfeld Mosaic Test was originated by Margaret Lowenfeld during the 1930s, and has been standardised in its present form since 1951. It consists of a box containing 456 pieces, made of sturdy plastic, in five different geometrical shapes each of which is available in six colours – red, blue, green, yellow, black and white. The shapes are inter-related and are based on a square. They are:

1. Squares with 2 cm. sides (8 in each colour)
2. Diamonds with 2 cm. sides and 45° angles (16 in each colour)
3. Isosceles triangles produced by bisecting the square on the diagonal (16 in each colour)

4. Equilateral triangles produced by erecting a triangle on the hypotenuse of the isosceles triangle (12 in each colour)
5. Scalene triangles produced by bisecting the equilateral triangle by dropping a perpendicular from the apex (24 in each colour)

A subject being tested is first shown the different shapes and colours available and is then invited to "make something with them" on a tray $12\frac{3}{8}'' \times 10\frac{1}{4}''$ (31·5cm × 26cm), with a low rim, and lined with an exactly-fitting sheet of white paper. His response can be recorded either by tracing around the pieces onto the paper with a sharp pencil and later colouring it in, or by colour photography.

The Lowenfeld Mosaic Test requires the subject to organise the material into something meaningful. In so doing he reveals aspects of his personality and principles or organisation in a way that is different to the information provided by other projective techniques.

The test material is obtainable from the Institute of Child Psychology, 6, Pembridge Villas, London W11 2SU, England.

Full details of the test, its administration, interpretation and areas of usefulness can be found in Lowenfeld, M.F. The Mosaic Test, Newman Neame, London 1954, pp 349 plus 144 coloured plates illustrating Mosaic Test responses. This is also obtainable from the Institute of Child Psychology.

Lowenfeld Poleidoblocs

Poleidoblocs were designed by Margaret Lowenfeld during the 1940s and finally completed during the 1950s.

The material consists of two sets:– Poleidoblocs G and A.

Poleidoblocs G is a set of 54 wooden blocks, coloured red, green, blue and yellow, packed in a solid wooden box with a slide-on lid. The blocks present six basic shapes:– cubes, cuboids, cylinders, triangular prisms, cones and pyramids, all interrelated in a number of ways, the basic shape being the 2-unit cube.

Poleidoblocs A contains 140 blocks in plain wood, packed in a solid wooden box with a slide-on lid. The shapes consist of cubes, cuboids, and right-angled triangles in various sizes, all interrelated, and the blocks of Poleidoblocs G can, with the exception of the cylinders, cones and pyramids, be constructed with the blocks of Poleidoblocs A.

Poleidoblocs G and A were designed by Dr. Lowenfeld to enable children through construction and experiment to discover the basic structure of mathematics: reversability, composition and decomposition, equivalence, etc. It all begins with the child's imaginative handling, tactile and visual experimentation in what is termed Free Construction.

Poleidoblocs are used widely in schools, and also in clinics, where the three-dimensional constructions by a child (or adult) are comparable with the two-dimensional responses with the Lowenfeld Mosaic Test.

The material is available from ESA Creative Learning, Limited, Pinnacles, P.O. Box 22, Harlow, Essex CM19 5AY, England.

In 1973 a booklet was produced by the ESA on the use of Poleidoblocs with an Introduction by Margaret Lowenfeld. This handbook is supplied with the material, but can also be bought separately.

Lowenfeld Kaleidoblocs

Kaleidoblocs are designed to act in the reverse direction to normal testing procedures and so to supplement them. Where in standard testing procedures endeavour is made to limit the variables and sharpen the testing objective, the aim in Kaleidoblocs is to present an invariable and closely integrated and interrelated set of objects to be used in two ways.

A. Spontaneous manipulation by the subject (in a manner parallel to the use of the Lowenfeld Mosaic Test material).

B. The posing of problems concerned largely with space perception; practical reasoning; memory of concrete objects and ability to see them in many positions; creative understanding of relations.

Kaleidoblocs consist of 26 blocks of brightly coloured wood cut in such a way as to contain in themselves simple but basic mathematical relationships.

The blocks are packed in a strong wooden box with sliding lid with a diagram of the blocks on the back of the lid. Size of the box approximately $28 \times 6 \times 6$ cm.

(From Margaret Lowenfeld's Introduction to Kaleidoblocs Aug. 1966).

The material with a Tester's Handbook is available from The Institute of Child Psychology, 6 Pembridge Villas, London W11 2SU, England.

Bridge

In Dr. Lowenfeld's method of therapy the children are introduced to the situation with an explanation on the following lines:

Having discussed with the child the reasons for his referral, she would then use a metaphor of adults and children living on opposite banks of a river, i.e., separated by a very real gap in understanding. The I.C.P. is a place where we attempt to build a bridge to link the world of the adult with the world of the child, so that each can understand the other better.

Picture Thinking

The child, when asked, always replies that he does not know why he, e.g., wets the bed, steals, has nightmares, etc. The therapist does not know either and suggests that together they can find out, that the reason is "in his head somewhere" and goes on to say how the child has lots of pictures in his head that are difficult or impossible to talk about. To this the child agrees. That pictures can convey meaning is illustrated by reference to comic strips, cartoons, actions, and some advertisements. It is then said to the child that the I.C.P. is a place where he can make all kinds of pictures in all kinds of different ways. He is then introduced to the World material.

Notes on the Newspaper Game Technique

This is a form of a word association test but in which care is taken to break up habitual associations as far as possible so as to make significant proto-system connections more accessible.

The technique of administration is as follows:

The subject is presented usually with a box of twenty-six compartments each containing separate letters in alphabetical order and a number of simple "racks" in which the letters fit in lines. The Subject is asked to set out a newspaper heading which must not be "actual", i.e., must not have been seen in an actual newspaper, and a sub-heading. The Tester makes a note of the heading, copying carefully the exact arrangement (which is sometimes revealing). The Tester then takes out each letter of the heading in turn and places it on the table before the Subject, arranging the letters as they come in a single long line in alphabetical order. The Subject is then asked to give as quickly as possible a word beginning with the letter as it is presented and the word given is written down, the words being arranged in five columns of five words each, with one over, so as to check quickly the completion of the twenty-six. (No duplicate letters are used.)

When the letters composing the heading and subheading have been used up, the Subject is asked to supply one by one the missing letters from the alphabet and these are arranged in their proper places on the table but on a lower line (these details of arrangement seem fussy when the test is used with normal Subjects but are essential if an ordered result is to be obtained when used with schizophrenic subjects). As soon as the twenty-six words have been obtained, the Subject is asked to replace the letters in their proper order in the box, which keeps him occupied and his thoughts off the words already given while the Tester quickly groups the words on his record sheet, arranging them as follows:

Groups

1. People – this includes all names of individual people
2. Kinds of people – here come words indicating a group of people such as parent, policeman, airman, teacher, etc.
3. Places – here come all words which indicate an area whether large or small, e.g., Egypt, island, schoolroom, farm
4. Animals – includes insects, etc.
5. Things – this sounds like an elementary substitute for nouns but is not – what is meant is all words indicating substantial objects
6. Verbs – any part of any verb
7. Adjectives and Adverbs
8. Abstract ideas

Often a ninth group is necessary, called Miscellaneous, for words like interjections or nonsense words, etc.

The arrangement of the words into these groups often brings out facts of which the Subject is quite unaware, e.g., all adjectives or adverbs can be violently aggressive or negative without this fact being observable to the Subject when mixed with other words.

When grouping is complete, the words are taken one by one with the Subject and the Subject is asked to "say something" about the word, the Tester taking down what is said. Quite often the Subject's remarks *about* the word will mean transferring of a word from one group to another, as for example when a name put in the People group turns out to be that of an animal or a toy, or the word "mother" not mean mothers in general but my particular mother.

Origin of the "World".

When the Clinic moved to The Quest in March 1929 Dr. Lowenfeld had added new features to the equipment of the playroom. Amongst them were two zinc trays placed on tables, one with sand and one with water. It will be remembered that at the Telford Road Clinic a "bowl with water" was available for play with rubber toys, but no sand. Now *sand* was added and also the use of clay. It was at this point that the origin of what came to be known as the "World" began.

Dr. Lowenfeld had conceived the idea of adding to the equipment a collection of such small toy models of ordinary people and objects as could at that time be found. The chance existence of an old birds' eggs collecting cabinet with small drawers was made use of as the place where those objects were kept. The cabinet itself stood on one of the playroom tables, was called "The World", and the children were encouraged to play with it.

The following are extracts* from the actual case sheets, which give the earliest references to the use of the sand tray and "the World" objects.

Case No. 24/29. E.— C.—, a girl age 7, referred 18.4.29. for backwardness and nervous of going downstairs.

Report 18.4.29. " .... Good idea of making a village, very particular about putting the front of the house. Made an avenue with trees down between the houses which she put in straight rows; 4 little figures she put dancing in couples (2 men together and 2 women together) .... Then played farms. Very careful to put everything in its right place and anxious if she could not find a suitable place for all the animals. ..." (S.B.)

Report 25.4.29. *Sand Tray* – made the sand into hills and planted the trees on them – soon got tired of it and preferred filling little metal dishes with sand and putting them on the table.... (S.B.)

Case 25/29. M.— S.—, girl age 5½, referred on 25.4.29. for disobedience and premature mind.

Report 25.4.29. I tried to persuade her to play with the other children who were playing with "the World" with sand and clay, but she would not. A little later she said "Look how dirty those children are". (C.G.T.)

Report 29.4.29. "M. started with 'the World' but had no idea of arranging it. She would not touch the sand much and did not use the clay at all".... (C.G.T.)

Case 27/29. D.— M.—, a boy age 6½, referred on 2.5.29 for fits.

Report 2.5.29. "Also playing with the World, helped P. to make a village, but seemed very quiet, rather shy".... (R.P.)

---

*Each worker signed their reports with their initials; these will appear in brackets after the excerpts of the reports.

278

From these extracts it will be noted that the objects in the cabinet in which they were arranged were at that time referred to as "the World". The children using these arranged them either on the table or in the sand tray. Furthermore it is to be noted that the children seemed to be expected to use the objects in a reality setting.

The first story picture told by a child in connection with his construction in the sand tray was recorded in the following case:—

Case 26/29. P.— B.—, a boy age 9, referred 2.5.29. for enuresis and nervousness.

Report 2.5.29. "I found him playing with the World. He had everything out in a chaotic mess, so I suggested he should start again and build a village, this seemed to please him so he put everything away and started again. He put all the houses in a straight line round three sides of the square and an avenue of trees straight down the middle, all sizes being mixed up anyhow; he did not seem to have any idea of grouping or arranging. He was very enthusiastic about the toys and admired them. When he had filled up all the available space he said the king of the town had said it was to be torn up because it was so windy, and nobody could possibly live in its safely, he then put everything away. He then started again with the clay, modelling it into caves, etc., and said 'what fun getting our hands messy'. He seemed to be thoroughly enjoying himself. He had the cave and I said, "what will live there ?" and he said "robbers"." (R.P.)
P. was now taken over by another worker whose report runs,
" . . . Showed great enjoyment in playing with clay and moulding it. - He made a story picture on the sand tray – modelling boat, cave-rocks, cave, etc. – Story, 'A band of robbers live in the cave on the edge of the lake. At the other end of the lake is the 'hidden treasure'. This is covered at night by a cloth which is the same colour as the rock under which the treasure lies. – The captain of the gang, chosen for his stoutness – stands at the entrance to the treasure. – Another robber is in the boat on the lake. – Others are round the cave entrance. – Two dogs belonging to the robbers are lost on the other side of the lake. – The only thing on the island which the robbers are afraid of is a wild animal. They make an attempt to get him (or shoot him ?) but fail. – They are being hunted, but they do not know it. There are men and horses and wagons after them (but too far off to come into the picture). The robbers' drinking water is beside the lake but separated from it by the bank. Their food is fish from the lake." – (S.B.)

It is regrettable that at this stage the idea of making a sketch of the construction had not occurred to anybody. Comparing this boy's second construction in the sand tray with the early Worlds of William Carter, one finds a striking resemblance in content with this boy's "story picture" in the sand and William's Worlds Nos. 4 and 6. In both cases there are island, rocks, hidden treasure, boat, wild animal which is shot at, drinking water and food. Both boys were of approximately the same age, both suffered from enuresis and "nervousness" yet there is a gap in time of 24 years between them. But one would very much now have liked to know if there was any resemblance in the lay-out and the groupings of the objects in the tray.*

The first record of a World

One month after the date of the report quoted above, we find the first record of a World in a case (21/29) of a girl N.— S.—., age 13½, referred 25.3.29 for being backward, delicate, very passionate, and untruthful.

It is a pencil drawing, quite competent and intelligible, made on a white sheet of paper 12½ × 20 cm. It carries the signatures of 2 workers (C.G.T. and E.G.M.) so we do not know which of these made the drawing; the only reference to it in the playroom report is, . . . "after playing with World, went on to . . ." (S.B.).

But the next important feature of this record is written in pencil on the back; it reads,

N.— S.—'s World 3.6.29.

This is the first time that the construction in the sand tray was called *World* in the playroom reports.

Three days after this we find the term applied by another worker to a construction of another child.

Case 25/29 M.— S.—., (see above)†

Report 6.6.29. "Straight to sand and water. Taking no notice of me. Made a 'World' in sand tray – animals behind a fence – zoo. Row of people going to see it. Tree with apple on it, and vegetables on the ground. Went out to fetch water on her own. (L.B.)

From then on, according to the playroom reports, the term "World" seems to have been adopted throughout to describe the construction made in the sand tray. The date can be fixed, but there is no means of saying who of the staff at the Clinic first used the term that to us of today seems so obvious and natural, and which has been adopted by many workers all over the world who have never visited this Institute nor had any training in the use of the technique.

It is clear by reading these old playroom reports, that as soon as the workers (by chance or by intention?) refrained from expecting something realistic and from interfering or suggesting to the children, then something new and excitingly creative grew out of the children's constructions.

To sum up the surprising development.

Less than three months after a metal tray with mouldable sand placed on a table and a cabinet containing small miniature objects

---

*The case of P.B. from 1929 was unfortunately discontinued, so no complete research in this case is possible.
†This was the same child who 6 weeks earlier on refused to play with the World objects or touch sand or clay.

280

were included in the playroom equipment, a spontaneous new technique had developed, created *by the children themselves*.

Dr. Lowenfeld and the staff began to observe this phenomenon and to pay special attention to what the children made. Some Worlds were recorded in drawings, others described in the text.*

During the autumn of 1929, R. G. Collingwood, late Professor of Metaphysics at Magdalen College, Oxford, sometimes looked in at the Clinic, and if a World happened to be about, drew it for filing. Two of these drawings have been preserved.

The real discoverers of the World (in the sense it is now used), therefore, were the children themselves.

We need to pause and to look back on the original goal set before herself by Dr. Lowenfeld in designing the Children's Clinic. She described one of these goals in the following way:—

"to find a medium which would in itself be instantly attractive to children and which would give them and the observer a 'language', as it were, through which communication could be established. Furthermore, once such a medium had been discovered and its use tested, it would be necessary to devise means for the study and evaluation of the material collected".

That is to say that the foundation of the whole concept of the treatment of children was that if given the right tools they would find their way to communication of their interior experience.

This is exactly what happened.

Looking back over those 30 years from 1959 to the children's work in 1929, a striking similarity appears between what the children did with the toys of the World cabinet and the sand in the tray and what they do now with the fully developed technique of the present day.

---

*8 Worlds from 1929 are drawn; 53 Worlds (or equivalent play with sand) were reported more or less in detail; total 61 Worlds by the end of 1929.